P9-CRU-249

27 Evaluating sources 94
28 Managing information; avoiding plagiarism 102

MLA Papers 106 e ✓

29 Supporting a thesis 107
30 Avoiding plagiarism 110
31 Integrating sources 113
32 Integrating literary quotations 121
33 MLA documentation style 124
34 MLA manuscript format; sample pages 167

APA Papers 174 e ✓

35 Supporting a thesis 175
36 Avoiding plagiarism 177
37 Integrating sources 180
38 APA documentation style 184
39 APA manuscript format; sample pages 217

Chicago Papers 230 e

40 Supporting a thesis 231
41 Avoiding plagiarism 233
42 Integrating sources 236
43 Chicago documentation style 240
44 Chicago manuscript format; sample pages 262

CSE Papers 270 e

45 CSE documentation style 271
46 CSE manuscript format 284

Appendixes 287

Glossary of usage 288
Glossary of grammatical terms 298
Checklist for global revision 306
Checklist for visiting the writing center 307

Index 308
Revision symbols

How to Use This Book and Its Media

A Pocket Style Manual is your quick reference for writing and research. You can turn to it for advice on revising sentences for clarity, grammar, and punctuation—as well as for help with finding, evaluating, integrating, and citing sources. The following reference aids make *A Pocket Style Manual* a useful companion in any course where writing is assigned.

- **The brief and detailed contents** inside the front and back covers allow you to quickly spot the help you need.

- **The index** at the back of the book includes user-friendly terms like *"I* vs. *me"* to point to common problems like pronoun case.

- **Color-coded MLA, APA, *Chicago*, and CSE** sections give discipline-specific advice for working with sources. Directories at the beginning of each section list documentation models.

- **The glossaries** in the Appendixes offer useful definitions and help with commonly confused or misused words such as *affect/effect*.

If your instructor has assigned this book with LaunchPad Solo, use the activation code to access exercises, model papers, and LearningCurve game-like quizzing. Visit **hackerhandbooks.com/pocket** to log in.

- **150 grammar and research exercises** help you improve your writing and integrate sources.

- **30 model papers** in 5 documentation styles provide guidance in writing and formatting your work in any course.

- **22 LearningCurve quizzes** offer game-like sentence-level practice and let you track your progress.

10a Words between subject and verb

Word groups often come between the subject and the verb. Such word groups, usually modifying the subject, may contain a noun that at first appears to be the subject. By mentally stripping a~~~~ late the noun that is in ~

The *samples* on the tr~

▶ High levels of air po~

respiratory tract.

The subject is *levels*, not *pollution*.

▶ The slaughter of pandas for their pelts ~~have~~ caused
                                                    ^has
the panda population to decline drastically.

The subject is *slaughter*, not *pandas* or *pelts*.

hackerhandbooks.com/pocket
🄴 Grammar > Exercises: 10–1 to 10–4
☑ Grammar > LearningCurve: Subject-verb agreement

> **hackerhandbooks.com/pocket**
> 🄴 Grammar > Exercises: 10–1 to 10–4
> ☑ Grammar > LearningCurve: Subject-verb agreement

References to additional online support appear throughout *A Pocket Style Manual*.

A Pocket Style Manual

SEVENTH EDITION

Diana Hacker

Nancy Sommers
Harvard University

Bedford/St. Martin's
Boston ◆ New York

For Bedford/St. Martin's

Publisher for Composition: Leasa Burton
Editorial Director, English and Music: Karen S. Henry
Executive Editor: Michelle M. Clark
Senior Editors: Barbara G. Flanagan and Mara Weible
Associate Editor: Kylie Paul
Editorial Assistants: Amanda Legee and Stephanie Thomas
Senior Production Editors: Rosemary R. Jaffe and Gregory Erb
Production Manager: Joe Ford
Marketing Manager: Jane Helms
Copyeditor: Barbara Jatkola
Indexer: Ellen Kuhl Repetto
Photo Researcher: Sheri Blaney
Senior Art Director: Anna Palchik
Text Design: Claire Seng-Niemoeller
Cover Design: Donna Lee Dennison and William Boardman
Composition: Cenveo Publisher Services
Printing and Binding: RR Donnelley and Sons

Printed in China.

9   8   7   6   5

f   e   d   c   b

For information, write: Bedford/St. Martin's, 75 Arlington Street, Boston, MA 02116   (617-399-4000)

ISBN 978-1-4576-4232-6

Acknowledgments

Lousie Bogan, excerpt from "Women" from *The Blue Estuaries*. Copyright © 1968 by Louise Bogan. Copyright renewed 1996 by Ruth Limmer. Reprinted by permission of Farrar, Straus and Giroux, LLC.

Robert Frost, excerpt from "Fire and Ice" from *The Poetry of Robert Frost*, edited by Edward Connery Lathem. Copyright © 1916, 1936, 1942, 1944, 1951, 1956, 1958 by Robert Frost. Copyright © 1964, 1967, 1970, 1975 by Lesley Frost Ballantine. Copyright © 1916, 1923, 1928, 1930, 1939, 1947, 1969 by Henry Holt and Co., Ltd. Reprinted with permission of Henry Holt, LLC, and Random House, Ltd.

Acknowledgments and copyrights for images appear on the same page as the selections they cover; these acknowledgments and copyrights constitute an extension of the copyright page. It is a violation of the law to reproduce these selections by any means whatsoever without the written permission of the copyright holder.

Photograph by Mara Weible.

Introduction

Dear Students:

One of the pleasures of writing is seeing your ideas change and take shape on the page. You may find that the writing process leads in unexpected directions—the more you read about a topic, the more questions arise for you to consider; new questions may lead you to challenge your initial assumptions. It is in the process of writing—of working in depth with your own ideas and those of others—that you discover what's compelling to you and your audience. *A Pocket Style Manual* will be your companion throughout the writing process, helping you to develop your authority as a thoughtful and effective writer.

College offers abundant opportunities to write across disciplines and enter research conversations. As you take positions in academic debates or propose solutions to complex problems, you'll have questions about how to engage with other writers and thinkers who have written about your topic, how to support your ideas with well-documented evidence, and how to communicate your points clearly and correctly. *A Pocket Style Manual* provides the guidance you'll need to enter research conversations and write successful college papers in all of your courses.

As you flip through *A Pocket Style Manual*, you'll see that it's easy to use and convenient to keep with you as you draft and revise. You'll find help for forming and testing a thesis; finding, evaluating, and integrating

1

sources; and managing information to avoid plagiarism. You'll find documentation models and formatting advice in MLA, APA, *Chicago*, and CSE. You'll also find answers to your questions about grammar, punctuation, and mechanics—how to tighten wordy sentences, for example, or how to use commas appropriately. And the book's glossary of usage offers help with commonly confused or misused words.

Start a good habit by making *A Pocket Style Manual* an essential part of your writing process. For each assignment, flag sections that contain information you need to write an effective paper. And when assignments are returned with your instructors' comments, flag sections to help you address writing challenges that your instructor has commented on. The more you rely on your handbook and learn from its lessons, the more successful you'll be as a college writer.

A Pocket Style Manual is your writing and research guide. Being a successful college writer starts here.

With all good wishes,

Nancy Sommers

Clarity

1 Wordy sentences 4

2 Active verbs 5

3 Parallelism 7

4 Needed words 8

5 Shifts 10

6 Mixed constructions 11

7 Misplaced and dangling modifiers 12

8 Sentence variety 15

9 Appropriate voice 17

1   Tighten wordy sentences.

Long sentences are not necessarily wordy, nor are short sentences always concise. A sentence is wordy if it can be tightened without loss of meaning.

1a Redundancies

Redundancies such as *cooperate together*, *yellow in color*, and *basic essentials* are a common source of wordiness. There is no need to say the same thing twice.

▶   Daniel ~~is employed~~ at a private rehabilitation center ~~working~~ as a physical therapist.

(works inserted above "is employed")

Modifiers are redundant when their meanings are suggested by other words in the sentence.

▶   Sylvia ~~very hurriedly~~ scribbled her name and phone number on the back of a greasy napkin.

1b Empty or inflated phrases

An empty word or phrase can be cut with little or no loss of meaning. An inflated phrase can be reduced to a word or two.

▶   ~~In my opinion,~~ Their current immigration policy is misguided.

▶   Funds are limited ~~at this point in time.~~ *now.*

INFLATED	CONCISE
along the lines of	like
at the present time	now, currently
because of the fact that	because
by means of	by
due to the fact that	because
for the reason that	because
in order to	to
in spite of the fact that	although, though

hackerhandbooks.com/pocket
ⓔ Clarity > Exercises: 1–1 to 1–5
☑ Clarity > LearningCurve: Word choice and appropriate language

INFLATED	CONCISE
in the event that	if
until such time as	until

1c Needlessly complex structures

In a rough draft, sentence structures are often more complex than they need to be.

▶ Researchers ~~were involved in examining~~ *examined* the effect of classical music on unborn babies.

▶ ~~It is imperative that~~ *A*ll night managers *must* follow strict procedures when locking the safe.

▶ The analyst claimed that because of volatile market conditions she could not ~~make an~~ estimate ~~of~~ the company's future profits.

2 Prefer active verbs.

As a rule, active verbs express meaning more vigorously than forms of the verb *be* or verbs in the passive voice. Forms of *be* (*be, am, is, are, was, were, being, been*) lack vigor because they convey no action. Passive verbs lack strength because their subjects receive the action instead of doing it.

Forms of *be* and passive verbs have legitimate uses, but choose an active verb whenever possible.

BE VERB A surge of power *was* responsible for the destruction of the pumps.

PASSIVE The pumps *were destroyed* by a surge of power.

ACTIVE A surge of power *destroyed* the pumps.

2a When to replace *be* verbs

Not every *be* verb needs replacing. The forms of *be* (*be, am, is, are, was, were, being, been*) work well when you want to link a subject to a noun that clearly renames it or to

hackerhandbooks.com/pocket
🄴 Clarity > Exercises: 2–1 to 2–5
☑ Clarity > LearningCurve: Active and passive voice

a vivid adjective that describes it: *Orchard House was the home of Louisa May Alcott. The harvest will be bountiful after the summer rains.*

If a *be* verb makes a sentence needlessly wordy, however, consider replacing it. Often a phrase following the verb will contain a word (such as *violation, resistant*) that suggests a more vigorous, active verb (*violate, resisted*).

▶ **Burying nuclear waste in Antarctica would ~~be in~~** *violate*

   ~~violation of~~ **an international treaty.**

▶ **When Rosa Parks ~~was resistant to~~** *resisted* **giving up her**

   seat on the bus, she became a civil rights hero.

NOTE: When used as helping verbs with present participles to express ongoing action, *be* verbs are fine: *She was swimming when the whistle blew.* (See 11b.)

2b When to replace passive verbs

In the active voice, the subject of the sentence performs the action; in the passive, the subject receives the action.

ACTIVE   The committee *reached* a decision.

PASSIVE   A decision *was reached* by the committee.

In passive sentences, the actor (in this case *committee*) frequently does not appear: *A decision was reached.*

In most cases, you will want to emphasize the actor, so you should use the active voice. To replace a passive verb with an active one, make the actor the subject of the sentence.

▶ *Investigators*   *samples*
   ~~Samples were~~ collected daily from the stagnant pond.

▶ *The settlers stripped the land of timber before realizing*
   ~~The land was stripped of timber before the settlers~~

   ~~realized~~ the consequences of their actions.

The passive voice is appropriate when you wish to emphasize the receiver of the action or to minimize the importance of the actor. In the following sentence, for example, the writer wished to focus on the tobacco plants, not on the people spraying them: *As the time for harvest approaches, the tobacco plants are sprayed with a chemical to retard the growth of suckers.*

3 Balance parallel ideas.

If two or more ideas are parallel, they should be expressed in parallel grammatical form.

A kiss can be a comma, a question mark, or an

exclamation point. —Mistinguett

This novel is not to be tossed lightly aside, but to

be hurled with great force. —Dorothy Parker

3a Items in a series

Balance all items in a series by presenting them in parallel grammatical form.

► **Cross-training involves a variety of exercises,**
   lifting
   such as running, swimming, and weights.
                                   ∧

► **Children who study music also learn confidence,**
   creativity.
   discipline, and ~~they are creative.~~
                   ∧

► **Racing to work, Sam drove down the middle of the**
   ignored
   road, ran one red light, and two stop signs.
                                ∧

3b Paired ideas

When pairing ideas, underscore their connection by expressing them in similar grammatical form. Paired ideas are usually connected in one of three ways: (1) with a coordinating conjunction such as *and*, *but*, or *or*; (2) with a pair of correlative conjunctions such as *either...or*,

hackerhandbooks.com/pocket
e Clarity > Exercises: 3–1 to 3–5
✔ Clarity > LearningCurve: Parallelism

neither . . . nor, not only . . . but also, or *whether . . . or;* or (3) with a word introducing a comparison, usually *than* or *as.*

▶ Many states are reducing property taxes for home
  owners and ~~extend~~ *extending* financial aid in the form of tax
                     ^
  credits to renters.

  The coordinating conjunction *and* connects two *-ing* verb
  forms: *reducing . . . extending.*

▶ Thomas Edison was not only a prolific inventor

  but also ~~was~~ a successful entrepreneur.

  The correlative conjunction *not only . . . but also* connects two
  noun phrases: *a prolific inventor* and *a successful entrepreneur.*

▶ It is easier to speak in abstractions than ~~grounding~~ *to ground*
                                                        ^
  one's thoughts in reality.

  The comparative term *than* links two infinitive phrases: *to
  speak . . . to ground.*

NOTE: Repeat function words such as prepositions (*by, to*)
and subordinating conjunctions (*that, because*) to make
parallel ideas easier to grasp.

▶ Our study revealed that left-handed students were

  more likely to have trouble with classroom desks
  that
  and rearranging desks for exam periods was useful.
  ^

4   Add needed words.

Sometimes writers leave out words intentionally, without
affecting meaning. But the result is often a confusing
or an ungrammatical sentence. Readers need to see at a
glance how the parts of a sentence are connected.

4a Words in compound structures

In compound structures, words are often omitted for
economy: *Tom is a man who means what he says and [who]*

says what he means. Such omissions are acceptable as long as the omitted word is common to both parts of the compound structure.

If a sentence is ungrammatical because an omitted word is not common to both parts of the compound structure, the word must be put back in.

▶ **Some of the regulars are acquaintances whom we**
                                                                  who
see at work or live in our community.
                             ^

The word *who* must be included because *whom live in our community* is not grammatically correct.

                                                accepted
▶ **Mayor Davidson never has and never will accept a**
                                                         ^
bribe.

Has ... accept is not grammatically correct.

                                                            in
▶ **Many South Pacific tribes still believe and live by**
                                                              ^
ancient laws.

Believe ... by is not idiomatic English.

4b The word *that*

Add the word *that* if there is any danger of misreading without it.

▶ **In his obedience experiments, psychologist Stanley**
                                          that
Milgram discovered ordinary people were willing to
                                    ^
inflict physical pain on strangers.

Milgram didn't discover people; he discovered that people were willing to inflict pain on strangers.

4c Words in comparisons

Comparisons should be between items that are alike. To compare unlike items is illogical and distracting.

▶ **The forests of North America are much more**
                                    those of
extensive than Europe.
                        ^

Comparisons should be complete so that readers will understand what is being compared.

INCOMPLETE   Brand X is less salty.

COMPLETE   Brand X is less salty than Brand Y.

Also, comparisons should leave no ambiguity about meaning. In the following sentence, two interpretations are possible.

AMBIGUOUS   Kai helped me more than my roommate.

CLEAR   Kai helped me more than *he helped* my roommate.

CLEAR   Kai helped me more than my roommate *did*.

5 Eliminate confusing shifts.

5a Shifts in point of view

The point of view of a piece of writing is the perspective from which it is written: first person (*I* or *we*), second person (*you*), or third person (*he*, *she*, *it*, *one*, or *they*). The *I* (or *we*) point of view, which emphasizes the writer, is a good choice for writing based primarily on personal experience. The *you* point of view, which emphasizes the reader, works well for giving advice or explaining how to do something. The third-person point of view, which emphasizes the subject, is appropriate in most academic and professional writing.

Writers who have difficulty settling on an appropriate point of view sometimes shift confusingly from one to another. The solution is to choose a suitable perspective and then stay with it. (See also 12a.)

▶ **Our class practiced rescuing a victim trapped in a**
    wrecked car. ~~You~~ *We* were graded on ~~your~~ *our* speed and
    ~~your~~ *our* skill.

▶ ~~Travelers~~ *You* need a signed passport for trips abroad.
    You should also fill out the emergency information

    page in the passport.

hackerhandbooks.com/pocket
e Clarity > Exercises: 5–1 to 5–7
✓ Clarity > LearningCurve: Shifts

5b Shifts in tense

Consistent verb tenses clearly establish the time of the actions being described. When a passage begins in one tense and then shifts without warning and for no reason to another, readers are distracted and confused.

▶ There was no way I could fight the current and
                                         jumped
    win. Just as I was losing hope, a stranger ~~jumps~~
                  swam
    off a passing boat and ~~swims~~ toward me.

Writers often shift verb tenses when writing about literature. The literary convention is to describe fictional events consistently in the present tense. (See p. 31.)

6   Untangle mixed constructions.

A mixed construction contains sentence parts that do not sensibly fit together. The mismatch may be a matter of grammar or of logic.

6a Mixed grammar

You should not begin a sentence with one grammatical plan and then switch without warning to another.

           M
▶ ~~For~~ most drivers who have a blood alcohol level

of .05 percent increase their risk of causing an

accident.

The prepositional phrase beginning with *For* cannot serve as the subject of the verb *increase*. The revision makes *drivers* the subject.

▶ Although the United States is a wealthy nation, ~~but~~

more than 20 percent of our children live in poverty.

The coordinating conjunction *but* cannot link a subordinate clause (*Although . . .*) with an independent clause (*more than 20 percent . . .*).

hackerhandbooks.com/pocket
e Clarity > Exercises: 6–1 to 6–4

6b Illogical connections

A sentence's subject and verb should make sense together.

▶   Under the revised plan, the elderly, ~~who now receive~~
     the double personal exemption for
     ^
     ~~a double personal exemption,~~ will be abolished.

The exemption, not the elderly, will be abolished.

▶   The court decided that ~~Tiffany's welfare~~ would not be
     Tiffany
     ^
     safe living with her abusive parents.

Tiffany, not her welfare, would not be safe.

6c *Is when*, *is where*, and *reason . . . is because* constructions

In formal English, readers sometimes object to *is when*, *is where*, and *reason . . . is because* constructions on grammatical or logical grounds.

▶   Anorexia nervosa is ~~where people~~ think they are too
     a disorder suffered by people who
     ^
     fat and diet to the point of starvation.

Anorexia nervosa is a disorder, not a place.

▶   ~~The reason~~ ṭhe experiment failed ~~is~~ because
     T
     ^
     conditions in the lab were not sterile.

7   Repair misplaced and dangling modifiers.

Modifiers should point clearly to the words they modify. As a rule, related words should be kept together.

7a Misplaced words

The most commonly misplaced words are limiting modifiers such as *only*, *even*, *almost*, *nearly*, and *just*. They should

hackerhandbooks.com/pocket
e Clarity > Exercises: 7–1 to 7–8
☑ Clarity > LearningCurve: Modifiers

appear in front of a verb only if they modify the verb. If
they limit the meaning of some other word in the sentence, they should be placed in front of that word.

▶ Lasers ~~only~~ destroy the target, leaving the *only*
   surrounding healthy tissue intact.

▶ I couldn't ~~even~~ save a dollar out of my paycheck. *even*

When the limiting modifier *not* is misplaced, the sentence usually suggests a meaning the writer did not intend.

▶ In the United States in 1860, all black southerners *not*

   were ~~not~~ slaves.

The original sentence means that no black southerners were
slaves. The revision makes the writer's real meaning clear.

7b Misplaced phrases and clauses

Although phrases and clauses can appear at some distance
from the words they modify, make sure your meaning is
clear. When phrases or clauses are oddly placed, absurd
misreadings can result.

▶ ~~There~~ are many pictures of comedians who have *On the walls*

   performed at Gavin's. ~~on the walls.~~

The comedians weren't performing on the walls; the pictures
were on the walls.

▶ The robber was described as a six-foot-tall man *170-pound,*

   with a mustache. ~~weighing 170 pounds.~~

The robber, not the mustache, weighed 170 pounds.

7c Dangling modifiers

A dangling modifier fails to refer logically to any word in
the sentence. Dangling modifiers are usually introductory
word groups (such as verbal phrases) that suggest but do
not name an actor. When a sentence opens with such a

modifier, readers expect the subject of the next clause to name the actor. If it doesn't, the modifier dangles.

DANGLING   Upon entering the doctor's office, a skeleton caught my attention.

This sentence suggests—absurdly—that the skeleton entered the doctor's office.

To repair a dangling modifier, you can revise the sentence in one of two ways:

1. Name the actor in the subject of the sentence.
2. Name the actor in the modifier.

▶   Upon entering the doctor's office, a skeleton.
    I noticed
    ^   ^

    ~~caught my attention.~~

▶   *As I entered*
    ~~Upon entering~~ the doctor's office, a skeleton
    ^

    caught my attention.

You cannot repair a dangling modifier simply by moving it: *A skeleton caught my attention upon entering the doctor's office.* The sentence still suggests that the skeleton entered the doctor's office.

▶   **Wanting to create checks and balances on power,**
    the framers of
    the Constitution divided the government into three
    ^

    branches.

    The framers (not the Constitution itself) wanted to create checks and balances.

▶   **After completing seminary training,**
    women were often denied
    ~~women's~~
    ^

    access to the priesthood. ~~was often denied.~~
    ^

    The women (not their access to the priesthood) completed the training. The writer has revised the sentence by making *women* (not *women's access*) the subject.

7d Split infinitives

An infinitive consists of *to* plus a verb: *to think, to dance.* When a modifier appears between its two parts, an infinitive is said to be "split": *to slowly drive.* If a split infinitive is awkward, move the modifier to another position in the sentence.

▶ Cardiologists encourage their patients to ~~more carefully~~ watch their cholesterol levels. *more carefully.*

Attempts to avoid split infinitives sometimes result in awkward sentences. When alternative phrasing sounds unnatural, most experts allow—and even encourage—splitting the infinitive. *We decided to actually enforce the law* is a natural construction in English. *We decided actually to enforce the law* is not.

8 Provide sentence variety.

When a rough draft is filled with too many same-sounding sentences, try to inject some variety—as long as you can do so without sacrificing clarity or ease of reading.

8a Combining choppy sentences

If a series of short sentences sounds choppy, consider combining sentences. Look for opportunities to tuck some of your ideas into subordinate clauses. A subordinate clause, which contains a subject and a verb, begins with a word such as *after, although, because, before, if, since, that, unless, until, when, where, which,* or *who.* (See p. 304.)

▶ We keep our use of insecticides to a minimum. *because we* ~~We~~ are concerned about the environment.

Also look for opportunities to tuck some of your ideas into phrases, word groups without subjects or verbs (or both). You will usually see more than one way to combine choppy sentences; the method you choose should depend on the details you want to emphasize.

▶ The Chesapeake and Ohio Canal, ~~is~~ a 184-mile waterway constructed in the 1880s, ~~It~~ was a major source of transportation for goods during the Civil War.

hackerhandbooks.com/pocket
e Clarity > Exercises: 8–1 to 8–4
☑ Clarity > LearningCurve: Coordination and subordination

The revision on the bottom of page 15 emphasizes the significance of the canal during the Civil War. The first sentence, about the age of the canal, has been made into a phrase modifying *Chesapeake and Ohio Canal.*

▶ *Used as a major source of transportation for goods during the Civil War, the*
~~The~~ Chesapeake and Ohio Canal is a 184-mile
ʌ

waterfall constructed in the 1880s. ~~It was a major~~

~~source of transportation for goods during the Civil War.~~

This revision emphasizes the age of the canal. The second sentence, about its use for transportation of goods, has become a participial phrase modifying *Chesapeake and Ohio Canal.*

When short sentences contain ideas of equal importance, it is often effective to combine them with *and*, *but*, or *or*.

                                                    and
▶ Shore houses were flooded up to the first floor/,
                                                    ʌ
Brant's Lighthouse was swallowed by the sea.

8b Varying sentence openings

Most sentences in English begin with the subject, move to the verb, and continue to an object, with modifiers tucked in along the way or put at the end. For the most part, such sentences are fine. Put too many of them in a row, however, and they become monotonous.

Words, phrases, or clauses modifying the verb can often be inserted ahead of the subject.

   Eventually a
▶ A few drops of sap ~~eventually~~ began to trickle into
   ʌ
the pail.

   Just as the sun was coming up, a
▶ A pair of black ducks flew over the pond. ~~just as the~~
   ʌ   ʌ
~~sun was coming up.~~

Participial phrases (beginning with verb forms such as *driving* or *exhausted*) can frequently be moved to the start of a sentence without loss of clarity.

▶ ~~The committee,~~ discouraged by the researchers'
D
∧ *the committee*
apparent lack of progress, nearly withdrew funding
∧
for the prizewinning experiments.

NOTE: In a sentence that begins with a participial phrase, the subject of the sentence must name the person or thing being described. If it doesn't, the phrase dangles. (See 7c.)

9 Find an appropriate voice.

An appropriate voice is one that suits your subject, engages your audience, and conforms to the conventions of the genre in which you are writing, such as lab reports, informal essays, research papers, business memos, and so on.

In academic and professional writing, certain language is generally considered inappropriate: jargon, clichés, slang, and sexist or biased language.

9a Jargon

Jargon is specialized language used among members of a trade, profession, or group. Use jargon only when readers will be familiar with it; even then, use it only when plain English will not do as well.

JARGON   We outsourced the work to an outfit in Ohio because we didn't have the bandwidth to tackle it in-house.

REVISED   We hired a company in Ohio because we had too few employees to do the work.

Broadly defined, jargon includes puffed-up language designed more to impress readers than to inform them. The following are common examples from business, government, higher education, and the military, with plain English translations in parentheses.

commence (begin)	finalize (finish)
components (parts)	impact (v.) (affect)
endeavor (try)	indicator (sign)
facilitate (help)	optimal (best)

hackerhandbooks.com/pocket
🅴 Clarity > Exercises: 9–1 to 9–7
☑ Clarity > LearningCurve: Word choice and appropriate language

parameters (boundaries, limits) utilize (use)
prior to (before) viable (workable)

Sentences filled with jargon are hard to read and often wordy.

► The CEO should ~~dialogue~~ *talk* with investors about
working ∧
~~partnering~~ with clients to buy land in ~~economically~~
∧ *poor*
neighborhoods. ∧
~~deprived zones.~~
∧

► All ~~employees functioning in the capacity of~~
must prove that they are
work-study students ~~are required to give evidence of~~
currently enrolled. ∧
~~current enrollment.~~
∧

9b Clichés

The pioneer who first announced that he had "slept like a log" no doubt amused his companions with a fresh and unlikely comparison. Today, however, that comparison is a cliché, a saying that can no longer add emphasis or surprise. To see just how predictable clichés are, put your hand over the right-hand column below and then finish the phrases given on the left.

beat around the	bush
busy as a	bee, beaver
cool as a	cucumber
crystal	clear
light as a	feather
like a bull	in a china shop
nutty as a	fruitcake
playing with	fire
selling like	hotcakes
water under the	bridge
white as a	sheet, ghost
avoid clichés like the	plague

The solution for clichés is simple: Just delete them. Sometimes you can write around a cliché by adding an element of surprise. One student who had written that she had butterflies in her stomach revised her cliché like this:

If all of the action in my stomach is caused by butterflies, there must be a horde of them, with horseshoes on.

The image of butterflies wearing horseshoes is fresh and unlikely, not predictable like the original cliché.

9c Slang

Slang is an informal and sometimes private vocabulary that expresses the solidarity of a group such as teenagers, rap musicians, or sports fans. Although it does have a certain vitality, slang is a code that not everyone understands, and it is too informal for most written work.

▶ When the server crashed, *we lost* three hours of unsaved data. ~~went down the tubes.~~

9d Sexist language

Sexist language excludes, stereotypes, or demeans women or men and should be avoided.

In your writing, avoid referring to any one profession as exclusively male or exclusively female (teachers as women or engineers as men, for example). Also avoid using different conventions when identifying women and men.

▶ All executives' *spouses* ~~wives~~ are invited to the picnic.

▶ Boris Stotsky, attorney, and ~~Mrs.~~ Cynthia Jones, *graphic designer,* ~~mother of three,~~ are running for city council.

Traditionally, *he, him,* and *his* were used to refer generically to persons of either sex: *A journalist is motivated by his deadline.* You can avoid such sexist usage in one of three ways: substitute a pair of pronouns (*he or she, his or her*); reword in the plural; or revise the sentence to avoid the problem.

▶ A journalist is motivated by his *or her* deadline.

▶ *Journalists are* ~~A journalist is~~ motivated by ~~his deadline.~~ *their deadlines.*

▶ A journalist is motivated by ~~his~~ *a* deadline.

Like *he* and *his*, the nouns *man* and *men* and related words were once used generically to refer to persons of either sex. Use gender-neutral terms instead.

INAPPROPRIATE	APPROPRIATE
chairman	chairperson, chair
congressman	representative, legislator
fireman	firefighter
mailman	mail carrier, postal worker
mankind	people, humans
to man	to operate, to staff
weatherman	meteorologist, forecaster

9e Offensive language

Your writing should be respectful and free of stereotypical, biased, or other offensive language. Be especially careful when describing or labeling people. Labels can become inappropriate over time, and it is important to recognize when their continued use is not acceptable. When naming groups of people, choose labels that the groups currently use to describe themselves. For example, *Negro* is not an acceptable label for African Americans; instead of *Indian*, use *Native American* or, better, the name of the specific group.

▶ North Dakota takes its name from the ~~Indian~~ word
        ^*Lakota*

    meaning "friend" or "ally."

▶ Many ~~Oriental~~ immigrants have recently settled in
      ^*Asian*

    our small town.

Avoid stereotyping a person or a group even if you believe your generalization to be positive.

▶ It was no surprise that Greer, ~~a Chinese American,~~
                      ^*an excellent math and science student,*

    was selected for the honors chemistry program.

Grammar

10 Subject-verb agreement 22

11 Other problems with verbs 26

12 Pronouns 32

13 Adjectives and adverbs 40

14 Sentence fragments 42

15 Run-on sentences 44

16 Grammar concerns for multilingual writers 47

10 Make subjects and verbs agree.

In the present tense, verbs agree with their subjects in number (singular or plural) and in person (first, second, or third). The present-tense ending -s is used on a verb if its subject is third-person singular; otherwise the verb takes no ending. Consider, for example, the present-tense forms of the verb *give*.

	SINGULAR	**PLURAL**
FIRST PERSON	I give	we give
SECOND PERSON	you give	you give
THIRD PERSON	he/she/it gives	they give
	Yolanda gives	parents give

The verb *be* varies from this pattern; it has special forms in *both* the present and the past tense.

PRESENT-TENSE FORMS OF *BE*		**PAST-TENSE FORMS OF *BE***	
I am	we are	I was	we were
you are	you are	you were	you were
he/she/it is	they are	he/she/it was	they were

This section describes particular situations that can cause problems with subject-verb agreement.

10a Words between subject and verb

Word groups often come between the subject and the verb. Such word groups, usually modifying the subject, may contain a noun that at first appears to be the subject. By mentally stripping away such modifiers, you can isolate the noun that is in fact the subject.

The *samples* on the tray in the lab *need* testing.

▶ High levels of air pollution damages the

respiratory tract.

The subject is *levels*, not *pollution*.

▶ The slaughter of pandas for their pelts ~~have~~ caused
                                                   has
the panda population to decline drastically.

The subject is *slaughter*, not *pandas* or *pelts*.

hackerhandbooks.com/pocket
🄴 Grammar > Exercises: 10–1 to 10–4
☑ Grammar > LearningCurve: Subject-verb agreement

NOTE: Phrases beginning with the prepositions *as well as, in addition to, accompanied by, together with,* and *along with* do not make a singular subject plural: *The governor as well as his aide was* [not *were*] *on the plane.*

10b Subjects joined with *and*

Compound subjects joined with *and* are nearly always plural.

► Bleach and ammonia creates a toxic gas when mixed.

EXCEPTION: If the parts of the subject form a single unit, you may treat the subject as singular: *Bacon and eggs is always on the menu.*

10c Subjects joined with *or* or *nor*

With compound subjects joined with *or* or *nor,* make the verb agree with the part of the subject nearer to the verb.

► If an infant or a child ~~are~~ is having difficulty breathing,

seek medical attention immediately.

► Neither the lab assistant nor the students ~~was~~ were able

to download the program.

10d Indefinite pronouns such as *someone*

Indefinite pronouns refer to nonspecific persons or things. The following indefinite pronouns are singular: *anybody, anyone, anything, each, either, everybody, everyone, everything, neither, nobody, no one, somebody, someone, something.*

► Nobody who participated in the taste tests ~~were~~ was paid.

► Each of the essays ~~have~~ has been graded.

A few indefinite pronouns (*all, any, none, some*) may be singular or plural depending on the noun or pronoun they refer to: *Some of our luggage was lost. Some of the rocks were slippery. None of his advice makes sense. None of the eggs were broken.*

10e Collective nouns such as *jury*

Collective nouns such as *jury*, *committee*, *audience*, *crowd*, *class*, *family*, and *couple* name a group. In American English, collective nouns are usually treated as singular: They emphasize the group as a unit.

> *meets*
> The board of trustees ~~meet~~ in Denver twice a year.
> ^

Occasionally, to draw attention to the individual members of the group, a collective noun may be treated as plural: *The class are debating among themselves.* Many writers prefer to add a clearly plural noun such as *members*: *The class members are debating among themselves.*

NOTE: In general, when fractions or units of measurement are used with a singular noun, treat them as singular; when they are used with a plural noun, treat them as plural: *Three-fourths of the pie has been eaten. One-fourth of the drivers were texting.*

10f Subject after verb

Verbs ordinarily follow subjects. When this normal order is reversed, it is easy to be confused.

> *are*
> Of particular concern ~~is~~ penicillin and tetracycline,
> ^
> antibiotics used to make animals more resistant
> to disease.

The subject, *penicillin and tetracycline*, is plural.

The subject always follows the verb in sentences beginning with *there is* or *there are* (or *there was* or *there were*).

> *were*
> There ~~was~~ a turtle and a snake in the tank.
> ^

The subject, *turtle and snake*, is plural, so the verb must be *were*.

10g *Who, which,* and *that*

Like most pronouns, the relative pronouns *who*, *which*, and *that* have antecedents, nouns or pronouns to which they refer. Relative pronouns used as subjects of subordinate clauses take verbs that agree with their antecedents.

ANT   PN   V

Take a *train that arrives* before 6:00.

Constructions such as *one of the students who* (or *one of the things that*) may cause problems for writers. Do not assume that the antecedent must be *one*. Instead, consider the logic of the sentence.

▶ **Our ability to use language is one of the things**
            set
that ~~sets~~ us apart from animals.
       ^

The antecedent of *that* is *things*, not *one*. Several things set us apart from animals.

When the phrase *the only* comes before *one*, you are safe in assuming that *one* is the antecedent of the relative pronoun.

                                     lives
▶ **Carmen is the only one of my friends who ~~live~~**
                                    ^

in my building.

The antecedent of *who* is *one*, not *friends*. Only one friend lives in the building.

10h Plural form, singular meaning

Words such as *athletics, economics, mathematics, physics, politics, statistics, measles,* and *news* are usually singular, despite their plural form.

     is
▶ **Politics ~~are~~ among my mother's favorite pastimes.**
   ^

EXCEPTION: Occasionally some of these words, especially *economics, mathematics, politics,* and *statistics,* have plural meanings: *Office politics often affect decisions about hiring and promotion. The economics of the building plan are prohibitive.*

10i Titles, company names, and words mentioned as words

Titles, company names, and words mentioned as words are singular.

▶ *Lost Cities* ~~describe~~ the discoveries of fifty
               describes
                    ^
ancient civilizations.

▶ Delmonico Brothers ~~specialize~~ in organic produce
                   specializes
and additive-free meats.

▶ *Controlled substances* ~~are~~ a euphemism for illegal
                 is
drugs.

11 Be alert to other problems with verbs.

Section 10 deals with subject-verb agreement. This section
describes a few other potential problems with verbs.

11a Irregular verbs

For all regular verbs, the past-tense and past-participle
forms are the same, ending in *-ed* or *-d*, so there is no danger of confusion. This is not true, however, for irregular
verbs, such as the following.

BASE FORM	PAST TENSE	PAST PARTICIPLE
begin	began	begun
fly	flew	flown
ride	rode	ridden

The past-tense form, which never has a helping verb,
expresses action that occurred entirely in the past. The
past participle is used with a helping verb—either with
has, *have*, or *had* to form one of the perfect tenses or with
be, *am*, *is*, *are*, *was*, *were*, *being*, or *been* to form the passive
voice.

PAST TENSE	Last July, we *went* to Paris.
PAST PARTICIPLE	We have *gone* to Paris twice.

When you aren't sure which verb form to choose
(*went* or *gone*, *began* or *begun*, and so on), consult the list

hackerhandbooks.com/pocket
e Grammar > Exercises: 11–1 to 11–9
✓ Grammar > LearningCurve: Verbs

that begins at the bottom of this page. Choose the past-tense form if your sentence doesn't have a helping verb; choose the past-participle form if it does.

▶ Yesterday we ~~seen~~ *saw* a film about rain forests.

Because there is no helping verb, the past-tense form *saw* is required.

▶ By the end of the day, the stock market had ~~fell~~ *fallen*

two hundred points.

Because of the helping verb *had*, the past-participle form *fallen* is required.

Distinguishing between *lie* and *lay*   Writers often confuse the forms of *lie* (meaning "to recline or rest on a surface") and *lay* (meaning "to put or place something"). The intransitive verb *lie* does not take a direct object: *The tax forms lie on the table.* The transitive verb *lay* takes a direct object: *Please lay the tax forms on the table.*

In addition to confusing the meanings of *lie* and *lay*, writers are often unfamiliar with the Standard English forms of these verbs.

BASE FORM	PAST TENSE	PAST PARTICIPLE	PRESENT PARTICIPLE
lie	lay	lain	lying
lay	laid	laid	laying

Elizabeth was so exhausted that she *lay* down for a nap. [Past tense of *lie*, meaning "to recline"]

The prosecutor *laid* the photograph on a table close to the jurors. [Past tense of *lay*, meaning "to place"]

Letters dating from the Civil War were *lying* in the corner of the chest. [Present participle of *lie*]

The patient had *lain* in an uncomfortable position all night. [Past participle of *lie*]

Common irregular verbs

BASE FORM	PAST TENSE	PAST PARTICIPLE
arise	arose	arisen
awake	awoke, awaked	awaked, awoke
be	was, were	been

BASE FORM	PAST TENSE	PAST PARTICIPLE
beat	beat	beaten, beat
become	became	become
begin	began	begun
bend	bent	bent
bite	bit	bitten, bit
blow	blew	blown
break	broke	broken
bring	brought	brought
build	built	built
burst	burst	burst
buy	bought	bought
catch	caught	caught
choose	chose	chosen
cling	clung	clung
come	came	come
cost	cost	cost
deal	dealt	dealt
dig	dug	dug
dive	dived, dove	dived
do	did	done
draw	drew	drawn
dream	dreamed, dreamt	dreamed, dreamt
drink	drank	drunk
drive	drove	driven
eat	ate	eaten
fall	fell	fallen
fight	fought	fought
find	found	found
fly	flew	flown
forget	forgot	forgotten, forgot
freeze	froze	frozen
get	got	gotten, got
give	gave	given
go	went	gone
grow	grew	grown
hang (suspend)	hung	hung
hang (execute)	hanged	hanged
have	had	had
hear	heard	heard
hide	hid	hidden
hurt	hurt	hurt
keep	kept	kept
know	knew	known
lay (put)	laid	laid
lead	led	led
lend	lent	lent
let (allow)	let	let
lie (recline)	lay	lain

BASE FORM	PAST TENSE	PAST PARTICIPLE
lose	lost	lost
make	made	made
prove	proved	proved, proven
read	read	read
ride	rode	ridden
ring	rang	rung
rise (get up)	rose	risen
run	ran	run
say	said	said
see	saw	seen
send	sent	sent
set (place)	set	set
shake	shook	shaken
shoot	shot	shot
shrink	shrank	shrunk, shrunken
sing	sang	sung
sink	sank	sunk
sit (be seated)	sat	sat
slay	slew	slain
sleep	slept	slept
speak	spoke	spoken
spin	spun	spun
spring	sprang	sprung
stand	stood	stood
steal	stole	stolen
sting	stung	stung
strike	struck	struck, stricken
swear	swore	sworn
swim	swam	swum
swing	swung	swung
take	took	taken
teach	taught	taught
throw	threw	thrown
wake	woke, waked	waked, woken
wear	wore	worn
win	won	won
wring	wrung	wrung
write	wrote	written

11b Tense

Tenses indicate the time of an action in relation to the time of the speaking or writing about that action. The most common problem with tenses—shifting from one tense to another—is discussed in 5b. Other problems with tenses are detailed in this section, after the following survey of tenses.

Survey of tenses   Tenses are classified as present, past, and future, with simple, perfect, and progressive forms for each.

The simple tenses indicate relatively simple time relations. The *simple present* tense is used primarily for actions occurring at the time they are being discussed or for actions occurring regularly. The *simple past* tense is used for actions completed in the past. The *simple future* tense is used for actions that will occur in the future. In the following table, the simple tenses are given for the regular verb *walk*, the irregular verb *ride*, and the highly irregular verb *be*.

SIMPLE PRESENT

SINGULAR		PLURAL	
I	walk, ride, am	we	walk, ride, are
you	walk, ride, are	you	walk, ride, are
he/she/it	walks, rides, is	they	walk, ride, are

SIMPLE PAST

SINGULAR		PLURAL	
I	walked, rode, was	we	walked, rode, were
you	walked, rode, were	you	walked, rode, were
he/she/it	walked, rode, was	they	walked, rode, were

SIMPLE FUTURE

I, you, he/she/it, we, they   will walk, ride, be

A verb in one of the perfect tenses (a form of *have* plus the past participle) expresses an action that was or will be completed at the time of another action.

PRESENT PERFECT

I, you, we, they	have walked, ridden, been
he/she/it	has walked, ridden, been

PAST PERFECT

I, you, he/she/it, we, they   had walked, ridden, been

FUTURE PERFECT

I, you, he/she/it, we, they   will have walked, ridden, been

Each of the six tenses has a progressive form used to describe actions in progress. A progressive verb consists of a form of *be* followed by the present participle.

PRESENT PROGRESSIVE

I	am walking, riding, being
he/she/it	is walking, riding, being
you, we, they	are walking, riding, being

PAST PROGRESSIVE

| I, he/she/it | was walking, riding, being |
| you, we, they | were walking, riding, being |

FUTURE PROGRESSIVE

| I, you, he/she/it, we, they | will be walking, riding, being |

PRESENT PERFECT PROGRESSIVE

| I, you, we, they | have been walking, riding, being |
| he/she/it | has been walking, riding, being |

PAST PERFECT PROGRESSIVE

| I, you, he/she/it, we, they | had been walking, riding, being |

FUTURE PERFECT PROGRESSIVE

| I, you, he/she/it, we, they | will have been walking, riding, being |

Special uses of the present tense   Use the present tense when writing about literature or when expressing general truths.

▶ The scarlet letter ~~was~~ ^{*is*} a punishment placed on Hester's breast by the community, and yet it ~~was~~ ^{*is*} an imaginative product of Hester's own needlework.

▶ Galileo taught that the earth ~~revolved~~ ^{*revolves*} around the sun.

The past perfect tense   The past perfect tense is used for an action already completed by the time of another past action. This tense consists of a past participle preceded by *had* (*had worked, had gone*).

▶ We built our cabin forty feet above an abandoned quarry that ~~was~~ ^{*had been*} flooded in 1920 to create a lake.

▶ By the time dinner was served, the guest of honor ^{*had*} left.

11c Mood

There are three moods in English: the *indicative*, used for facts, opinions, and questions; the *imperative*, used for orders or advice; and the *subjunctive*, used to express wishes, requests, or conditions contrary to fact. For many writers, the subjunctive is especially challenging.

For wishes and in *if* clauses expressing conditions contrary to fact, the subjunctive is the past-tense form of the verb; in the case of *be*, it is always *were* (not *was*), even if the subject is singular.

> I wish that Jamal *drove* more slowly late at night.

> If I *were* a member of Congress, I would vote for the bill.

TIP: Do not use the subjunctive mood in *if* clauses expressing conditions that exist or may exist: *If Danielle passes* [not *passed*] *the test, she will become a lifeguard.*

Use the subjunctive mood in *that* clauses following verbs such as *ask, insist, recommend,* and *request.* The subjunctive in such cases is the base form of the verb.

> Dr. Chung insists that her students *be* on time.

> We recommend that Dawson *file* form 1050 soon.

12 Use pronouns with care.

Pronouns are words that substitute for nouns: *he, it, them, her, me,* and so on. Pronoun errors are typically related to the four topics discussed in this section:

a. pronoun-antecedent agreement (singular vs. plural)
b. pronoun reference (clarity)
c. pronoun case (personal pronouns such as *I* vs. *me*)
d. pronoun case (*who* vs. *whom*)

12a Pronoun-antecedent agreement

The antecedent of a pronoun is the word the pronoun refers to. A pronoun and its antecedent agree when they are both singular or both plural.

---

hackerhandbooks.com/pocket

🄴 Grammar > Exercises: 12–1 to 12–4

☑ Grammar > Learning Curve: Pronoun agreement and pronoun reference

SINGULAR The *doctor* finished *her* rounds.

PLURAL The *doctors* finished *their* rounds.

Indefinite pronouns Indefinite pronouns refer to nonspecific persons or things. Even though some of the following indefinite pronouns may seem to have plural meanings, treat them as singular in formal English: *anybody, anyone, anything, each, either, everybody, everyone, everything, neither, nobody, no one, nothing, somebody, someone, something.*

In this class *everyone* performs at *his or her* [not *their*] own fitness level.

When *they* or *their* refers mistakenly to a singular antecedent such as *everyone,* you will usually have three options for revision:

1. Replace *they* with *he or she* (or *their* with *his or her*).
2. Make the antecedent plural.
3. Rewrite the sentence to avoid the problem.

▶ If anyone wants to audition, ~~they~~ *he or she* should sign up.

▶ If ~~anyone wants~~ *singers want* to audition, they should sign up.

▶ ~~If~~ *Anyone who* anyone wants to audition / ~~they~~ should sign up.

Because the *he or she* construction is wordy, often the second or third revision strategy is more effective.

NOTE: The traditional use of *he* (or *his*) to refer to persons of either sex is now widely considered sexist. (See p. 19.)

Generic nouns A generic noun represents a typical member of a group, such as *a student,* or any member of a group, such as *any lawyer.* Although generic nouns may seem to have plural meanings, they are singular.

Every *runner* must train rigorously if *he or she wants* [not *they want*] to excel.

When a plural pronoun refers mistakenly to a generic noun, you will usually have the same revision options as for indefinite pronouns.

he or she wants

▶ A medical student must study hard if ~~they want~~ to

  succeed.
  ^

Medical students

▶ ~~A medical student~~ must study hard if they want to
  ^

  succeed.

▶ A medical student must study hard ~~if they want~~ to

  succeed.

Collective nouns   Collective nouns such as *jury, committee, audience, crowd, family,* and *team* name a group. In American English, collective nouns are usually singular because they emphasize the group functioning as a unit.

The planning *committee* granted *its* [not *their*] permission to build.

If the members of the group function individually, however, you may treat the noun as plural: *The family put their signatures on the document.* Or you might add a plural antecedent such as *members* to the sentence: *The family members put their signatures on the document.*

12b Pronoun reference

In the sentence *When Andrew got home, he went straight to bed*, the noun *Andrew* is the antecedent of the pronoun *he*. A pronoun should refer clearly to its antecedent.

Ambiguous reference   Ambiguous reference occurs when the pronoun could refer to two possible antecedents.

The cake collapsed when Aunt Harriet put it

▶ ~~When Aunt Harriet put the cake~~ on the table~~,~~/. ~~it~~
  ^   ^
  ~~collapsed.~~

"You have

▶ Tom told James, ~~that he had~~ won the lottery."
  ^   ^

What collapsed—the cake or the table? Who won the lottery—Tom or James? The revisions eliminate the ambiguity.

hackerhandbooks.com/pocket
🅔 Grammar > Exercises: 12–5 to 12–8
☑ Grammar > LearningCurve: Pronoun agreement and pronoun reference

Implied reference A pronoun must refer to a specific antecedent, not to a word that is implied but not actually stated.

▶ After braiding Ann's hair, Sue decorated ~~them~~ with
 the braids
 ∧

 ribbons.

Vague reference of *this*, *that*, or *which* The pronouns *this*, *that*, and *which* should ordinarily refer to specific antecedents rather than to whole ideas or sentences. When a pronoun's reference is too vague, either replace the pronoun with a noun or supply an antecedent to which the pronoun clearly refers.

▶ Television advertising has created new demands for
 prescription drugs. People respond to ~~this~~ by asking
 the ads
 ∧

 for drugs they may not need.

▶ Romeo and Juliet were both too young to have
 acquired much wisdom, ~~and~~ that accounts for
 a fact
 ∧

 their rash actions.

Indefinite reference of *they*, *it*, or *you* The pronoun *they* should refer to a specific antecedent. Do not use *they* to refer indefinitely to persons who have not been specifically mentioned.

▶ ~~They~~ announced an increase in sports fees for all
 The board
 ∧

 student athletes.

The word *it* should not be used indefinitely in constructions such as *In the article, it says that....*

▶ ~~In the~~ encyclopedia ╱ ~~it~~ states that male moths can
 The
 ∧

 smell female moths from several miles away.

The pronoun *you* is appropriate only when the writer is addressing the reader directly: *Once you have kneaded the dough, let it rise in a warm place.* Except in informal contexts, however, *you* should not be used to mean "anyone in general."

▶ Ms. Pickersgill's *Guide to Etiquette* stipulates that
  a guest
  ~~you~~ should not arrive at a party too early or leave
  ∧
  too late.

12c Case of personal pronouns (*I* vs. *me* etc.)

The personal pronouns in the following list change what is
known as *case form* according to their grammatical function
in a sentence. Pronouns functioning as subjects or subject
complements appear in the *subjective* case; those functioning as objects appear in the *objective* case; and those showing ownership appear in the *possessive* case.

SUBJECTIVE CASE	OBJECTIVE CASE	POSSESSIVE CASE
I	me	my
we	us	our
you	you	your
he/she/it	him/her/it	his/her/its
they	them	their

For the most part, you know how to use these forms
correctly. The structures discussed in this section may
tempt you to choose the wrong pronoun.

Compound word groups You may sometimes be confused when a subject or an object appears as part of a compound structure. To test for the correct pronoun, mentally
strip away all of the compound structure except the pronoun in question.

                                    she
▶ While diving for pearls, Ikiko and ~~her~~ found a
                                      ∧
  sunken boat.

  Ikiko and she is the subject of the verb *found*. Strip away the
  words *Ikiko and* to test for the correct pronoun: *she found*
  [not *her found*].

▶ The most traumatic experience for her father and
  me
  ~~I~~ occurred long after her operation.
  ∧
  Her father and me is the object of the preposition *for*. Strip
  away the words *her father and* to test for the correct pronoun:
  for me [not *for I*].

When in doubt about the correct pronoun, some writers try to evade the choice by using a reflexive pronoun such as *myself*. Using a reflexive pronoun in such situations is nonstandard.

► The cabdriver gave my husband and ~~myself~~ *me* some

good tips on traveling in New Delhi.

> *My husband and me* is the indirect object of the verb *gave*.

Appositives   Appositives are noun phrases that rename nouns or pronouns. A pronoun used as an appositive has the same function (usually subject or object) as the word(s) it renames.

► The chief strategists, Dr. Bell and ~~me,~~ *I,* could not

agree on a plan.

> The appositive *Dr. Bell and I* renames the subject, *strategists.* Test: *I could not agree on a plan* [not *me could not agree on a plan*].

► The reporter interviewed only two witnesses, the

shopkeeper and ~~I.~~ *me.*

> The appositive *the shopkeeper and me* renames the direct object, *witnesses.* Test: *interviewed me* [not *interviewed I*].

Subject complements   Use subjective-case pronouns for subject complements, which rename or describe the subject and usually follow *be, am, is, are, was, were, being,* or *been.*

► During the Lindbergh trial, Bruno Hauptmann

repeatedly denied that the kidnapper was ~~him.~~ *he.*

> If *kidnapper was he* seems too stilted, rewrite the sentence: *During the Lindbergh trial, Bruno Hauptmann repeatedly denied that he was the kidnapper.*

***We* or *us* before a noun**   When deciding whether *we* or *us* should precede a noun, choose the pronoun that would be appropriate if the noun were omitted.

► ~~Us~~ *We* tenants would rather fight than move.

> Test: *We would rather fight* [not *Us would rather fight*].

► Management is shortchanging ~~we~~ tenants.

   us

Test: *Management is shortchanging us* [not *Management is shortchanging we*].

Pronoun after *than* or *as*   When a comparison begins with *than* or *as*, your choice of pronoun will depend on your meaning. To test for the correct pronoun, finish the sentence.

► My brother is six years older than ~~me.~~

   I.

Test: *older than I* [*am*].

► We respected no other candidate for city council as
      her.
much as ~~she.~~

Test: *as much as* [*we respected*] *her.*

Pronoun before or after an infinitive   An infinitive is the word *to* followed by a verb. Both subjects and objects of infinitives take the objective case.

                me
► Ms. Wilson asked John and ~~I~~ to drive the senator
  her
and ~~she~~ to the airport.

John and me is the subject and *senator and her* is the object of the infinitive *to drive*.

Pronoun or noun before a gerund   If a pronoun modifies a gerund, use the possessive case: *my, our, your, his, her, its, their*. A gerund is a verb form ending in *-ing* that functions as a noun.

     your
► The chances of ~~you~~ being hit by lightning are about

two million to one.

Nouns as well as pronouns may modify gerunds. To form the possessive case of a noun, use an apostrophe and *-s* (*victim's*) for a singular noun or just an apostrophe (*victims'*) for a plural noun. (See also 19a.)

▶ The old order in France paid a high price for the

  aristocracy's

  ~~aristocracy~~ exploiting the lower classes.
  ^

12d *Who* or *whom*

Who, a subjective-case pronoun, is used for subjects and subject complements. *Whom*, an objective-case pronoun, is used for objects. The words *who* and *whom* appear primarily in subordinate clauses or in questions.

In subordinate clauses   When deciding whether to use *who* or *whom* in a subordinate clause, check for the word's function within the clause.

                             whoever
▶ He tells that story to ~~whomever~~ will listen.
                         ^

  Whoever is the subject of *will listen*. The entire subordinate clause *whoever will listen* is the object of the preposition *to*.

                                              whom
▶ You will work with our senior engineers, ~~who~~ you
                                            ^
  will meet later.

  Whom is the direct object of the verb *will meet*. This becomes clear if you restructure the clause: *you will meet whom later.*

In questions   When deciding whether to use *who* or *whom* in a question, check for the word's function within the question.

  Who
▶ ~~Whom~~ was responsible for creating that computer
  ^
  virus?

  Who is the subject of the verb *was.*

  Whom
▶ ~~Who~~ would you nominate for council president?
  ^
  Whom is the direct object of the verb *would nominate*. This becomes clear if you restructure the question: *You would nominate whom?*

13   Use adjectives and adverbs appropriately.

Adjectives modify nouns or pronouns; adverbs modify verbs, adjectives, or other adverbs.

Many adverbs are formed by adding *-ly* to adjectives (*formal, formally*). But don't assume that all words ending in *-ly* are adverbs or that all adverbs end in *-ly*. Some adjectives end in *-ly* (*lovely, friendly*), and some adverbs don't (*always, here*). When in doubt, consult a dictionary.

13a Adjectives

Adjectives ordinarily precede the nouns they modify. But they can also function as subject complements following linking verbs (usually a form of *be*: *be, am, is, are, was, were, being, been*). When an adjective functions as a subject complement, it describes the subject.

Justice is *blind*.

Verbs such as *smell, taste, look, appear, grow*, and *feel* may also be linking. If the word following one of these verbs describes the subject, use an adjective; if the word modifies the verb, use an adverb.

ADJECTIVE   The detective looked *cautious*.

ADVERB   The detective looked *cautiously* for the
                  fingerprints.

Linking verbs usually suggest states of being, not actions. For example, to look *cautious* suggests the state of being cautious, whereas to look *cautiously* is to perform an action in a cautious way.

▶ Lori looked ~~well~~ *good* in her new raincoat.

▶ All of us on the debate team felt ~~badly~~ *bad* about our

performance.

The verbs *looked* and *felt* suggest states of being, not actions, so they should be followed by adjectives.

---

hackerhandbooks.com/pocket
Ⓔ Grammar > Exercises: 13–1 to 13–3
✓ Grammar > LearningCurve: Verbs, adjectives, and adverbs

13b Adverbs

Use adverbs to modify verbs, adjectives, and other adverbs. Adverbs usually answer one of these questions: When? Where? How? Why? Under what conditions? How often? To what degree?

Adjectives are often used incorrectly in place of adverbs in casual or nonstandard speech.

▶ The manager must ensure that the office runs
smoothly   *efficiently.*
~~smooth~~ and ~~efficient.~~
   ∧   ∧

▶ The chance of recovering any property lost in the
         really
fire looks ~~real~~ slim.
           ∧

The incorrect use of the adjective *good* in place of the adverb *well* is especially common in casual or nonstandard speech.

                                            well
▶ We were delighted that Nomo had done so ~~good~~
                                            ∧

on the exam.

13c Comparatives and superlatives

Most adjectives and adverbs have three forms: the positive, the comparative, and the superlative.

POSITIVE	COMPARATIVE	SUPERLATIVE
soft	softer	softest
fast	faster	fastest
careful	more careful	most careful
bad	worse	worst
good	better	best

Comparative vs. superlative Use the comparative to compare two things, the superlative to compare three or more.

                                            better?
▶ Which of these two brands of toothpaste is ~~best?~~
                                             ∧

      most
▶ Jia is the ~~more~~ qualified of the three applicants.
             ∧

Form of comparatives and superlatives To form comparatives and superlatives of one-syllable adjectives, use the endings *-er* and *-est*: *smooth, smoother, smoothest*. For adjectives with three or more syllables, use *more* and *most* (or *less* and *least*): *exciting, more exciting, most exciting*. Two-syllable adjectives form comparatives and superlatives in both ways: *lovely, lovelier, loveliest; helpful, more helpful, most helpful.*

Some one-syllable adverbs take the endings *-er* and *-est* (*fast, faster, fastest*), but longer adverbs and all of those ending in *-ly* use *more* and *most* (or *less* and *least*).

Double comparatives or superlatives When you have added *-er* or *-est* to an adjective or an adverb, do not also use *more* or *most* (or *less* or *least*).

▶   All the polls indicated that Gore was more
    likely
    ~~likelier~~ to win than Bush.
    ∧

Absolute concepts Do not use comparatives or superlatives with absolute concepts such as *unique* or *perfect*. Either something is unique or it isn't. It is illogical to suggest that absolute concepts come in degrees.

　　　　　　　　　　unusual
▶   That is the most ~~unique~~ wedding gown I have
    　　　　　　　　∧
    ever seen.

14   Repair sentence fragments.

As a rule, do not treat a piece of a sentence as if it were a sentence. When you do, you create a fragment. To be a sentence, a word group must consist of at least one full independent clause. An independent clause has a subject and a verb, and it either stands alone as a sentence or could stand alone.

You can repair a fragment in one of two ways: Either pull the fragment into a nearby sentence, punctuating the new sentence correctly, or rewrite the fragment as a complete sentence.

14a Fragmented clauses

A subordinate clause is patterned like a sentence, with both a subject and a verb, but it begins with a word that tells readers it cannot stand alone—a word such as *after, although, because, before, if, so that, that, though, unless, until, when, where, who,* or *which.* (For a longer list, see p. 304.)

Most fragmented clauses beg to be pulled into a sentence nearby.

▶ We fear the West Nile virus. ~~Because~~ it is transmitted
   because

   by the common mosquito.

If a fragmented clause cannot be combined gracefully with a nearby sentence, try rewriting it. The simplest way to turn a fragmented clause into a sentence is to delete the opening word or words that mark it as subordinate.

▶ Uncontrolled development is taking a deadly toll on
   the environment. ~~So that in~~ many parts of the world,
   In

   fragile ecosystems are collapsing.

14b Fragmented phrases

Like subordinate clauses, certain phrases are sometimes mistaken for sentences. They are fragments if they lack a subject, a verb, or both. Frequently a fragmented phrase may simply be pulled into a nearby sentence.

▶ The archaeologists worked slowly. ~~Examining~~ and
   examining

   labeling hundreds of pottery shards.

   The word group beginning with *Examining* is a verbal
   phrase, not a sentence.

▶ Many adults suffer silently from agoraphobia. ~~A~~
   a

   fear of the outside world.

   A fear of the outside world is an appositive phrase, not a
   sentence.

▶ It has been said that there are only three

indigenous American art forms ̂/ː J̶a̶z̶z̶, musical *jazz,*

comedy, and soap operas.

The list is not a sentence. Notice how easily a colon corrects the problem. (See 18b.)

If the fragmented phrase cannot be attached to a nearby sentence, turn the phrase into a sentence. You may need to add a subject, a verb, or both.

▶ Jamie explained how to access the database. A̶l̶s̶o̶ *She also taught us*

how to submit reports and request vendor payments.

The revision turns the fragmented phrase into a sentence by adding a subject and a verb.

14c Acceptable fragments

Skilled writers occasionally use sentence fragments for emphasis. Although fragments are sometimes appropriate, writers and readers do not always agree on when they are appropriate. Therefore, you will find it safer to write in complete sentences.

15 Revise run-on sentences.

Run-on sentences are independent clauses that have not been joined correctly. An independent clause is a word group that stands alone or could stand alone as a sentence. When two or more independent clauses appear in one sentence, they must be joined in one of these ways:

- with a comma and a coordinating conjunction (*and, but, or, nor, for, so, yet*)
- with a semicolon (or occasionally a colon or a dash)

There are two types of run-on sentences. When a writer puts no mark of punctuation and no coordinating conjunction between independent clauses, the result is a *fused sentence.*

hackerhandbooks.com/pocket
e Grammar > Exercises: 15–1 to 15–6
✓ Grammar > LearningCurve: Run-on sentences

FUSED

Air pollution poses risks to all humans it can be deadly
for people with asthma.

A far more common type of run-on sentence is the
comma splice—two or more independent clauses joined
with a comma and no coordinating conjunction. In some
comma splices, the comma appears alone.

COMMA SPLICE

Air pollution poses risks to all humans, it can be deadly
for people with asthma.

In other comma splices, the comma is accompanied by a
joining word, such as *however*, that is not a coordinating
conjunction. (See 15b.)

COMMA SPLICE

Air pollution poses risks to all humans, however, it can
be deadly for people with asthma.

To correct a run-on sentence, you have four choices:

1. Use a comma and a coordinating conjunction.
2. Use a semicolon (or, if appropriate, a colon or a dash).
3. Make the clauses into separate sentences.
4. Restructure the sentence, perhaps by subordinating
   one of the clauses.

CORRECTED WITH COMMA AND COORDINATING CONJUNCTION

Air pollution poses risks to all humans, but it can be
deadly for people with asthma.

CORRECTED WITH SEMICOLON

Air pollution poses risks to all humans; it can be deadly
for people with asthma.

CORRECTED WITH SEPARATE SENTENCES

Air pollution poses risks to all humans. It can be deadly
for people with asthma.

CORRECTED BY RESTRUCTURING

Although air pollution poses risks to all humans, it can
be deadly for people with asthma.

One of these revision techniques will usually work better
than the others for a particular sentence. The fourth tech-
nique, the one requiring the most extensive revision, is
often the most effective.

15a Revision with a comma and a coordinating conjunction

When a coordinating conjunction (*and*, *but*, *or*, *nor*, *for*, *so*, *yet*) joins independent clauses, it is usually preceded by a comma.

▶ Most of his friends had made plans for their
   retirement, *but* Tom had not.

15b Revision with a semicolon (or a colon or a dash)

When the independent clauses are closely related and their relation is clear without a coordinating conjunction, a semicolon is an acceptable method of revision.

▶ Tragedy depicts the individual confronted with the

   fact of death ; comedy depicts the adaptability

   of human society.

A semicolon is required between independent clauses that have been linked with a conjunctive adverb such as *however* or *therefore* or a transitional phrase such as *in fact* or *of course*. (See p. 65 for longer lists.)

▶ The timber wolf looks like a large German

   shepherd ; however, the wolf has longer legs,

   larger feet, and a wider head.

If the first independent clause introduces a quoted sentence, use a colon.

▶ Scholar and crime writer Carolyn Heilbrun says this

   about the future : "Today's shocks are tomorrow's

   conventions."

Either a colon or a dash may be appropriate when the second clause summarizes or explains the first. (See 18b and 21d.)

15c Revision by separating sentences

If both independent clauses are long—or if one is a question and the other is not—consider making them separate sentences.

▶ Why should we spend money on space exploration,/[?]
   We
   ~~we~~ have enough underfunded programs here on
   ∧
   Earth.

15d Revision by restructuring the sentence

For sentence variety, consider restructuring the run-on sentence, perhaps by turning one of the independent clauses into a subordinate clause or a phrase.

▶ One of the most famous advertising slogans is
                                           which
   Wheaties cereal's "Breakfast of Champions," ~~it~~
                                                 ∧
   was penned in 1933.

▶ Mary McLeod Bethune, ~~was~~ the seventeenth child
                        ∧
   of former slaves, ~~she~~ founded the National Council
   of Negro Women in 1935.

16   Review grammar concerns for multilingual writers.

16a Verbs

This section offers a brief review of English verb forms and tenses and the passive voice.

Verb forms   Every main verb in English has five forms (except *be*, which has eight). These forms are used to create all of the verb tenses in Standard English. The following list shows these forms for the regular verb *help* and the irregular verbs *give* and *be*.

hackerhandbooks.com/pocket
e Grammar > Exercises: 16–1 to 16–6
✓ Grammar > LearningCurve: Verbs for multilingual writers

	REGULAR (*HELP*)	IRREGULAR (*GIVE*)	IRREGULAR (*BE*)*
BASE FORM	help	give	be
PAST TENSE	helped	gave	was, were
PAST PARTICIPLE	helped	given	been
PRESENT PARTICIPLE	helping	giving	being
***-S* FORM**	helps	gives	is

Be also has the forms *am* and *are*, which are used in the present tense. (See also p. 30.)

Verb tense   Here are descriptions of the tenses and progressive forms in Standard English. See also 11b.

The simple tenses show general facts, states of being, and actions that occur regularly.

Simple present tense (base form or -s form) expresses general facts, constant states, habitual or repetitive actions, or scheduled future events: *The sun rises in the east. The plane leaves tomorrow at 6:30.*

Simple past tense (base form + -ed or -d or irregular form) is used for actions that happened at a specific time or during a specific period in the past or for repetitive actions that have ended: *She drove to Montana three years ago. When I was young, I walked to school.*

Simple future tense (will + base form) expresses actions that will occur at some time in the future and promises or predictions of future events: *I will call you next week.*

The simple progressive forms show continuing action.

Present progressive (am, is, are + present participle) shows actions in progress that are not expected to remain constant or future actions (with verbs such as *go, come, move*): *We are building our house at the shore. They are moving tomorrow.*

Past progressive (was, were + present participle) shows actions in progress at a specific past time or a continuing action that was interrupted: *Roy was driving his new car yesterday. When she walked in, we were planning her party.*

Future progressive (will + be + present participle) expresses actions that will be in progress at a certain time in the future: *Nan will be flying home tomorrow.*

TIP: Certain verbs are not normally used in the progressive: *appear, believe, belong, contain, have, hear, know, like, need, see, seem, taste, think, understand,* and *want.* There are exceptions, however, that you must notice as you encounter them: *We are thinking of buying a summer home.*

The perfect tenses show actions that happened or will happen before another time.

Present perfect tense (*have, has* + past participle) expresses actions that began in the past and continue to the present or actions that happened at an unspecific time in the past: *She has not spoken of her grandfather in a long time. They have traveled to Africa twice.*

Past perfect tense (*had* + past participle) expresses an action that began or occurred before another time in the past: *By the time Hakan was fifteen, he had learned to drive. I had just finished my walk when my brother drove up.* (See also p. 31.)

Future perfect tense (*will* + *have* + past participle) expresses actions that will be completed before or at a specific future time: *By the time I graduate, I will have taken five film study classes.*

The perfect progressive forms show continuous past actions before another present or past time.

Present perfect progressive (*have, has* + *been* + present participle) expresses continuous actions that began in the past and continue to the present: *My sister has been living in Oregon since 2008.*

Past perfect progressive (*had* + *been* + present participle) conveys actions that began and continued in the past until some other past action: *By the time I moved to Georgia, I had been supporting myself for five years.*

Future perfect progressive (*will* + *have* + *been* + present participle) expresses actions that are or will be in progress before another specified time in the future: *By the time we reach the cashier, we will have been waiting in line for an hour.*

Modal verbs   The nine modal verbs—*can, could, may, might, must, shall, should, will,* and *would*—are used with the base form of verbs to show certainty, necessity, or possibility. Modals do not change form to indicate tense.

> *launch*
> The art museum will ~~launches~~ its fundraising
>   ∧
>
> campaign next month.

> *speak*
> We could ~~spoke~~ Portuguese when we were young.
>   ∧

Passive voice When a sentence is written in the passive voice, the subject receives the action instead of doing it. To form the passive voice, use a form of *be—am, is, are, was, were, being, be,* or *been*—followed by the past participle of the main verb. (For appropriate uses of the passive voice, see 2b.)

> *written*
> *Dreaming in Cuban* was ~~writing~~ by Cristina García.
>   ∧

> *be*
> Senator Dixon will defeated.
>   ∧

NOTE: Verbs that do not take direct objects—such as *occur, happen, sleep, die,* and *fall*—do not form the passive voice.

16b Articles (*a, an, the*)

Articles and other noun markers Articles (*a, an, the*) are part of a category of words known as *noun markers* or *determiners*. Noun markers identify the nouns that follow them. Besides articles, noun markers include possessive nouns (*Elena's, child's*); possessive pronoun/adjectives (*my, your, their*); demonstrative pronoun/adjectives (*this, that*); quantifiers (*all, few, neither, some*); and numbers (*one, twenty-six*).

> ART N
> Felix is reading a book about mythology.

> ART ADJ N
> We took an exciting trip to Alaska last summer.

When to use *a* or *an* Use *a* or *an* with singular count nouns that refer to one unspecific item (not a whole category). *Count nouns* refer to persons, places, things, or ideas that can be counted: *one girl, two girls; one city, three cities; one goose, four geese.*

> *a*
> My professor asked me to bring dictionary to class.
>   ∧

hackerhandbooks.com/pocket
🅴 Grammar > Exercises: 16–7 to 16–10
✅ Grammar > LearningCurve: Articles and nouns for multilingual writers

                          an
▶ We want to rent apartment close to the lake.
                          ∧

When to use *the*   Use *the* with most nouns that the reader can identify specifically. Usually the identity will be clear to the reader for one of the following reasons.

1. The noun has been previously mentioned.

                                  the
▶ A truck cut in front of our van. When truck
                                ∧

   skidded a few seconds later, we almost crashed

   into it.

2. A phrase or clause following the noun restricts its identity.

                   the
▶ Bryce warned me that GPS in his car was not
                  ∧

   working.

3. A superlative adjective such as *best* or *most intelligent* makes the noun's identity specific. (See also 13c.)

         the
▶ Brita had best players on her team.
         ∧

4. The noun describes a unique person, place, or thing.

                                        the
▶ During an eclipse, one should not look directly at sun.
                                        ∧

5. The context or situation makes the noun's identity clear.

               the
▶ Please don't slam door when you leave.
               ∧

6. The noun is singular and refers to a class or category of items (most often animals, musical instruments, and inventions).

   The tin
▶ ~~Tin~~ whistle is common in traditional Irish music.
   ∧

When not to use articles   Do not use *a* or *an* with noncount nouns. *Noncount nouns* refer to things or abstract ideas that cannot be counted or made plural: *salt, silver, air, furniture, patience, knowledge*. (See the chart at the bottom of this page.)

To express an approximate amount of a noncount noun, use a quantifier such as *some* or *more*: *some water, enough coffee, less violence*.

▶ Ava gave us ~~an~~ information about the Peace Corps.

▶ Claudia said she had ~~a~~ *some* news that would surprise

her parents.

Do not use articles with nouns that refer to all of something or something in general.

▶ ~~The kindness~~ *Kindness* is a virtue.

▶ In some parts of the world, ~~the~~ rice is preferred to

all other grains.

Commonly used noncount nouns

Food and drink

beef, bread, butter, candy, cereal, cheese, cream, meat, milk, pasta, rice, salt, sugar, wine

Nonfood substances

air, cement, coal, dirt, gasoline, gold, paper, petroleum, plastic, rain, silver, snow, soap, steel, wood, wool

Abstract nouns

advice, anger, beauty, confidence, courage, employment, fun, happiness, health, honesty, information, intelligence, knowledge, love, poverty, satisfaction, wealth

Other

biology (and other areas of study), clothing, equipment, furniture, homework, jewelry, luggage, machinery, mail, money, news, poetry, pollution, research, scenery, traffic, transportation, violence, weather, work

NOTE: A few noncount nouns can also be used as count nouns: *He had two loves: music and archery.*

When to use articles with proper nouns Do not use articles with most singular proper nouns: *Prime Minister Cameron, Jamaica, Lake Huron, Ivy Street, Mount Everest.* Use *the* with most plural proper nouns: *the McGregors, the Bahamas, the Finger Lakes, the United States.* Also use *the* with large regions, oceans, rivers, and mountain ranges: *the Sahara, the Indian Ocean, the Amazon River, the Rocky Mountains.*

There are, however, many exceptions, especially with geographic names. Note exceptions when you encounter them or consult a native speaker or an ESL dictionary.

16c Sentence structure

This section focuses on the major challenges that multilingual students face when writing sentences in English.

Omitted verbs Some languages do not use linking verbs (*am, is, are, was, were*) between subjects and complements (nouns or adjectives that rename or describe the subject). Every English sentence, however, must include a verb.

▶ Jim $\overset{is}{\wedge}$ intelligent.

▶ Many streets in San Francisco $\overset{are}{\wedge}$ very steep.

Omitted subjects Some languages do not require a subject in every sentence. Every English sentence, however, needs a subject.

▶ Your aunt is very energetic. $\overset{She\ seems}{\underset{\wedge}{\text{Seems}}}$ young for her age.

EXCEPTION: In commands, the subject *you* is understood but not present in the sentence: *Give me the book.*

The word *it* is used as the subject of a sentence describing the weather or temperature, stating the time, indicating distance, or suggesting an environmental fact. Do not omit *it* in such sentences.

It is raining in the valley and snowing in the mountains.

It is 9:15 a.m.

hackerhandbooks.com/pocket
🄴 Grammar > Exercises: 16–11 to 16–14
✅ Grammar > LearningCurve: Sentence structure for multilingual writers

It is three hundred miles to Chicago.

In July, *it* is very hot in Arizona.

In some English sentences, the subject comes after the verb, and a placeholder (called an expletive)—*there* or *it*—comes before the verb.

EXP   V ┌──— S ──┐   ┌──— S ──┐ V
There are many people here today. (Many people are

here today.)

EXP V   ┌─ S ─┐   ┌─ S ─┐ V
It is important to study daily. (To study daily is important.)

▶ As you know, many religious sects in India.
                     there are ∧

Repeated subjects, objects, and adverbs English does not allow a subject to be repeated in its own clause.

▶ The doctor ~~she~~ advised me to cut down on salt.

Do not add a pronoun even when a word group comes between the subject and the verb.

▶ The car that had been stolen ~~it~~ was found.

Do not repeat an object or an adverb in an adjective clause. Adjective clauses begin with relative pronouns (*who, whom, whose, which, that*) or relative adverbs (*when, where*). Relative pronouns usually serve as subjects or objects in the clauses they introduce; another word in the clause cannot serve the same function. Relative adverbs should not be repeated by other adverbs later in the clause.

▶ The cat ran under the car that ~~it~~ was parked on

the street.

The relative pronoun *that* is the subject of the adjective clause, so the pronoun *it* cannot be added as the subject.

If the clause begins with a relative adverb, do not use another adverb with the same meaning later in the clause.

▶ The office where I work ~~there~~ is close to home.

The adverb *there* cannot repeat the relative adverb *where*.

16d Prepositions showing time and place

The chart on this page is limited to three prepositions that show time and place: *at*, *on*, and *in*. Not every possible use is listed in the chart, so don't be surprised when you encounter exceptions and idiomatic uses that you must learn one at a time. For example, in English, we ride *in* a car but *on* a bus, plane, train, or subway.

At, *on*, and *in* to show time and place

Showing time

AT   *at* a specific time: *at* 7:20, *at* dawn, *at* dinner

ON   *on* a specific day or date: *on* Tuesday, *on* June 4

IN   *in* a part of a day: *in* the afternoon, *in* the daytime [but *at* night]

   in a year or month: *in* 1999, *in* July

   in a period of time: finished *in* three hours

Showing place

AT   *at* a meeting place or location: *at* home, *at* the club

   at a specific address: living *at* 10 Oak Street

   at the edge of something: sitting *at* the desk

   at the corner of something: turning *at* the intersection

   at a target: throwing the snowball *at* Lucy

ON   *on* a surface: placed *on* the table, hanging *on* the wall

   on a street: the house *on* Spring Street

   on an electronic medium: *on* television, *on* the Internet

IN   *in* an enclosed space: *in* the garage, *in* an envelope

   in a geographic location: *in* San Diego, *in* Texas

   in a print medium: *in* a book, *in* a magazine

---

hackerhandbooks.com/pocket
Grammar > Exercises: 16–15 and 16–16
Grammar > LearningCurve: Prepositions for Multilingual Writers

Punctuation

17 The comma 57

18 The semicolon and the colon 64

19 The apostrophe 67

20 Quotation marks 70

21 Other marks 74

17   The comma

The comma was invented to help readers. Without it, sentence parts can collide into one another unexpectedly, causing misreadings.

CONFUSING   If you cook Elmer will do the dishes.

CONFUSING   While we were eating a rattlesnake approached our campsite.

Add commas in the logical places (after *cook* and *eating*), and suddenly all is clear. No longer is Elmer being cooked, the rattlesnake being eaten.

Various rules have evolved to prevent such misreadings and to guide readers through complex grammatical structures. According to most experts, you should use a comma in the situations described in sections 17a–17i. (Section 17j explains when not to use a comma.)

17a Before a coordinating conjunction joining independent clauses

When a coordinating conjunction connects two or more independent clauses—word groups that could stand alone as separate sentences—a comma must precede the conjunction. There are seven coordinating conjunctions in English: *and*, *but*, *or*, *nor*, *for*, *so*, and *yet*.

A comma tells readers that one independent clause has come to a close and that another is about to begin.

▶   **Jake has no talent for numbers, so he hires someone**

   to prepare his taxes.
   ^

EXCEPTION: If the two independent clauses are short and there is no danger of misreading, the comma may be omitted.

   The plane took off and we were on our way.

TIP: Do *not* use a comma with a coordinating conjunction that joins only two words, phrases, or subordinate clauses. (See 17j. See also 17c for commas with coordinating conjunctions joining three or more elements.)

17b After an introductory word group

Use a comma after an introductory clause or phrase. A comma tells readers that the introductory word group has come to a close and that the main part of the sentence is about to begin. The most common introductory word groups are adverb clauses, prepositional phrases, and participial phrases.

▶ **When Arthur ran his first marathon, he was pleased**
                                        ∧
  to finish in under four hours.

▶ **During the past decade, scientists have made**
                          ∧
  important discoveries about how humans form

  memories.

▶ **Buried under layers of younger rocks, the earth's**
                                      ∧
  oldest rocks contain no fossils.

EXCEPTION: The comma may be omitted after a short clause or phrase if there is no danger of misreading.

In no time we were at 2,800 feet.

NOTE: Other introductory word groups include transitional expressions and absolute phrases (see 17f).

17c Between items in a series

In a series of three or more items (words, phrases, or clauses), use a comma between all items, including the last two.

▶ **Bubbles of air, leaves, ferns, bits of wood, and**
                                              ∧
  insects are often found trapped in amber.

Although some writers view the last comma in a series as optional, most experts advise using it because its omission can result in ambiguity or misreading.

17d Between coordinate adjectives

Use a comma between coordinate adjectives, those that each modify a noun separately.

▶ **Should patients with severe, irreversible brain**
    ∧
damage be put on life support systems?

Adjectives that can be connected with *and* are coordinate:
severe and irreversible.

NOTE: Do not use a comma between cumulative adjectives, those that do not each modify the noun separately.

Three large gray shapes moved slowly toward us.

Cumulative adjectives cannot be joined with *and* (not *three and large and gray shapes*).

17e To set off a nonrestrictive element, but not a restrictive element

A *restrictive* element defines or limits the meaning of the word it modifies; it is therefore essential to the meaning of the sentence and is not set off with commas. A *nonrestrictive* element describes a word whose meaning is clear without it. Because it is not essential to the meaning of the sentence, it is set off with commas.

RESTRICTIVE (NO COMMAS)
The campers need clothes *that are durable.*

NONRESTRICTIVE (WITH COMMAS)
The campers need sturdy shoes, *which are expensive.*

If you remove a restrictive element from a sentence, the meaning changes significantly, becoming more general than intended. The writer of the first sample sentence does not mean that the campers need clothes in general. The meaning is more restricted: The campers need *durable* clothes.

If you remove a nonrestrictive element from a sentence, the meaning does not change significantly. Some information may be lost, but the defining characteristics of the person or thing described remain the same: The campers need *sturdy shoes*, and these happen to be expensive.

Elements that may be restrictive or nonrestrictive include adjective clauses, adjective phrases, and appositives.

Adjective clauses   Adjective clauses, which usually follow the noun or pronoun they describe, begin with a relative pronoun (*who, whom, whose, which, that*) or a relative adverb (*when, where*). When an adjective clause is nonrestrictive, set it off with commas; when it is restrictive, omit the commas.

NONRESTRICTIVE CLAUSE (WITH COMMAS)

▶   The Kyoto Protocol, which was adopted in 1997,

aims to reduce greenhouse gases.

RESTRICTIVE CLAUSE (NO COMMAS)

▶   A corporation/that has government contracts/must

maintain careful personnel records.

NOTE: Use *that* only with restrictive clauses. Many writers use *which* only with nonrestrictive clauses, but usage varies.

Adjective phrases   Prepositional or verbal phrases functioning as adjectives may be restrictive or nonrestrictive. Nonrestrictive phrases are set off with commas; restrictive phrases are not.

NONRESTRICTIVE PHRASE (WITH COMMAS)

▶   The helicopter, with its million-candlepower

spotlight illuminating the area, circled above.

RESTRICTIVE PHRASE (NO COMMAS)

▶   One corner of the attic was filled with newspapers/

dating from the 1920s.

Appositives   An appositive is a noun or pronoun that renames a nearby noun. Nonrestrictive appositives are set off with commas; restrictive appositives are not.

NONRESTRICTIVE APPOSITIVE (WITH COMMAS)

▶   Darwin's most important book, *On the Origin of*

Species, was the result of many years of research.

RESTRICTIVE APPOSITIVE (NO COMMAS)

▶ Selections from the book/ *Democracy and Education*/

were read aloud in class.

17f To set off transitional and parenthetical expressions, absolute phrases, and contrasted elements

Transitional expressions Transitional expressions serve as bridges between sentences or parts of sentences. They include conjunctive adverbs such as *however, therefore,* and *moreover* and transitional phrases such as *for example* and *as a matter of fact.* For a longer list, see page 65.

When a transitional expression appears between independent clauses in a compound sentence, it is preceded by a semicolon and usually followed by a comma.

▶ Minh did not understand our language; moreover,
                                                       ^
he was unfamiliar with our customs.

When a transitional expression appears at the beginning of a sentence or in the middle of an independent clause, it is usually set off with commas.

▶ In fact, stock values rose after the company's press
        ^
release.

▶ Natural foods are not always salt-free; celery, for
                                                       ^
example, is relatively high in sodium.
         ^

Parenthetical expressions Expressions that are distinctly parenthetical, interrupting the flow of a sentence, should be set off with commas.

▶ Evolution, so far as we know, doesn't work this way.
            ^   ^

Absolute phrases An absolute phrase consists of a noun followed by a participle or participial phrase. It modifies the whole sentence and should be set off with commas.

```
┌────────ABSOLUTE PHRASE────────┐
    N   ┌──────PARTICIPLE──────┐
```
Our grant having been approved, we were at last

able to begin the archaeological dig.

Contrasted elements   Sharp contrasts beginning with words such as *not* and *unlike* are set off with commas.

▶ The Epicurean philosophers sought mental, not bodily, pleasures.

17g To set off nouns of direct address, the words *yes* and *no*, interrogative tags, and mild interjections

▶ Forgive me, Angela, for forgetting our meeting.

▶ Yes, the loan will probably be approved.

▶ The film was faithful to the book, wasn't it?

▶ Well, cases like this are difficult to decide.

17h To set off direct quotations introduced with expressions such as *he said*

▶ Gladwell asserts, "Those who are successful . . . are most likely to be given the kinds of special opportunities that lead to further success" (30).

17i With dates, addresses, and titles

Dates   In dates, the year is set off from the rest of the sentence with commas.

▶ On December 12, 1890, orders were sent out for the arrest of Sitting Bull.

EXCEPTIONS: Commas are not needed if the date is inverted or if only the month and year are given: *The 15 April 2014 deadline is approaching. May 2009 was a surprisingly cold month.*

Addresses   The elements of an address or a place name are separated by commas. A zip code, however, is not preceded by a comma.

▶ The teen group met at 708 Spring Street ͜ Washington ͜
IL 61571.

Titles   If a title follows a name, set off the title with a pair of commas.

▶ Sandra Barnes ͜ MD ͜ was appointed to the board.

17j Misuses of the comma

Do not use commas unless you have good reasons for using them. In particular, avoid using commas in the following situations.

WITH A COORDINATING CONJUNCTION JOINING ONLY TWO ELEMENTS

▶ Marie Curie discovered radium / and later applied
her work on radioactivity to medicine.

TO SEPARATE A VERB FROM ITS SUBJECT

▶ Zoos large enough to give the animals freedom to
roam / are becoming more popular.

BETWEEN CUMULATIVE ADJECTIVES (See p. 59.)

▶ We found an old / maroon hatbox.

TO SET OFF RESTRICTIVE ELEMENTS (See pp. 59–61.)

▶ Drivers / who think they own the road / make
cycling a dangerous sport.

▶ Margaret Mead's book / *Coming of Age in Samoa* /
caused controversy when it was published.

AFTER A COORDINATING CONJUNCTION

▶ TV talk shows are sometimes performed live,
but / more often they are taped.

AFTER *SUCH AS* OR *LIKE*

▶ Bacterial infections such as / methicillin-resistant
Staphylococcus aureus (MRSA) have become a serious
concern in hospitals.

BEFORE *THAN*

▶   Touring Crete was more thrilling for us/than

visiting the Greek islands frequented by the rich.

BEFORE A PARENTHESIS

▶   At InterComm, Sylvia began at the bottom/(with

only a cubicle and a swivel chair), but within three

years she had been promoted to supervisor.

TO SET OFF AN INDIRECT (REPORTED) QUOTATION

▶   Samuel Goldwyn once said/that a verbal contract

isn't worth the paper it's written on.

WITH A QUESTION MARK OR AN EXCLAMATION POINT

▶   "Why don't you try it?/" she coaxed.

18   The semicolon and the colon

18a   The semicolon

The semicolon is used between independent clauses not joined with a coordinating conjunction. It can also be used between items in a series containing internal punctuation.

The semicolon is never used between elements of unequal grammatical rank.

Between independent clauses   When two independent clauses appear in one sentence, they are usually linked with a comma and a coordinating conjunction (*and, but, or, nor, for, so, yet*). The coordinating conjunction signals the relation between the clauses. If the relation is clear without a conjunction, a writer may choose to connect the clauses with a semicolon instead.

> In film, a low-angle shot makes the subject look powerful; a high-angle shot does just the opposite.

hackerhandbooks.com/pocket
e Punctuation > Exercises: 18–1 to 18–6
☑ Punctuation > LearningCurve: Colons and semicolons

A writer may also connect the clauses with a semicolon and a conjunctive adverb such as *however* or a transitional phrase such as *for example.*

> Many corals grow very gradually; in fact, the creation of a coral reef can take centuries.

CONJUNCTIVE ADVERBS

accordingly, also, anyway, besides, certainly, consequently, conversely, finally, furthermore, hence, however, incidentally, indeed, instead, likewise, meanwhile, moreover, nevertheless, next, nonetheless, now, otherwise, similarly, specifically, still, subsequently, then, therefore, thus

TRANSITIONAL PHRASES

after all, as a matter of fact, as a result, at any rate, at the same time, even so, for example, for instance, in addition, in conclusion, in fact, in other words, in the first place, on the contrary

NOTE: A semicolon must be used whenever a coordinating conjunction does not appear between independent clauses. To use merely a comma—or to use a comma and a conjunctive adverb or transitional expression—creates an error known as a *comma splice.* (See 15.)

Between items in a series containing internal punctuation Three or more items in a series are usually separated by commas. If one or more of the items contain internal punctuation, a writer may use semicolons for clarity.

> Classic science fiction sagas include *Star Trek*, with Captain Kirk, Dr. McCoy, and Mr. Spock; *Battlestar Galactica*, with its Cylons; and *Star Wars*, with Han Solo, Luke Skywalker, and Darth Vader.

Misuses of the semicolon Do not use a semicolon in the following situations.

BETWEEN AN INDEPENDENT CLAUSE AND A SUBORDINATE CLAUSE

▶ The media like to portray my generation as lazy;,

   although polls show that we work as hard as the

   twentysomethings before us.

BETWEEN AN APPOSITIVE AND THE WORD IT REFERS TO

▶ We were fascinated by the species *Argyroneta*

   aquatica;, a spider that lives underwater.

TO INTRODUCE A LIST

▶ Some birds are flightless: emus, penguins, and

ostriches.

BETWEEN INDEPENDENT CLAUSES JOINED BY *AND*, *BUT*, *OR*, *NOR*, *FOR*, *SO*, OR *YET*

▶ Five of the applicants had used spreadsheets,

but only one was familiar with databases.

18b The colon

Main uses of the colon A colon can be used after an independent clause to direct readers' attention to a list, an appositive, or a quotation.

A LIST

The routine includes the following: twenty knee bends, fifty leg lifts, and five minutes of running in place.

AN APPOSITIVE

My roommate is guilty of two of the seven deadly sins: gluttony and sloth.

A QUOTATION

Consider the words of Benjamin Franklin: "There never was a good war or a bad peace."

For other ways of introducing quotations, see pages 72–73.

A colon may also be used between independent clauses if the second clause summarizes or explains the first clause.

Faith is like love: It cannot be forced.

When an independent clause follows a colon, begin the independent clause with a capital letter. Some disciplines use a lowercase letter; see 34a, 39a, and 44a for variations.

Conventional uses Use a colon after the salutation in a formal letter, to indicate hours and minutes, to show proportions, between a title and a subtitle, to separate city and publisher in bibliographic entries, and between chapter and verse in citations of sacred texts.

Dear Editor:

5:30 p.m.

The ratio of women to men was 2:1.

Alvin Ailey: A Life in Dance

Boston: Bedford, 2014

Luke 2:14, Qur'an 67:3

NOTE: MLA recommends a period in citations of sacred texts: Luke 2.14, Qur'an 67.3.

Misuses of the colon A colon must be preceded by an independent clause. Therefore, avoid using it in the following situations.

BETWEEN A VERB AND ITS OBJECT OR COMPLEMENT

► Some important vitamins found in vegetables are: vitamin A, thiamine, niacin, and vitamin C.

BETWEEN A PREPOSITION AND ITS OBJECT

► The heart's two pumps each consist of: an upper chamber, or atrium, and a lower chamber, or ventricle.

AFTER *SUCH AS*, *INCLUDING*, OR *FOR EXAMPLE*

► The NCAA regulates college athletic teams, including: basketball, baseball, softball, and football.

19 The apostrophe

The apostrophe indicates possession and marks contractions. In addition, it has a few conventional uses.

hackerhandbooks.com/pocket
e Punctuation > Exercises: 19–1 to 19–3
☑ Punctuation > LearningCurve: Apostrophes

19a To indicate possession

The apostrophe is used to indicate that a noun or an indefinite pronoun is possessive. Possessives usually indicate ownership, as in *Tim's hat*, *the writer's desk*, or *someone's gloves*. Frequently, however, ownership is only loosely implied: *the tree's roots*, *a day's work*. If you are not sure whether a word is possessive, try turning it into an *of* phrase: *the roots of the tree*, *the work of a day*.

When to add -'s   Add -'s if the noun does not end in -s or if the noun is singular and ends in -s or an s sound.

> Luck often propels a rock musician's career.

> Thank you for refunding the children's money.

> Lois's sister spent last year in India.

> Her article presents an overview of Marx's teachings.

EXCEPTION: If pronunciation would be awkward with an apostrophe and an -s, some writers use only the apostrophe: *Sophocles'*.

When to add only an apostrophe   If the noun is plural and ends in -s, add only an apostrophe.

> Both diplomats' briefcases were searched by guards.

Joint possession   To show joint possession, use -'s (or -s') with the last noun only; to show individual possession, make all nouns possessive.

> Have you seen Joyce and Greg's new camper?

> Hernando's and Maria's expectations were quite different.

Compound nouns   If a noun is compound, use -'s (or -s') with the last element.

> Her father-in-law's sculpture won first place.

Indefinite pronouns such as *someone*   Use -'s to indicate that an indefinite pronoun is possessive. Indefinite pronouns refer to no specific person or thing: *anyone*, *everyone*, *someone*, *no one*, and so on.

> This diet will improve almost anyone's health.

NOTE: Possessive pronouns (*its*, *his*, and so on) do not use an apostrophe. (See 19d.)

19b To mark contractions

In a contraction, an apostrophe takes the place of missing letters.

> It's a shame that Frank can't go on the tour.

It's stands for *it is*, *can't* for *cannot*.
The apostrophe is also used to mark the omission of the first two digits of a year (*the class of '13*) or years (*the '60s generation*).

19c Conventional uses

An apostrophe typically is not used to pluralize numbers, abbreviations, letters, or words mentioned as words. Note the few exceptions and be consistent in your writing.

Plural numbers and abbreviations   Do not use an apostrophe in the plural of any numbers (including decades) or of any abbreviations.

> Peggy skated nearly perfect figure 8s.

> We've paid only four IOUs out of six.

Plural letters   Italicize the letter and use roman (regular) font style for the *-s* ending.

> Two large *J*s were painted on the door.

To avoid misreading, you may use an apostrophe with some letters: *A*'s.

NOTE: MLA recommends an apostrophe for the plural of all letters: *J*'s.

Plural of words mentioned as words   Italicize the word and use roman (regular) font style for the *-s* ending.

> We've heard enough *maybe*s.

Words mentioned as words may also appear in quotation marks. When you choose this option, use the apostrophe and no italics.

> We've heard enough "maybe's."

19d Misuses of the apostrophe

Do not use an apostrophe in the following situations.

WITH NOUNS THAT ARE PLURAL BUT NOT POSSESSIVE

► Some ~~outpatient's~~ *outpatients* have special parking permits.

IN THE POSSESSIVE PRONOUNS *ITS, WHOSE, HIS, HERS, OURS, YOURS,* AND *THEIRS*

► Each area has ~~it's~~ *its* own conference room.

► We attended a reading by Junot Díaz, ~~who's~~ *whose* work

focuses on the Dominican immigration experience.

It's means "it is"; *who's* means "who is" (see 19b). Possessive pronouns such as *its* and *whose* contain no apostrophes.

20 Quotation marks

Quotation marks are used to enclose direct quotations. They are also used around some titles and to set off words used as words.

20a To enclose direct quotations

Direct quotations of a person's words, whether spoken or written, must be in quotation marks.

> "The contract negotiations are stalled," the mediator told reporters, "but I'll bring both sides together."

Use single quotation marks to enclose a quotation within a quotation.

> Megan Marshall notes that Peabody's school focused on "not merely 'teaching' but 'educating children morally and spiritually as well as intellectually from the first'" (107).

EXCEPTIONS: Do not use quotation marks around indirect quotations, which report what a person said without using the person's exact words: *The mediator pledged to find a compromise even though contract negotiations had broken down.*

When a long quotation has been set off from the text by indenting, quotation marks are not needed. (See pp. 122–23, 181–82, and 237.)

20b Around titles of short works

Use quotation marks around titles of short works such as articles, poems, short stories, songs, television and radio episodes, and chapters or subdivisions of long works.

> The poem "Mother to Son" is by Langston Hughes.

NOTE: Titles of long works such as books, plays, television and radio programs, films, magazines, and so on are put in italics. (See pp. 84–85.)

20c To set off words used as words

Although words used as words are ordinarily italicized (see p. 85), quotation marks are also acceptable. Use one method or the other consistently.

> The words "affect" and "effect" are frequently confused.

20d Other punctuation with quotation marks

This section describes the conventions to observe in placing various marks of punctuation inside or outside quotation marks. It also explains how to punctuate when introducing quoted material.

Periods and commas   Place periods and commas inside quotation marks.

> "I'm here for my service-learning project," I told the teacher. "I'd like to become a reading specialist."

This rule applies to single and double quotation marks, and it applies to quotation marks around words, phrases, and clauses.

EXCEPTION: In MLA and APA parenthetical in-text citations, the period follows the citation in parentheses. MLA: *According to Cole, "The instruments of science have vastly extended our senses" (53).* APA: *According to Cole (1999), "The instruments of science have vastly extended our senses" (p. 53).*

Colons and semicolons   Put colons and semicolons outside quotation marks.

> Harold wrote, "I regret that I cannot attend the fundraiser for AIDS research"; his letter, however, contained a contribution.

Question marks and exclamation points   Put question marks and exclamation points inside quotation marks unless they apply to the whole sentence.

> On the first day of class, Professor Abram always poses the question "What three goals do you have for the course?"

> Have you heard the old proverb "Do not climb the hill until you reach it"?

In the first sentence, the question mark applies only to the quoted question. In the second sentence, the question mark applies to the whole sentence.

Introducing quoted material   After a word group introducing a quotation, use a colon, a comma, or no punctuation at all, whichever is appropriate in context.

If a quotation has been formally introduced, a colon is appropriate. A formal introduction is a full independent clause, not just an expression such as *he said* or *she writes.*

> Thomas Friedman provides a challenging yet optimistic view of the future: "We need to get back to work on our country and on our planet. The hour is late, the stakes couldn't be higher, the project couldn't be harder, the payoff couldn't be greater" (25).

If a quotation is introduced or followed by an expression such as *he said* or *she writes*, use a comma.

> About New England's weather, Mark Twain once declared, "In the spring I have counted one hundred and thirty-six different kinds of weather within four and twenty hours" (55).

"Unless another war is prevented it is likely to bring destruction on a scale never before held possible," Einstein predicted in 1947 (29).

When you blend a quotation into your own sentence, use either a comma or no punctuation, depending on the way the quotation fits into your sentence structure.

The champion could, as he put it, "float like a butterfly and sting like a bee."

Virginia Woolf wrote in 1928 that "a woman must have money and a room of her own if she is to write fiction" (4).

If a quotation appears at the beginning of a sentence, use a comma after it unless the quotation ends with a question mark or an exclamation point.

"I've always thought of myself as a reporter," American poet Gwendolyn Brooks stated (162).

"What is it?" I asked, bracing myself.

If a quoted sentence is interrupted by explanatory words, use commas to set off the explanatory words.

"With regard to air travel," Stephen Ambrose notes, "Jefferson was a full century ahead of the curve" (53).

If two successive quoted sentences from the same source are interrupted by explanatory words, use a comma before the explanatory words and a period after them.

"Everyone agrees journalists must tell the truth," Bill Kovach and Tom Rosenstiel write. "Yet people are befuddled about what 'the truth' means" (37).

20e Misuses of quotation marks

Avoid using quotation marks in the following situations.

FAMILIAR SLANG, TRITE EXPRESSIONS, OR HUMOR

▶ The economist emphasized that 5 percent was a

   ⁄ballpark figure.⁄

INDIRECT QUOTATIONS

▶ After finishing the exam, Chuck said that ⁄he was

   due for a coffee break.⁄

21 Other marks

21a The period

Use a period to end all sentences except direct questions or genuine exclamations.

> Celia asked whether the picnic would be canceled.

A period is conventionally used with personal titles, Latin abbreviations, and designations for time.

Mr.	i.e.	a.m. (or AM)
Ms.	e.g.	p.m. (or PM)
Dr.	etc.	

NOTE: If a sentence ends with a period marking an abbreviation, do not add a second period.

A period is not used for most other abbreviations.

| CA | UNESCO | FCC | NATO | BS | BC |
| NY | AFL-CIO | IRS | USA | PhD | BCE |

21b The question mark

Use a question mark after a direct question.

> What is the horsepower of a 747 engine?

NOTE: Use a period, not a question mark, after an indirect question, one that is reported rather than asked directly.

> He asked me who was teaching the mythology course.

21c The exclamation point

Use an exclamation point after a sentence that expresses exceptional feeling or deserves special emphasis.

> We yelled to the police officer, "He's not drunk! He's in diabetic shock!"

Do not overuse the exclamation point.

▶ **In the fisherman's memory, the fish lives on,**

   increasing in length and weight each year, until it is

   big enough to shade a fishing boat!
                                      ⌃

This sentence doesn't need to be pumped up with an exclamation point. It is emphatic enough without it.

21d The dash

The dash may be used to set off parenthetical material that deserves special emphasis. When typing, use two hyphens to form a dash (--), with no spaces before or after the dash. If your word processing program has what is known as an "em-dash" (—), you may use it instead, with no space before or after it.

Use a dash to introduce a list, to signal a restatement or an amplification, or to indicate a striking shift in tone or thought.

> Along the wall are the bulk liquids—sesame seed oil, honey, safflower oil, and half-liquid peanut butter.

> Peter decided to focus on his priorities—applying to graduate school, getting financial aid, and finding a roommate.

> Kiere took a few steps back, came running full speed, kicked a mighty kick—and missed the ball.

In the first two examples, the writer could also use a colon. (See 18b.) The colon is more formal than the dash and not quite as dramatic.

Use a pair of dashes to set off parenthetical material that deserves special emphasis or to set off an appositive that contains commas.

> Everything in the classroom—from the pencils on the desks to the books on the shelves—was in perfect order.

> In my hometown, people's basic needs—food, clothing, and shelter—are less costly than in Denver.

TIP: Unless you have a specific reason for using the dash, avoid it. Unnecessary dashes create a choppy effect.

21e Parentheses

Parentheses have several conventional uses.

Use parentheses to enclose supplemental material, minor digressions, and afterthoughts.

> Nurses record patients' vital signs (temperature, pulse, and blood pressure) several times a day.

Use parentheses around an abbreviation following the spelled-out form the first time you mention the term. Use the abbreviation alone in subsequent references.

> Data from the Uniform Crime Reports (UCR) indicate that homicide rates have been declining. Because most murders are reported to the police, the data from the UCR are widely viewed as a valid indicator of homicide rates.

Use parentheses to enclose letters or numbers labeling items in a series.

> Freudians recognize three parts to a person's psyche: (a) the unconscious id, where basic drives reside; (b) the ego, which controls many of our conscious decisions; and (c) the superego, which regulates behavior according to internalized societal expectations.

Parentheses are used around page numbers in in-text citations and, in APA style, around dates in in-text citations and the reference list. (See also 33a and 38a.)

TIP: Do not overuse parentheses. Often a sentence reads more gracefully without them.

▶ **Research shows that seventeen million** ~~(estimates~~ ^{from}

~~run as high as~~ **twenty-three million)** ^{to} **Americans**

have diabetes.

21f Brackets

Use brackets to enclose any words or phrases you have inserted into an otherwise word-for-word quotation.

> *Audubon* reports that "if there are not enough young to balance deaths, the end of the species [California condor] is inevitable" (4).

The *Audubon* article did not contain the words *California condor* in the sentence quoted.

The Latin word "sic" in brackets indicates that an error in a quoted sentence appears in the original source.

> According to the review, the book was "an important contribution to gender studies, suceeding [sic] where others have fallen short."

NOTE: APA and *Chicago* use italics for the word "sic" (but not for the brackets). MLA uses regular (roman) font. See pages 181, 237, and 115, respectively.

21g The ellipsis mark

Use an ellipsis mark, three spaced periods, to indicate that you have deleted material from an otherwise word-for-word quotation.

> Harmon (2011) noted, "During hibernation, heart rate would drop to nine beats per minute between breaths...and then speed up with each inhale."

If you delete a full sentence or more in the middle of a quoted passage, use a period before the three ellipsis dots.

NOTE: Do not use the ellipsis mark at the beginning of a quotation; do not use it at the end of a quotation unless you have cut some words from the end of the final sentence quoted.

21h The slash

Use the slash to separate two or three lines of poetry that have been run into your text. Add a space both before and after the slash.

> In the opening lines of "Jordan," George Herbert pokes fun at popular poems of his time: "Who says that fictions only and false hair / Become a verse? Is there in truth no beauty?"

Use the slash sparingly, if at all, to separate options: *pass/fail, producer/director.* Put no space around the slash. Avoid using expressions such as *he/she* and *his/her* and the awkward construction *and/or.*

Mechanics

22 Capitalization 79

23 Abbreviations, numbers, and italics 82

24 Spelling and the hyphen 86

22 Capitalization

In addition to the following guidelines, a good dictionary can tell you when to use capital letters.

22a Proper vs. common nouns

Proper nouns and words derived from them are capitalized; common nouns are not. Proper nouns name specific persons, places, and things. All other nouns are common nouns.

The following types of words are usually capitalized: names of deities, religions, religious followers, and sacred books; words of family relationships used as names; particular places; nationalities and their languages, races, and tribes; educational institutions, departments, and particular courses; government departments, organizations, and political parties; historical movements, periods, events, and documents; and trade names.

PROPER NOUNS	COMMON NOUNS
God (used as a name)	a god
Book of Common Prayer	a sacred book
Uncle Pedro	my uncle
Dad (used as a name)	my dad
Lake Superior	a lake
the Capital Center	a center for the arts
the South	a southern state
Wrigley Field	a baseball stadium
University of Wisconsin	a good university
Geology 101	a geology course
Veterans Administration	a federal agency
Phi Kappa Psi	a fraternity
the Democratic Party	a political party
the Enlightenment	the eighteenth century
the Great Depression	a recession
the Treaty of Versailles	a treaty
Advil	a painkiller

Months, holidays, and days of the week are capitalized: *May, Labor Day, Monday*. The seasons and numbers of the days of the month are not: *summer, the fifth of June*.

Names of school subjects are capitalized only if they are names of languages: *geology, history, English, French*.

Names of particular courses are capitalized: *Geology 101, Principles of Economics.*

The terms *Web* and *Internet* are typically capitalized, but related common nouns are not: *home page, search engine.* Usage varies widely, however, so check with your instructor about whether you should follow the guidelines for MLA, APA, or *Chicago* style (34a, 39a, or 44a, respectively).

NOTE: Do not capitalize common nouns to make them seem important: *Our company is currently hiring technical support staff* [not *Company, Technical Support Staff*].

22b Titles with proper names

Capitalize a title when used as part of a proper name but usually not when used alone.

> Prof. Margaret Burnes; Dr. Sinyee Sein; John Scott Williams Jr.; Anne Tilton, LLD

> District Attorney Mill was ruled out of order.

> The district attorney was elected for a two-year term.

Usage varies when the title of an important public figure is used alone: *The president* [or *President*] *vetoed the bill.*

22c Titles of works

In the text of a paper, major words should be capitalized in both titles and subtitles. Minor words—articles, prepositions, and coordinating conjunctions—are not capitalized unless they are the first or last word of a title or subtitle. (In APA style, capitalize all words of four or more letters in titles. See 39a.)

> *The Impossible Theater: A Manifesto*

> "Man in the Middle"

> "I Want to Hold Your Hand"

Titles of works are handled differently in the APA reference list. See "Preparing the list of references" in 39a.

22d First word of a sentence or quoted sentence

The first word of a sentence should be capitalized. Capitalize the first word of a quoted sentence but not a quoted phrase.

> Loveless writes, "If failing schools are ever to be turned around, much more must be learned about how schools age as institutions" (25).

> Russell Baker has written that sports are "the opiate of the masses" (46).

If a quoted sentence is interrupted by explanatory words, do not capitalize the first word after the interruption.

> "When we all think alike," he said, "no one is thinking."

When a sentence appears within parentheses, capitalize the first word unless the parentheses appear within another sentence.

> Early detection of breast cancer increases survival rates. (See table 2.)

> Early detection of breast cancer increases survival rates (see table 2).

22e First word following a colon

Capitalize the first word after a colon if it begins an independent clause.

> I came to a startling conclusion: The house must be haunted.

NOTE: Preferences vary among academic disciplines. See 34a, 39a, and 44a, respectively.

22f Abbreviations

Capitalize abbreviations for departments and agencies of government, other organizations, and corporations; capitalize trade names and the call letters of radio and television stations.

> EPA, FBI, DKNY, IBM, WERS, KNBC-TV

23 Abbreviations, numbers, and italics

23a Abbreviations

Use abbreviations only when they are clearly appropriate.

Appropriate abbreviations Use standard abbreviations for titles immediately before and after proper names.

TITLES BEFORE PROPER NAMES	TITLES AFTER PROPER NAMES
Ms. Nancy Linehan	Thomas Hines Jr.
Dr. Margaret Simmons	Anita Lor, PhD
Rev. John Stone	Robert Simkowski, MD
St. Joan of Arc	William Lyons, MA
Prof. James Russo	Polly Stern, DDS

Do not abbreviate a title if it is not used with a proper name: *My history professor* [not *prof.*] *was an expert on naval warfare.*

Familiar abbreviations for the names of organizations, corporations, and countries are also acceptable: *CIA, FBI, NAACP, EPA, YMCA, NBC, USA.*

When using an unfamiliar abbreviation (such as NAB for National Association of Broadcasters) throughout a paper, write the full name followed by the abbreviation in parentheses at the first mention of the name. Then use just the abbreviation in the rest of the paper.

Other commonly accepted abbreviations include *BC, AD, a.m., p.m., No.,* and *$.* The abbreviation *BC* ("before Christ") follows a date, and *AD* ("*anno Domini*") precedes a date. Acceptable alternatives are *BCE* ("before the common era") and *CE* ("common era").

40 BC (or 40 BCE)	4:00 a.m. (or AM)	No. 12 (or no. 12)
AD 44 (or 44 CE)	6:00 p.m. (or PM)	$150

Inappropriate abbreviations In formal writing, abbreviations for the following are not commonly accepted.

DAYS OF THE WEEK Monday (*not* Mon.)

HOLIDAYS Christmas (*not* Xmas)

MONTHS January, February (*not* Jan., Feb.)

COURSES OF STUDY   political science (*not* poli. sci.)

STATES AND COUNTRIES   Florida (*not* FL or Fla.)

Use abbreviations for units of measurement when they are preceded by numerals, as in most scientific writing (*13 cm, 5 ft*). Do not abbreviate them when they are used alone (*The results were measured in millimeters*) or when they appear with spelled-out numbers (*The plant grew five inches in one week*). (See also 23b.)

Although Latin abbreviations are appropriate in footnotes and bibliographies and in informal writing, use the appropriate English phrases in formal writing.

e.g. (Latin *exempli gratia*, "for example")

et al. (Latin *et alii*, "and others")

etc. (Latin *et cetera*, "and so forth")

i.e. (Latin *id est*, "that is")

N.B. (Latin *nota bene*, "note well")

23b Numbers

Spell out numbers of one or two words. Use numerals for numbers that require more than two words to spell out.

▶ **The 1980 eruption of Mount St. Helens blasted**
  sixteen   230
  ash ~~16~~ miles into the sky and devastated ~~two~~
          ∧   ∧
  ~~hundred thirty~~ square miles of land.

If a sentence begins with a number, spell out the number or rewrite the sentence.

  One hundred fifty
▶ **~~150~~ children in our program need expensive**
  ∧
  dental treatment.

Academic styles vary for handling numbers in the text of a paper. In the humanities, MLA and *Chicago* spell out numbers below 101 and large round numbers (*forty million*); they use numerals for specific numbers above one hundred (*234*). In the social sciences and the sciences, APA and CSE spell out the numbers one through nine and use numerals for all other numbers.

Generally, numerals are acceptable for the following.

DATES July 4, 1776; 56 BC; AD 30

ADDRESSES 77 Latches Lane, 519 West 42nd Street

PERCENTAGES 55 percent (or 55%)

FRACTIONS, DECIMALS ⁷/₈, 0.047

SCORES 7 to 3, 21–18

STATISTICS average age 37

SURVEYS 4 out of 5

EXACT AMOUNTS OF MONEY $105.37

DIVISIONS OF BOOKS volume 3, chapter 4, page 189

DIVISIONS OF PLAYS act 3, scene 3 (or act III, scene iii)

TIME OF DAY 4:00 p.m., 1:30 a.m.

23c Italics

This section describes conventional uses for italics: for titles of works; names of ships, aircraft, and spacecraft; foreign words; and words as words. (If your instructor prefers underlining, simply substitute underlining for italics in the examples in this section.)

Titles of works Titles of the following types of works are italicized.

TITLES OF BOOKS *The Known World, The Round House*

MAGAZINES *Time, Scientific American, Slate*

NEWSPAPERS the *Baltimore Sun,* the *Orlando Sentinel*

PAMPHLETS *Common Sense, Facts about Marijuana*

LONG POEMS *The Waste Land, Paradise Lost*

PLAYS *King Lear, Wicked*

FILMS *Casablanca, Argo*

TELEVISION PROGRAMS *American Idol, Frontline*

RADIO PROGRAMS *All Things Considered*

MUSICAL COMPOSITIONS *Porgy and Bess*

CHOREOGRAPHIC WORKS *Brief Fling*

WORKS OF VISUAL ART *American Gothic*

VIDEO GAMES   *Dragon Age, Call of Duty*

DATABASES [MLA]   *ProQuest*

WEB SITES [MLA]   *Salon, Google*

COMPUTER SOFTWARE OR APP [MLA]   *Photoshop, Instagram*

The titles of other works, such as short stories, essays, songs, and short poems, are enclosed in quotation marks. (See 20b.)

NOTE: Do not use italics when referring to the Bible; the titles of books in the Bible (Genesis, not *Genesis*); the titles of legal documents (the Constitution, not the *Constitution*); or the titles of your own papers.

Names of ships, aircraft, spacecraft   Italicize names of specific ships, aircraft, and spacecraft.

Queen Mary 2, Endeavour, Wright Flyer

Foreign words   Italicize foreign words used in an English sentence.

Caroline's *joie de vivre* should be a model for all of us.

EXCEPTION: Do not italicize foreign words that have become part of the English language—"laissez-faire," "fait accompli," "modus operandi," and "per diem," for example.

Words as words etc.   Italicize words used as words, letters mentioned as letters, and numbers mentioned as numbers.

Tomás assured us that the chemicals could probably be safely mixed, but his *probably* stuck in our minds.

Some toddlers have trouble pronouncing the letters *f* and *s.*

A big *3* was painted on the stage door.

NOTE: Quotation marks may be used instead of italics to set off words mentioned as words. (See 20c.)

Inappropriate italics   Italicizing to emphasize words or ideas is often ineffective and should be used sparingly.

24 Spelling and the hyphen

24a Spelling

A word processing program equipped with a spell checker is a useful tool, but be aware of its limitations. A spell checker will not tell you how to spell words not listed in its dictionary; nor will it help you catch words commonly confused, such as *accept* and *except*, or common typographical errors, such as *own* for *won*. You will still need to proofread, and for some words you may need to turn to the dictionary.

NOTE: To check for correct use of commonly confused words (*accept* and *except*, *its* and *it's*, and so on), consult the glossary of usage in the appendixes.

Major spelling rules If you need to improve your spelling, review the following rules and exceptions.

1. In general, use *i* before *e* except after *c* and except when sounded like "ay," as in *neighbor* and *weigh*.

I BEFORE *E*	relieve, believe, sieve, niece, fierce, frieze
E BEFORE *I*	receive, deceive, sleigh, freight, eight
EXCEPTIONS	seize, either, weird, height, foreign, leisure

2. Generally, drop a final silent *-e* when adding a suffix that begins with a vowel. Keep the final *-e* if the suffix begins with a consonant.

| desire, desiring | achieve, achievement |
| remove, removable | care, careful |

Words such as *changeable*, *judgment*, *argument*, and *truly* are exceptions.

3. When adding *-s* or *-ed* to words ending in *-y*, ordinarily change *-y* to *-i* when the *-y* is preceded by a consonant but not when it is preceded by a vowel.

| comedy, comedies | monkey, monkeys |
| dry, dried | play, played |

With proper names ending in *-y*, however, do not change the *-y* to *-i* even if it is preceded by a consonant: *the Dougherty family, the Doughertys.*

4. If a final consonant is preceded by a single vowel and the consonant ends a one-syllable word or a stressed syllable, double the consonant when adding a suffix beginning with a vowel.

bet, betting	occur, occurrence
commit, committed	

5. Add *-s* to form the plural of most nouns; add *-es* to singular nouns ending in *-s*, *-sh*, *-ch*, and *-x*.

table, tables	church, churches
paper, papers	dish, dishes
agenda, agendas	fox, foxes

Ordinarily add *-s* to nouns ending in *-o* when the *-o* is preceded by a vowel. Add *-es* when the *-o* is preceded by a consonant.

radio, radios	hero, heroes
video, videos	tomato, tomatoes

To form the plural of a hyphenated compound word, add the *-s* to the chief word even if it does not appear at the end.

mother-in-law, mothers-in-law

NOTE: English words derived from other languages such as Latin, Greek, or French sometimes form the plural as they would in their original language.

medium, media	chateau, chateaux
criterion, criteria	

Spelling variations   Following is a list of some common words spelled differently in American and British English. Consult a dictionary for others.

AMERICAN	BRITISH
canceled, traveled	cancelled, travelled
color, humor	colour, humour
judgment	judgement

AMERICAN	BRITISH
check	cheque
realize, apologize	realise, apologise
defense	defence
anemia, anesthetic	anaemia, anaesthetic
theater, center	theatre, centre
fetus	foetus
mold, smolder	mould, smoulder
civilization	civilisation
connection, inflection	connexion, inflexion

24b The hyphen

In addition to the following guidelines, a dictionary will help you make decisions about hyphenation.

Compound words   The dictionary will tell you whether to treat a compound word as a hyphenated compound (*water-repellent*), as one word (*waterproof*), or as two words (*water table*). If the compound word is not in the dictionary, treat it as two words.

▶   **The prosecutor did not cross-examine any witnesses.**

▶   **Imogen kept her sketches in a small note book.**

▶   **Alice walked through the looking-glass.**

Words functioning together as an adjective   When two or more words function together as an adjective before a noun, connect them with a hyphen. Generally, do not use a hyphen when such compounds follow the noun.

▶   **Pat Hobbs is not yet a well-known candidate.**

▶   **After our television campaign, Pat Hobbs will be well known.**

Do not use a hyphen to connect -*ly* adverbs to the words they modify.

▶   **A slowly moving truck tied up traffic.**

NOTE: In a series of hyphenated adjectives modifying the same noun, hyphens are suspended: *Do you prefer first-, second-, or third-class tickets?*

Conventional uses Hyphenate the written form of fractions and of compound numbers from twenty-one to ninety-nine. Also use the hyphen with the prefixes *all-*, *ex-*, and *self-* and with the suffix *-elect*.

▶ **One-fourth of my income goes for rent.**
   ^

▶ **The charity is funding more self-help projects.**
                                              ^

Hyphenation at ends of lines Set your word processing program to not hyphenate a word at the end of a line of text. This setting ensures that only words that already contain a hyphen may be broken at the end of a line.

E-mail addresses, URLs, and other electronic addresses need special attention when they occur at the end of a line of text. Do not insert a hyphen to divide electronic addresses. Instead, break an e-mail address after the @ symbol or before a period. It is common practice to break a URL before most marks of punctuation. (For specific documentation styles, see 34a, 39a, 44a, and 46b.)

Research

25 Posing a research question 91

26 Finding appropriate sources 92

27 Evaluating sources 94

28 Managing information; avoiding plagiarism 102

College research assignments ask you to pose questions worth exploring, read widely in search of possible answers, interpret what you read, draw reasoned conclusions, and support those conclusions with valid and well-documented evidence. They ask you to enter a conversation by engaging with the ideas of other writers and thinkers who have explored your topic.

This section and the color-coded sections that follow—MLA (orange), APA (turquoise), *Chicago* (green), and CSE (purple)—will help you write your paper and properly document your sources in the style your instructor requires.

25 Posing a research question

Working within the guidelines of your assignment, pose a few preliminary questions that seem worth researching—questions that you want to explore, that you feel would engage your audience, and about which there is a substantial debate. As you formulate possible questions, choose those that are focused (not too broad), challenging (not just factual), and grounded (not too speculative) as entry points in a research conversation.

25a Choosing a focused question

If your initial question is too broad, given the length of the paper you plan to write, look for ways to restrict your focus. Here, for example, is how two students refined their initial questions.

TOO BROAD	FOCUSED
What are the benefits of stricter auto emissions standards?	How will stricter auto emissions standards create new, more competitive auto industry jobs?
What causes depression?	How has the widespread use of antidepressant drugs affected teenage suicide rates?

25b Choosing a challenging question

Your research paper will be more interesting to both you and your audience if you base it on an intellectually challenging line of inquiry. Try to draft questions that provoke thought or engage readers in a debate.

TOO FACTUAL	CHALLENGING
Is autism on the rise?	Why is autism so difficult to treat?
Where is wind energy being used?	What makes wind farms economically viable?

You may need to address a factual question in the course of answering a more challenging one, but it would be unproductive to use the factual question as the focus for the entire paper.

25c Choosing a grounded question

Finally, you will want to make sure that your research question is grounded, not too speculative. Although speculative questions—such as those that address morality or beliefs—are worth asking in a research paper, they are unsuitable central questions. For most college courses, the central argument of a research paper should be grounded in evidence, not beliefs.

TOO SPECULATIVE	GROUNDED
Is it wrong to share pornographic personal photos by cell phone?	What role should the US government play in regulating mobile content?
Do scientists have the right to experiment on animals?	How have technological breakthroughs made medical experiments on animals increasingly unnecessary?

26 Finding appropriate sources

Before you begin looking for sources, think about what kinds of sources will be useful for your paper. For example, if your research question addresses a historical issue, you might focus on scholarly articles and primary sources, such as speeches. If your question addresses a current political issue, you might turn to magazine and newspaper articles.

Considering the kinds of sources you need will help you develop a research strategy—a systematic plan for tracking down sources. To create an appropriate strategy for your research question, you might want to consult a reference librarian and look at your library's Web site for an overview of available resources. Keep in mind that no single search strategy works for every topic. Effective researchers often use a combination of library databases and the Web when looking for sources.

26a Using the library

The Web site hosted by your college library links to databases and other references. Many libraries offer one-on-one help from research librarians, who can tell you what resources are available and show you ways to focus your search so that you don't spend a lot of time puzzling over sources that turn out to be unsuitable for your paper.

If your library database searches turn up too many potential sources, filter out unwanted results by adding additional search terms, limiting a search to recent publications, or selecting an option to look at only one type of source, such as peer-reviewed articles.

Your library's catalog can help you find books, which often provide more context for ideas than scholarly articles can offer. You may find that a single chapter or even a few pages are just what you need to understand issues surrounding a problem or debate. Unless your topic warrants the use of older sources, stick to books with recent publication dates. After you've identified a promising book on the library shelves, looking through the books on nearby shelves can help you find additional relevant sources.

26b Using the Web

When conducting searches, use terms that are as specific as possible and enclose search phrases in quotation marks. You can refine your search by domain; for example, *autism site:.gov* will search for information about autism on government Web sites. Many search engines offer advanced options for refining your search with filters for phrases that should or should not appear, date restrictions, and so on.

If you need current information, online news outlets such as the *New York Times* and the BBC, think tanks, government agencies, and advocacy groups may provide appropriate sources. Information or links on one site can lead you to other sites or can suggest other search terms.

As you examine a site, look for "about" links to learn about the site's author or sponsoring agency. Avoid sites that provide no explanation of who the authors are or why the site was created. For more on evaluating Web sites, see pages 100–01.

26c Using bibliographies and citations

Scholarly books and articles list the works the author has cited, usually at the end. These lists are useful shortcuts to additional reliable sources on your topic. Even popular sources such as news articles, videos, and interviews may refer to additional relevant sources that may be worth tracking down.

27 Evaluating sources

You can often locate dozens or even hundreds of potential sources for your topic—far more than you will have time to read. Your challenge will be to determine what kinds of sources you need, evaluate your options, and select a reasonable number of quality sources.

Whether you're just beginning to look for sources or you've already selected some, keeping the following criteria in mind can help you make sure that those sources are worth your time and are suitable for your paper.

Relevance   Is your source clearly related to your topic and your argument? Make sure your readers will understand *why* you've included the source in your paper. For example, you may disagree with the author's position, but citing and refuting the author's ideas should help you clarify or support your own position.

Currency   Check the publication date. How recent is the source? If you're writing about a contemporary issue that changes rapidly, such as social media, avoid sources with outdated information. If your paper is about something like technological innovations of World War I, a mix of older and newer sources may be appropriate.

Credibility   Where does the source come from? Who created it? Check for the author's credentials—what education or experience makes the author qualified to discuss your topic? If the source is authored by an organization rather than an individual, what research has the organization done to support its claims?

Length and depth   Check the word or page count. If the source is very short, it may not cover the topic thoroughly enough to be useful. If you find an abstract (a citation and summary of a text) that looks promising, use the citation to find the complete text. In most cases, abstracts themselves are not suitable sources.

Evaluate sources throughout your research and writing process. Read them with an open mind and a critical eye.

27a Selecting sources

Determining how sources contribute to your writing
How you plan to use sources affects how you evaluate them. Sources can have various functions in a paper. You can use them to

- provide background information or context for your topic
- explain terms or concepts that your readers might not understand
- provide evidence for your argument
- lend authority to your argument
- offer counterevidence and alternative interpretations your argument should address

For examples of how student writers use sources for a variety of purposes, see 31, 37, and 42.

Common features of a scholarly source

1   Formal presentation with abstract and research methods
2   Includes review of previous research studies
3   Reports original research
4   Includes references
5   Multiple authors with academic credentials

FIRST PAGE OF ARTICLE

Cyberbullying: Using Virtual Scenarios to Educate and Raise Awareness

Vivian H. Wright, Joy J. Burnham, Christopher T. Inman, and Heather N. Ogorchock   **5**

1

Abstract

This study examined cyberbullying in three distinct phases to facilitate a multifaceted understanding of cyberbullying. The phases included (a) a quantitative survey, (b) a qualitative focus group, and (c) development of educational scenarios/simulations (within the Second Life virtual environment). Phase III was based on adolescent feedback about cyberbullying from Phases I and II of this study. In all three phases, adolescent reactions to cyberbullying were examined and reported to raise awareness and to educate others about cyberbullying. Results from scenario development indicate that simulations created in a virtual environment are engaging and have the potential to be powerful tools in helping schools address problems such as cyberbullying education and prevention. (Keywords: cyberbullying, virtual worlds, Second Life, teacher education, counselor education)

Introduction

Cyberbullying has gained attention and recognition in recent years (Beale & Hall, 2007; Carney, 2008; Casey-Canon, Hayward, & Gowen, 2001; Kowalski & Limber, 2007; Li, 2007; Shariff, 2005). The increased interest and awareness of cyberbullying relates to such factors as the national media attention after several publicized cyberbullying tragedies (Maag, 2007; Stelter, 2008; Zifcak, 2006), the attenuation of communication boundaries because of ever-advancing technology use among youth. Now, with the convenience of technology and the easy access and popularity of the Internet among youth, presently there remains a crisis related to the prevalence of cyberbullying and its possible effects on adolescents. Because cyberbullying has infiltrated communication systems (i.e., home, school, and the community), "now more than ever before, school professionals" (Li, 2007, p. 1778), and mental health providers must not only be made aware of cyberbullying and its consequences, but must also have access to ways to deal with this growing concern.

Two years ago, cyberbullying was considered to be a "new territory" for exploration (Li, 2007, p. 1778) because there was limited information about bullying through "electronic means" (Li, p. 1780). In contrast, today studies on cyberbullying, including some descriptions of the newest cyberbullying incidences (Maag, 2007; Stelter, 2008; Zifcak, 2006), are becoming more prevalent (Beale & Hall, 2007; Carney, 2008; Kowalski & Limber, 2007; Li, 2007). At this time, there is a need to raise awareness about the effects of cyberbullying and to create educational opportunities to serve multiple audiences (i.e., teachers, teacher educators, school administrators, school counselors, mental health professionals, students, parents) in the quest to identify and hopefully prevent cyberbullying in the future. Consequently, to facilitate a multifaceted understanding of

cyberbullying, this study sought to examine cyberbullying through three phases: (a) a quantitative survey, (b) a qualitative focus group, and (c) development of the educational scenarios/simulations (i.e., using virtual world avatars similar to those used in Linden Lab's (1993) Second Life (SL; http://secondlife.com) based on adolescent feedback from Phases I and II of this study. Adolescent reactions to cyberbullying in all three phases of this study were examined and reported with two aims in mind: (a) to raise awareness of cyberbullying, and (b) to educate others about cyberbullying.

Defining Cyberbullying

Cyberbullying has been described as a traumatic experience that can lead to physical, cognitive, emotional, and social consequences (Carney, 2008; Casey-Canon et al., 2001; Patchin & Hinduja, 2006). Cyberbullying has been defined as "bullying through the e-mail, instant messaging, in a chat room, on a website, or through digital messages or images sent to a cell phone" (Kowalski & Limber, 2007, p. 822). There are numerous methods to engage in cyberbullying, including e-mail, instant messaging, online gaming, chat rooms, and text messaging (Beale & Hall, 2007; Li, 2007). In addition, cyberbullying appears in different forms than traditional bullying. For example, Beale and Hall (2007), Mason (2007), and Willard (2008) found that at least seven different types of cyberbullying exist, including:

- • [information]
- • Exclusion: excluding someone purposefully

Research suggests that cyberbullying has distinct gender and age differences. According to the literature, girls are more likely to be online and to cyberbully (Beale & Hall, 2007; Kowalski & Limber, 2007; Li, 2006, 2007). This finding is "opposite of what happens off-line," where boys are more likely to bully than girls (Beale & Hall, p. 8). Age also appears to be a factor in cyberbullying. Cyberbullying increases in the elementary years, peaks during the middle school years, and declines in the high school years (Beale & Hall). Based on the literature, cyberbullying is a growing concern among middle school-aged children (Beale & Hall; Hinduja & Patchin, 2008; Kowalski & Limber, 2007; Li, 2007; Pellegrini & Bartini, 2000; Smith, Mahdavi, Carvalho, & Tippett, 2006; Williams & Guerra, 2007). Of the middle school grades, 6th grade students are usually the

2   Research suggests that cyberbullying has distinct gender and age differences. According to the literature, girls are more likely to be online and to cyberbully (Beale & Hall, 2007; Kowalski & Limber, 2007; Li, 2006, 2007). This finding is "opposite of what happens off-line," where boys are

Volume 26/ Number 1 Fall 2009   Journal of Computing in Teacher Education   35

Copyright © 2009 ISTE (International Society for Technology in Education), 800.336.5191 (U.S. & Canada) or 541.302.3777 (Int'l), iste@iste.org, www.iste.org

EXCERPTS FROM OTHER PAGES

3

Table 2: Percentage of Students Who Experienced Cyberbullying through Various Methods

	E-mail	Facebook	MySpace	Cell Phone	Online Video	Chat Rooms
Victim	35.3%	11.8%	52.9%	50%	14.7%	11.8%
Bully	17.6%	0%	70.6%	47.1%	11.8%	5.9%

4
References

Bainbridge, W. S. (2007, July). The scientific research potential of virtual worlds. *Science, 317,* 472–476.

Beale, A., & Hall, K. (2007, September/October). Cyberbullying: What

5   *Vivian H. Wright is an associate professor of instructional technology at the Uni[versity] of Alabama. In addition to teaching in the graduate program, Dr. Wright works with teacher educators on innovative ways to infuse technology in the curriculu[m].*

Common features of a popular source

1 Eye-catching title
2 Written by a staff reporter, not an expert
3 Presents anecdotes about the topic
4 Sources are named, but no formal works cited list appears
5 Presents a summary of research but no original research

ONLINE ARTICLE

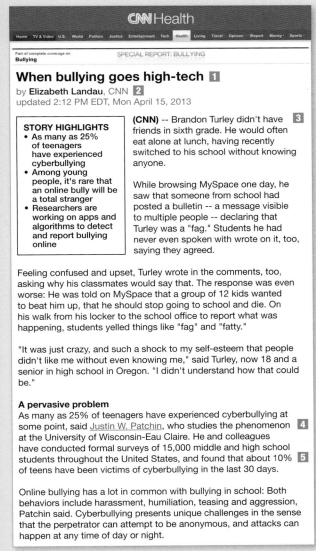

CNN Health

Home TV & Video U.S. World Politics Justice Entertainment Tech Health Living Travel Opinion iReport Money · Sports ·

Part of complete coverage on
Bullying   SPECIAL REPORT: BULLYING

When bullying goes high-tech 1

by **Elizabeth Landau**, CNN 2
updated 2:12 PM EDT, Mon April 15, 2013

STORY HIGHLIGHTS
- As many as 25% of teenagers have experienced cyberbullying
- Among young people, it's rare that an online bully will be a total stranger
- Researchers are working on apps and algorithms to detect and report bullying online

(CNN) -- Brandon Turley didn't have 3 friends in sixth grade. He would often eat alone at lunch, having recently switched to his school without knowing anyone.

While browsing MySpace one day, he saw that someone from school had posted a bulletin -- a message visible to multiple people -- declaring that Turley was a "fag." Students he had never even spoken with wrote on it, too, saying they agreed.

Feeling confused and upset, Turley wrote in the comments, too, asking why his classmates would say that. The response was even worse: He was told on MySpace that a group of 12 kids wanted to beat him up, that he should stop going to school and die. On his walk from his locker to the school office to report what was happening, students yelled things like "fag" and "fatty."

"It was just crazy, and such a shock to my self-esteem that people didn't like me without even knowing me," said Turley, now 18 and a senior in high school in Oregon. "I didn't understand how that could be."

A pervasive problem
As many as 25% of teenagers have experienced cyberbullying at some point, said Justin W. Patchin, who studies the phenomenon 4 at the University of Wisconsin-Eau Claire. He and colleagues have conducted formal surveys of 15,000 middle and high school students throughout the United States, and found that about 10% 5 of teens have been victims of cyberbullying in the last 30 days.

Online bullying has a lot in common with bullying in school: Both behaviors include harassment, humiliation, teasing and aggression, Patchin said. Cyberbullying presents unique challenges in the sense that the perpetrator can attempt to be anonymous, and attacks can happen at any time of day or night.

Determining if a source is scholarly

Many college assignments require you to use scholarly sources. Written by experts for a knowledgeable audience, these sources often go into more depth than books and articles written for a general audience. To determine if a source is scholarly, look for the following:

- Formal language and presentation
- Authors who are academics or scientists
- Footnotes or a bibliography documenting the works cited by the author in the source
- Original research and interpretation (rather than a summary of other people's work)
- Quotations from and analysis of primary sources (in the humanities)
- A description of research methods or a review of related research (in the sciences or social sciences)

See pages 96–97 for a sample scholarly source and popular source.

Evaluating search results   This section explains how to scan through search results for the most useful and reliable sources.

Databases   Most databases provide at least the following information to help you decide if a source is relevant, current, scholarly enough, and a suitable length.

Title and brief description (How relevant?)

Date (How current?)

Name of publication in which the source appears (How scholarly?)

Length (How extensive in coverage?)

Library catalogs   The title and date of publication of sources listed in catalogs are often your first clues as to whether a source is worth consulting. If a title looks interesting, you can click on it for further information about the subject matter and length.

Web search engines   Reliable and unreliable sources live side-by-side online. Look for the following clues about the probable relevance, currency, and reliability of a Web site.

Title, keywords, and lead-in text (How relevant?)

A date (How current?)

An indication of the site's sponsor or purpose (How reliable?)

The URL, especially the domain name extension: for example, .com, .edu, .gov, or .org (How relevant? How reliable?)

27b Reading with an open mind and a critical eye

As you begin reading the sources you have chosen, keep an open mind. Do not let your personal beliefs prevent you from listening to new ideas and opposing viewpoints. Be curious about the wide range of positions in the research conversation you are entering. Your research question—not a snap judgment about the question—should guide your reading.

Evaluating all sources

Checking for signs of bias

- Does the author or publisher endorse political or religious views that could affect objectivity?
- Is the author or publisher associated with a special-interest group, such as Greenpeace or the National Rifle Association, that might present a narrow view of an issue?
- Does the author present opposing views and treat them fairly?
- Does the author's language show signs of bias?

Assessing an argument

- What is the author's central claim or thesis?
- How does the author support this claim—with relevant and sufficient evidence or with anecdotes or emotional examples?
- Are statistics accurate and used fairly? Does the author explain where the statistics come from?
- Are any of the author's assumptions questionable?
- Does the author consider opposing arguments and refute them persuasively?

When you read critically, you are not necessarily judging an author's work harshly; you are simply examining its assumptions, assessing its evidence, and weighing its conclusions. Reading critically means understanding what the source says, determining whether the author's claims are valid or flawed, and figuring out how the source helps you make your argument. For a checklist on evaluating sources, see page 99.

27c Assessing Web sources with special care

Sources found on the Web can provide valuable information, but verifying their credibility may take time. Even sites that appear to be professional and fair-minded may contain questionable information. Before using a Web source in your paper, make sure you know who created the material and for what purpose. Sites with reliable information can stand up to scrutiny.

Even if you decide a particular Web source isn't credible, current, or relevant enough for your paper, it may contain links to sources that might be more suitable. For example, many instructors do not consider wikis, such as *Wikipedia*, to be appropriate sources for college research. Authorship on many wikis is not limited to experts—entries may be written or changed by anyone—and information is often general rather than critical or in-depth. Most wiki entries include a references section, however, that can point you to books, articles, and Web sites that may contain valuable information and ideas from credible sources.

Evaluating Web sources
Authorship

- Is there an author? You may need to do some clicking and scrolling to find the author's name. Check the home page or an "about this site" link.

- Can you tell whether an author is knowledgeable and credible? If the author's qualifications aren't listed on the site, look for links to the author's home page, which may provide evidence of his or her expertise.

Sponsorship

- Who, if anyone, sponsors the site? The sponsor of a site is often named and described on the home page.
- What does the URL tell you? The domain name extension often indicates the type of group hosting the site: commercial (.com), educational (.edu), nonprofit (.org), governmental (.gov), military (.mil), or network (.net). URLs may also indicate a country of origin: .uk (United Kingdom) or .jp (Japan), for instance.

Purpose and audience

- Why was the site created: To argue a position? To sell a product? To inform readers?
- Who is the site's intended audience?

Currency

- How current is the site? Check for the date of publication or the latest update.
- How current are the site's links? If many of the links to other sites no longer work, the site may be too dated for your purposes.

27d Annotating bibliography entries

At some point during your research process, or as a separate assignment, your instructor may ask you to write an annotated bibliography entry for one or more sources. When annotating a bibliography entry, you typically provide citation information for the source and, in your own words, a summary of its contents. Your instructor may ask that you evaluate its relevance and determine how the source relates to your argument and to your other sources. By noting the author's background or perspective, you can also evaluate the source for bias.

hackerhandbooks.com/pocket

e Research > Sample student writing
  > Orlov, "Online Monitoring: A Threat to Employee Privacy in the Wired Workplace: An Annotated Bibliography" (annotated bibliography; MLA)

e Research > Sample student writing
  > Niemeyer, "Keynesian Policy: Implications for the Current U.S. Economic Crisis" (annotated bibliography; APA)

SAMPLE ANNOTATED BIBLIOGRAPHY ENTRY (MLA STYLE)

Resnik, David. "Trans Fat Bans and Human Freedom." *American Journal of Bioethics* 10.3 (2010): 27-32. *Academic Search Premier.* Web. 17 Apr. 2013.

> In this scholarly article, bioethicist David Resnik argues **1** that bans on unhealthy foods threaten our personal freedom. He claims that researchers don't have enough evidence to **2** know whether banning trans fats will save lives or money; all we know is that such bans restrict dietary choices. Resnik explains why most Americans oppose food restrictions, noting our multiethnic and regional food traditions as well as our resistance to government limitations on personal freedoms. He acknowledges that few people would miss eating trans **3** fats, but he fears that bans on such substances could lead to widespread restrictions on red meat, sugary sodas, and other foods known to have harmful effects. Resnik offers a well-reasoned argument, but he goes too far by insisting that all proposed food restrictions will do more harm than good. This article contributes important perspectives on American **4** resistance to government intervention in food choice and counters arguments in other sources that support the idea of food legislation to advance public health.

1 Summarize the source using present tense.
2 Annotations should be three to seven sentences long.
3 Evaluate the source for bias and relevance.
4 Evaluate the source for its contribution to the research project.

28 Managing information; avoiding plagiarism

Whether you decide to keep records on paper or on your computer—or both—you will need methods for managing information: maintaining a working bibliography, keeping track of source materials, and taking notes without plagiarizing your sources. (For more on avoiding plagiarism, see 30 for MLA style, 36 for APA style, and 41 for *Chicago* style.)

28a Maintaining a working bibliography

Keep a record of each source you consider using. This record, called a *working bibliography*, will help you keep track of any sources you might use, so that you can refer to them throughout your research and writing process and cite them accurately if you use them in your final paper. The format for citations in your working bibliography depends on the documentation style you are using. (For MLA style, see 33b; for APA style, see 38b; for *Chicago* style, see 43c; for CSE style, see 45c.)

28b Keeping track of source materials

Save a copy of each potential source as you conduct your research. Many database services allow you to e-mail, save, or print citations or full texts, and you can download, copy, or take screen shots of information from the Web.

Working with photocopies, printouts, or electronic files—as opposed to relying on memory or notes without context—lets you annotate the source as you read. You also reduce the chances of unintentional plagiarism, since you will be able to compare your use of a source with the actual source, not just with your notes.

NOTE: Keep print or electronic copies of Web sources, which may change or become inaccessible over time. Include the site's URL and your date of access with your copy.

28c Taking notes responsibly: avoiding unintentional plagiarism

When you take notes, be very careful to put quotation marks around any borrowed words and phrases. Even if you half-copy the author's sentences—either by mixing the author's phrases with your own without using quotation marks or by plugging your synonyms into the author's sentence structure—you are committing plagiarism, a serious academic offense.

Summarizing and paraphrasing ideas and quoting exact language are three ways of taking notes. Be sure to include exact page references for all three types of notes, since you will need the page numbers later if you use the information in your paper. (See the chart on pages 104–5 for advice about avoiding plagiarism.)

Integrating and citing sources to avoid plagiarism

Source text

Our language is constantly changing. Like the Mississippi, it keeps forging new channels and abandoning old ones, picking up debris, depositing unwanted silt, and frequently bursting its banks. In every generation there are people who deplore changes in the language and many who wish to stop its flow. But if our language stopped changing it would mean that American society had ceased to be dynamic, innovative, pulsing with life — that the great river had frozen up.

— Robert MacNeil and William Cran, *Do You Speak American?*, p. 1

NOTE: The examples in this chart follow MLA style (see 33). For information on APA, *Chicago*, and CSE styles, see 38, 43, and 45, respectively.

If you are using an exact sentence from a source, with no changes . . .	→	. . . put quotation marks around the sentence. Use a signal phrase and include a page number in parentheses.
		MacNeil and Cran write, "Our language is constantly changing" (1).
If you are using a few exact words from the source but not an entire sentence . . .	→	. . . put quotation marks around the exact words that you have used from the source. Use a signal phrase and include a page number in parentheses.
		Some people, according to MacNeil and Cran, "deplore changes in the language" (1).
If you are using near-exact words from the source but changing some word forms (*I* to *she*, *walk* to *walked*) or adding words to clarify and make the quotation flow with your own text . . .	→	. . . put quotation marks around the quoted words and put brackets around the changes you have introduced. Include a signal phrase and follow the quotation with the page number in parentheses.
		MacNeil and Cran compare the English language to the Mississippi River, which "forg[es] new channels and abandon[s] old ones" (1).
		MacNeil and Cran write, "In every generation there are people who deplore changes in the [English] language and many who wish to stop its flow" (1).

| If you are para-phrasing or summarizing the source, using the author's ideas but not any of the author's exact words... | → | ...introduce the ideas with a signal phrase and put the page number at the end of your sentence. Do not use quotation marks. (See 30, 36, and 41.)

MacNeil and Cran argue that changes in the English language are natural and that they represent cultural progress (1). |
| If you have used the source's sentence structure but substituted a few synonyms for the author's words... | → | STOP! This is a form of plagiarism even if you use a signal phrase and a page number. Change your sentence by using one of the techniques given in this chart or in 31, 37, or 42.

PLAGIARIZED
MacNeil and Cran claim that, like a river, English creates new waterways and discards old ones.

INTEGRATED AND CITED CORRECTLY
MacNeil and Cran claim, "Like the Mississippi, [English] keeps forging new channels and abandoning old ones" (1). |

NOTE: Be especially careful when using copy and paste functions in electronic files. Some researchers unintentionally plagiarize their sources because they lose track of which words came from sources and which are their own. Put quotation marks around any source text that you copy during your research and include a note about where it came from.

MLA Papers

29 Supporting a thesis 107

30 Avoiding plagiarism 110

31 Integrating sources 113

32 Integrating literary quotations 121

33 MLA documentation style 124

Directory to MLA in-text citation models 125

Directory to MLA works cited models 134

34 MLA manuscript format 167

SAMPLE PAGES 170

Most English and some humanities instructors will ask you to document your sources with the Modern Language Association (MLA) system of citations described in section 33. When writing an MLA paper based on sources, you face three main challenges: (1) supporting a thesis, (2) citing your sources and avoiding plagiarism, and (3) integrating quotations and other source material.

29 Supporting a thesis

Most research assignments ask you to form a thesis, or main idea, and to support that thesis with well-organized evidence.

29a Forming a working thesis

Once you have read a variety of sources and considered your issue from different perspectives, you are ready to form a working thesis—a one-sentence (or occasionally a two-sentence) statement of your central idea. The thesis expresses your informed, reasoned judgment, not your opinion. Usually your thesis will appear at the end of the first paragraph (see p. 170).

As you learn more about your subject, your ideas may change, and your working thesis will evolve, too. You can revise your working thesis as you draft.

In your research paper, your thesis will answer the central question that you pose, as in the following examples.

PUBLIC POLICY QUESTION

Should the government enact laws to regulate healthy eating choices?

POSSIBLE THESIS

Government should regulate healthy eating choices because of the rise of chronic diseases.

LITERATURE QUESTION

What does Stephen Crane's short story "The Open Boat" reveal about the relationship between humans and nature?

POSSIBLE THESIS

In Stephen Crane's gripping tale "The Open Boat," four men lost at sea discover not only that nature is indifferent to their fate but also that their own particular talents make little difference as they struggle for survival.

MEDIA STUDIES QUESTION

What statement does the television show *House* make about the patient's right to choose or decline medical treatment?

POSSIBLE THESIS

On the television show *House,* Dr. House frequently accuses his patients of ignorance or deceit and sometimes manipulates them into undergoing treatment they do not want. Despite these negative qualities, Dr. House usually emerges as the hero, demonstrating that medical expertise is more valuable than a patient's right to make decisions about treatment.

Each of these thesis statements takes a stand on a debatable issue—an issue about which intelligent, well-meaning people might disagree. Each writer needs to convince such people that his or her view is worth taking seriously.

29b Testing your thesis

When drafting and revising a thesis statement, make sure that it's suitable for your writing purpose and that you can successfully develop it with the sources available to you. Keeping the following guidelines in mind will help you develop a successful thesis statement.

- A thesis should take a position that needs to be explained and supported. It should not be a fact or description.

- A thesis should be your answer to a question, your solution to a problem, or your position on a topic or debate. It should not simply present a question, problem, or topic.

- A thesis should match the scope of the assignment. If your thesis is too broad to cover in an essay, for example, explore a subtopic of your original topic. If your thesis is so narrow that you don't have much to say, find out what debates surround your topic and take a position.

- A thesis should be sharply focused. Avoid vague words such as *interesting* or *good*. Use concrete language and make sure your thesis lets readers know what you plan to discuss.

- A thesis should stand up to the "So what?" question. Ask yourself why readers should be interested in your essay and care about your thesis. If your thesis matters to you, your readers are more likely to find your ideas engaging.

29c Organizing your ideas

The body of your paper will consist of evidence in support of your thesis. To get started, list your key points, as student writer Sophie Harba did in this informal outline.

- Debates about the government's role in regulating food have a long history in the United States.

- Some experts argue that we should focus on the dangers of unhealthy eating habits and on preventing chronic diseases linked to diet.

- But food regulations are not a popular solution because many Americans object to government restrictions on personal choice.

- Food regulations designed to prevent chronic disease don't ask Americans to give up their freedom; they ask Americans to see health as a matter of public good.

After you have written a rough draft, a more formal outline can help you shape the complexities of your argument.

29d Using sources to inform and support your argument

Sources can play several different roles as you develop your points.

Providing background information or context   You can use facts and statistics to support generalizations or to establish the importance of your topic.

Explaining terms or concepts   Explain words, phrases, or ideas that might be unfamiliar to your readers. Quoting or paraphrasing a source can help you define terms and concepts in accessible language.

Supporting your claims   Back up your assertions with facts, examples, and other evidence from your research.

Lending authority to your argument   Expert opinion can give weight to your argument. But don't rely on experts to make your argument for you. Construct your argument in your own words and cite authorities in the field to support your position.

Anticipating and countering objections   Do not ignore sources that seem to contradict your position or that offer arguments different from your own. Instead, use them to give voice to opposing ideas and interpretations before you counter them.

30   Avoiding plagiarism

In a research paper, you draw on the work of other writers, and you must document their contributions by citing your sources. When you acknowledge your sources, you avoid plagiarism, a serious academic offense.

Three different acts are considered plagiarism: (1) failing to cite quotations and borrowed ideas, (2) failing to enclose borrowed language in quotation marks, and (3) failing to put summaries and paraphrases in your own words.

30a   Citing quotations and borrowed ideas

When you cite sources, you give credit to writers from whom you've borrowed words and ideas. You also let your readers know where your information comes from so that they can evaluate the original source.

You must cite anything you borrow from a source, including direct quotations; statistics and other specific facts; visuals such as cartoons, graphs, and diagrams; and any ideas you present in a summary or a paraphrase.

The only exception is common knowledge—information your readers could easily find in general sources. For example, most encyclopedias state that Joel Coen directed

hackerhandbooks.com/pocket
 MLA papers > Exercises: 30–1 to 30–6
✓ MLA papers > LearningCurve: Working with sources (MLA)

Fargo in 1996 and that Emily Dickinson published only a handful of her many poems during her lifetime.

When you have seen information repeatedly in your reading, you don't need to cite it. However, when information has appeared in only one or two sources, when it is highly specific (as with statistics), or when it is controversial, you should cite the source.

MLA recommends a system of in-text citations. Here, briefly, is how the MLA citation system usually works:

1. The source is introduced by a signal phrase that names its author.
2. The material being cited is followed by a page number in parentheses.
3. At the end of the paper, a list of works cited, arranged alphabetically by authors' last names (or by titles for works with no authors), gives complete publication information about the source.

IN-TEXT CITATION

Bioethicist David Resnik emphasizes that such policies "open the door to excessive government control over food, which could restrict dietary choices, interfere with cultural, ethnic, and religious traditions, and exacerbate socioeconomic inequalities" (31).

ENTRY IN THE LIST OF WORKS CITED

Resnik, David. "Trans Fat Bans and Human Freedom." *American Journal of Bioethics* 10.3 (2010): 27-32. *Academic Search Premier*. Web. 17 Apr. 2013.

This basic MLA format varies for different types of sources. For a detailed discussion of other models, see 33.

30b Enclosing borrowed language in quotation marks

To show that you are using a source's exact phrases or sentences, enclose them in quotation marks unless they have been set off from the text by indenting (see p. 115). To omit the quotation marks is to claim—falsely—that the language is your own. Such an omission is plagiarism even if you have cited the source.

ORIGINAL SOURCE

Although these policies may have a positive impact on human health, they open the door to excessive government control over food, which could restrict dietary choices, interfere with cultural, ethnic, and religious traditions, and exacerbate socioeconomic inequalities.

— David Resnik, "Trans Fat Bans and Human Freedom," p. 31

PLAGIARISM

Bioethicist David Resnik points out that policies to ban trans fat may protect human health, but they open the door to excessive government control over food, which could interfere with cultural, ethnic, and religious traditions (31).

BORROWED LANGUAGE IN QUOTATION MARKS

Bioethicist David Resnik points out that policies to ban trans fats may protect human health, but "they open the door to excessive government control over food, which could restrict dietary choices, interfere with cultural, ethnic, and religious traditions, and exacerbate socioeconomic inequalities" (31).

30c Putting summaries and paraphrases in your own words

A summary condenses information from a source; a paraphrase conveys the information using about the same number of words as in the original source. When you summarize or paraphrase, you must name the source and restate the source's meaning in your own words. You commit plagiarism if you half-copy, or patchwrite, the author's sentences, either by mixing the author's phrases with your own without using quotation marks or by plugging your synonyms into the author's sentence structure.

The first paraphrase on page 113 is plagiarized—even though the source is cited—because too much of its language is borrowed from the original. The highlighted strings of words have been copied exactly (without quotation marks). Also, the writer has echoed the sentence structure of the source, merely substituting some synonyms (*interfere with* for *paternalistic intervention into* and *decrease the feeling of* for *enfeeble the notion of*).

ORIGINAL SOURCE

[A]ntiobesity laws encounter strong opposition from some quarters on the grounds that they constitute paternalistic intervention into lifestyle choices and enfeeble the notion of personal responsibility. Such arguments echo those made in the early days of tobacco regulation.

— Michelle M. Mello, David M. Studdert, and Troyen A. Brennan, "Obesity—The New Frontier of Public Health Law," p. 2602

PLAGIARISM: UNACCEPTABLE BORROWING

Health policy experts Mello, Studdert, and Brennan argue that antiobesity laws encounter strong opposition from some people because they interfere with lifestyle choices and decrease the feeling of personal responsibility. These arguments mirror those made in the early days of tobacco regulation (2602).

To avoid plagiarizing an author's language, don't look at the source while you are summarizing or paraphrasing. After you've restated the author's idea in your own words, return to the source and check that you haven't used the author's language or sentence structure or misrepresented the author's ideas.

ACCEPTABLE PARAPHRASE

As health policy experts Mello, Studdert, and Brennan point out, opposition to food and beverage regulation is similar to the opposition to early tobacco legislation: the public views the issue as one of personal responsibility rather than one requiring government intervention (2602).

31 Integrating sources

Quotations, summaries, paraphrases, and facts will help you develop your argument, but they cannot speak for you. You can use several strategies to integrate information from sources into your paper while maintaining your own voice.

31a Using quotations appropriately

Limiting your use of quotations   In your writing, keep the emphasis on your own ideas. Do not quote excessively. Except for the following legitimate uses of quotations,

hackerhandbooks.com/pocket
e MLA papers > Exercises: 31–1 to 31–4
✓ MLA papers > LearningCurve: Working with sources (MLA)

use your own words to summarize and paraphrase your sources and to explain your points.

WHEN TO USE QUOTATIONS

- When language is especially vivid or expressive
- When exact wording is needed for technical accuracy
- When it is important to let the debaters of an issue explain their positions in their own words
- When the words of an authority lend weight to an argument
- When the language of a source is the topic of your discussion

It is not always necessary to quote full sentences from a source. Often you can integrate words or phrases from a source into your own sentence structure.

Resnik acknowledges that his argument relies on "slippery slope" thinking, but he insists that "social and political pressures" regarding food regulations make his concerns valid (31).

Using the ellipsis mark   To condense a quoted passage, you can use the ellipsis mark (three periods, with spaces between) to indicate that you have omitted words. What remains must be grammatically complete.

In Mississippi, legislators passed a ban on bans—"a law that forbids . . . local restrictions on food or drink" (Conly A23).

The writer has omitted *municipalities to place* before *local restrictions* to condense the quoted material.

If you want to omit a full sentence or more, use a period before the three ellipsis dots.

Legal scholars Gostin and Gostin argue that "individuals have limited willpower to defer immediate gratification for longer-term health benefits. . . . A person understands that high-fat foods or a sedentary lifestyle will cause adverse health effects, or that excessive spending or gambling will cause financial hardship, but it is not always easy to refrain" (217).

Ordinarily, do not use an ellipsis mark at the beginning or at the end of a quotation. Your readers will understand that you have taken the quoted material from a longer passage. The only exception occurs when you have dropped words at the end of the final quoted sentence. In such cases, put three ellipsis dots before the closing quotation mark and the parenthetical reference. Make sure omissions and ellipsis marks do not distort the meaning of your sentence.

Using brackets   Brackets allow you to insert your own words into quoted material—to clarify a confusing reference or to make the quoted words fit grammatically into the context of your writing.

Neergaard and Agiesta argue that "a new poll finds people are split on how much the government should do to help [solve the national health crisis]—and most draw the line at attempts to force healthier eating."

To indicate an error such as a misspelling, insert [sic], including the brackets, right after the error.

Setting off long quotations   When you quote more than four typed lines of prose or more than three lines of poetry, set off the quotation by indenting it one inch from the left margin. Use the normal right margin and double-space the quotation.

Long quotations should be introduced by an informative sentence, usually followed by a colon. Quotation marks are unnecessary because the indented format tells readers that the passage is taken word-for-word from the source.

In response to critics who claim that laws aimed at stopping us from eating whatever we want are an assault on our freedom of choice, Conly offers a persuasive counterargument:

> [L]aws aren't designed for each one of us individually. Some of us can drive safely at 90 miles per hour, but we're bound by the same laws as the people who can't, because individual speeding laws aren't practical. Giving up a little liberty is something we agree to when we agree to live in a democratic society that is governed by laws. (A23)

At the end of an indented quotation, the parenthetical citation goes outside the final punctuation mark.

31b Using signal phrases to integrate sources

When you include a paraphrase, summary, or direct quotation in your paper, introduce it with a *signal phrase* that names the author of the source and provides some context for the source material. (See the chart on page 118 for a list of verbs commonly used in signal phrases.)

Marking boundaries Readers need to move smoothly from your words to the words of a source. Avoid dropping quotations into the text without warning. Provide clear signal phrases, including at least the author's name, to indicate the boundary between your words and the source's words.

DROPPED QUOTATION

Laws designed to prevent chronic disease by promoting healthier food and beverage consumption also have potential economic benefits. "[A] 1% reduction in the intake of saturated fat across the population would prevent more than 30,000 cases of coronary heart disease annually and would save more than a billion dollars in health care costs" (Nestle 7).

QUOTATION WITH SIGNAL PHRASE

Laws designed to prevent chronic disease by promoting healthier food and beverage consumption also have potential economic benefits. Marion Nestle, New York University professor of nutrition and public health, notes that "a 1% reduction in the intake of saturated fat across the population would prevent more than 30,000 cases of coronary heart disease annually and would save more than a billion dollars in health care costs" (7).

Establishing authority The first time you mention a source, include in the signal phrase the author's title, credentials, or experience to help your readers recognize the source's authority and your own credibility as a responsible researcher who has located reliable sources.

SOURCE WITH NO CREDENTIALS

Michael Pollan notes that "[t]he Centers for Disease Control estimates that fully three quarters of US health care spending goes to treat chronic diseases, most of which are preventable and linked to diet: heart disease, stroke, type 2 diabetes, and at least a third of all cancers."

SOURCE WITH CREDENTIALS

Journalist Michael Pollan, who has written extensively about Americans' unhealthy eating habits, notes that "the Centers for Disease Control estimates that fully three quarters of US health care spending goes to treat chronic diseases, most of which are preventable and linked to diet: heart disease, stroke, type 2 diabetes, and at least a third of all cancers."

Introducing summaries and paraphrases Introduce most summaries and paraphrases with a signal phrase that names the author and places the material in the context of your argument. Readers will then understand that everything between the signal phrase and the parenthetical citation summarizes or paraphrases the cited source.

Without the signal phrase (highlighted) in the following example, readers might think that only the quotation at the end is being cited, when in fact the whole paragraph is based on the source.

To improve public health, advocates such as Bowdoin College philosophy professor Sarah Conly contend that it is the government's duty to prevent people from making harmful choices, whenever feasible and whenever public benefits outweigh the costs. In response to critics who claim that laws aimed at stopping us from eating whatever we want are an assault on our freedom of choice, Conly asserts that "laws aren't designed for each of us individually" (A23).

Sometimes a summary or a paraphrase does not require a signal phrase. When the context makes clear where the cited material begins, you may omit the signal phrase and include the author's last name in parentheses.

Integrating statistics and other facts When you cite a statistic or another specific fact, a signal phrase is often not necessary. In most cases, it is clear that the citation refers to the statistic or fact rather than the whole paragraph. (There is nothing wrong, however, with using a signal phrase to introduce statistics and other facts.)

Seventy-five percent of Americans are opposed to laws that restrict or put limitations on access to unhealthy foods (Neergaard and Agiesta).

Using signal phrases in MLA papers

To avoid monotony, try to vary both the language and the placement of your signal phrases.

Model signal phrases

According to researchers Neergaard and Agiesta, ". . ."

As journalist Michael Pollan has noted, ". . ."

The United States Department of Health and Human Services reports, ". . ."

". . . ," write health policy experts Mello, Studdert, and Brennan. ". . ."

". . . ," Bowdoin College philosophy professor Sarah Conly contends.

Bioethicist David Resnik offers a persuasive argument: ". . ."

Verbs in signal phrases

Are you providing background, explaining a concept, supporting a claim, lending authority, or refuting a belief? Choose a verb that is appropriate for the way you are using the source.

acknowledges	contends	insists
adds	declares	notes
admits	denies	observes
agrees	describes	points out
argues	disputes	refutes
asserts	emphasizes	rejects
believes	endorses	reports
claims	grants	responds
compares	illustrates	suggests
confirms	implies	writes

NOTE: In MLA style, use the present or present perfect tense (*argues* or *has argued*) to introduce source material unless you include a date that specifies the time of the original author's writing.

Putting source material in context   A signal phrase can help you connect your own ideas with those of another writer by clarifying how the source will contribute to your paper.

If you use another writer's words, you must explain how those words relate to your point; you must put the source in context. It's a good idea to embed a quotation between sentences of your own that interpret the source and link the quotation to your paper's argument. (See also 31c.)

QUOTATION WITH EFFECTIVE CONTEXT

In response to critics who claim that laws aimed at stopping us from eating whatever we want are an assault on our freedom of choice, Conly offers a persuasive counterargument:

> [L]aws aren't designed for each one of us individually. Some of us can drive safely at 90 miles per hour, but we're bound by the same laws as the people who can't, because individual speeding laws aren't practical. Giving up a little liberty is something we agree to when we agree to live in a democratic society that is governed by laws. (A23)

As Conly suggests, we need to change our either/or thinking (either we have complete freedom of choice *or* we have government regulations and lose our freedom) and instead see health as a matter of public good, not individual liberty.

31c Synthesizing sources

When you synthesize multiple sources in a research paper, you create a conversation about your research topic. You show readers how the ideas of one source relate to those of another by connecting and analyzing the ideas in the context of your argument. Keep the emphasis on your own writing. The thread of your argument should be easy to identify and to understand, with or without your sources.

In the sample synthesis on page 120, Sophie Harba uses her own analyses to shape the conversation among her sources. She does not simply string quotations together or allow sources to overwhelm her writing. In her final sentence, she delivers a key point of her own, supported by her sources.

SAMPLE SYNTHESIS (DRAFT)

1   Why is the public largely resistant to laws that would limit unhealthy choices or penalize those choices with so-called fat taxes? Many consumers and civil rights advocates find such laws to be an unreasonable restriction on individual freedom of **2** choice. As health policy experts Mello, Studdert, and Brennan point out, opposition to food and beverage regulation is similar to the opposition to early tobacco legislation: the public views the issue as one of personal responsibility rather than one requiring government intervention (2602).

Student writer

Source 1

3 In other words, if a person eats unhealthy food and becomes ill as a result, that is his or her choice. But those who favor legislation claim that freedom of choice is a myth because of the strong influence of food and beverage industry marketing on consumers' **4** dietary habits. According to one nonprofit health advocacy group, food and beverage companies spend roughly two billion dollars per year marketing directly to children. As a result, kids see about four thousand ads per year encouraging them to consume unhealthy food and drinks ("Facts on Junk Food"). As was the case with antismoking laws passed in recent decades, taxes and legal restrictions on junk food sales could help to counter the strong marketing messages that promote unhealthy products.

Student writer

Source 2

Student writer

     The United States has a history of state and local public health laws that have successfully promoted a particular behavior by punishing an undesirable behavior. The decline in tobacco use as a result of antismoking taxes and laws is perhaps the most obvious example. Another example is legislation requiring the use of seat belts, which have significantly reduced fatalities **5** in car crashes. One government agency reports that seat belt use saved an average of more than fourteen thousand lives per year in the United States between 2000 and 2010 (United States, Dept. of Transportation, Natl. Highway Traffic Safety Administration 231).

Source 3

Perhaps seatbelt laws have public support because
the cost of wearing a seatbelt is small, especially
when compared with the benefit of saving fourteen
thousand lives per year.

1 Student writer Sophie Harba sets up her synthesis with a question.

2 A signal phrase indicates how the source contributes to Harba's argument and shows that the idea that follows is not her own.

3 Harba interprets a paraphrased source.

4 Harba uses a source to support her counterargument.

5 Harba uses a statistic to extend the argument and follows the source with a closing thought of her own.

32 Integrating literary quotations

When you are writing about literary works, the advice in section 31 about integrating quotations generally applies. This section provides guidance for situations that are unique to literary quotations.

NOTE: The parenthetical citations at the ends of examples in this section tell readers where the quoted words can be found. They indicate the lines of a poem; the act, scene, and lines of a play; or the page number of a quotation from a short story or a novel. (For guidelines on citing literary works, see pp. 132–33.)

32a Introducing quotations from literary works

When writing about a single work of literature, you do not need to include the author's name each time you quote from the work. Mention the author's name in the introduction to your paper; then refer, as appropriate, to the narrator of a story, the speaker of a poem, or the characters in a play. Do not confuse the author of the work with the narrator, speaker, or characters.

INAPPROPRIATE

Poet Andrew Marvell describes his fear of death like this: "But at my back I always hear / Time's wingèd chariot hurrying near" (21-22).

APPROPRIATE

Addressing his beloved in an attempt to win her sexual favors, the speaker of the poem argues that death gives them no time to waste: "But at my back I always hear / Time's wingèd chariot hurrying near" (21-22).

For examples of quoted dialogue from a short story, see page 172.

32b Avoiding shifts in tense

Because it is conventional to write about literature in the present tense (see p. 31) and because literary works often use other tenses, you will need to exercise some care when weaving quotations into your own text. A first-draft attempt may result in an awkward shift, as it did for one student who was writing about Nadine Gordimer's short story "Friday's Footprint."

TENSE SHIFT

When Rita sees Johnny's relaxed attitude, "she blushed, like a wave of illness" (159).

To avoid the distracting shift from present tense (*sees*) to past tense (*blushed*), the writer decided to paraphrase the reference to Rita's blushing and reduce the length of the quotation.

REVISED

When Rita sees Johnny's relaxed attitude, she is overcome with embarrassment, "like a wave of illness" (159).

The writer could have changed the quotation to present tense, using brackets to indicate the change: *When Rita sees Johnny's relaxed attitude, "she blushe[s], like a wave of illness" (159).* (See also p. 115 for the use of brackets.)

32c Formatting and citing literary passages

MLA guidelines for formatting and citing quotations differ somewhat for short stories or novels, poems, and plays.

Short stories or novels   If a quotation from a short story or a novel takes up four or fewer typed lines in your paper, put it in quotation marks and run it into the text of your essay. Include a page number in parentheses after the quotation.

The narrator of Eudora Welty's "Why I Live at the P.O.," known to us only as "Sister," makes many catty remarks about her enemies. For example, she calls Mr. Whitaker "this photographer with the pop-eyes" (46).

If a quotation from a short story or a novel is five typed lines or longer in your paper, set the quotation off from the text by indenting it one inch from the left margin; do not use quotation marks. (See also p. 115.) Put the page number in parentheses after the final mark of punctuation.

Sister's tale begins with "I," and she makes every event revolve around herself, even her sister's marriage:

> I was getting along fine with Mama, Papa-Daddy, and Uncle Rondo until my sister Stella-Rondo just separated from her husband and came back home again. Mr. Whitaker! Of course I went with Mr. Whitaker first, when he first appeared here in China Grove, taking "Pose Yourself" photos, and Stella-Rondo broke us up. (46)

Poems   Enclose quotations of three or fewer lines of poetry in quotation marks within your text, and indicate line breaks with a slash with a space on each side. Include line numbers in parentheses at the end of the quotation. For the first reference, use the word "lines." Thereafter, use just numbers.

The opening of Frost's "Fire and Ice" strikes a conversational tone: "Some say the world will end in fire, / Some say in ice" (lines 1-2).

When you quote four or more lines of poetry, set the quotation off from the text by indenting one inch and omit the quotation marks. Put the line numbers in parentheses after the final mark of punctuation.

The opening stanza of Louise Bogan's "Women" startles readers by presenting a negative stereotype of women:

> Women have no wilderness in them,
> They are provident instead,
> Content in the tight hot cell of their hearts
> To eat dusty bread. (lines 1-4)

Plays   If a quotation from a play takes up four or fewer typed lines in your paper and is spoken by only one character, put quotation marks around it and run it into the text of your essay. Whenever possible, include the act number, scene number, and line numbers in parentheses at the end of the quotation. Separate the numbers with periods and use arabic numerals unless your instructor prefers roman numerals.

Two attendants silently watch as the sleepwalking Lady Macbeth subconsciously struggles with her guilt: "Here's the smell of blood still. All the perfumes of Arabia will not sweeten this little hand" (5.1.50-51).

33 MLA documentation style

In English and other humanities classes, you may be asked to use the MLA (Modern Language Association) system for documenting sources, which is set forth in the *MLA Handbook for Writers of Research Papers*, 7th ed. (New York: MLA, 2009).

MLA recommends in-text citations (33a) that refer readers to a list of works cited at the end of the paper (33b).

33a MLA in-text citations

MLA in-text citations are made with a combination of signal phrases and parenthetical references. A signal phrase introduces information taken from a source (a quotation, summary, paraphrase, or fact); usually the signal phrase includes the author's name. (See p. 118 about verbs in signal phrases.) The parenthetical reference comes after the cited material, often at the end of the sentence. It includes at least a page number (except for unpaginated sources). In the models in 33a, the elements of the in-text citation are highlighted in orange.

IN-TEXT CITATION

Resnik acknowledges that his argument relies on "slippery slope" thinking, but he insists that "social and political pressures" regarding food regulation make his concerns valid (31).

Readers can look up the author's last name in the alphabetized list of works cited, where they will learn the work's title and other publication information. If readers decide

Directory to MLA in-text citation models

GENERAL GUIDELINES FOR SIGNAL PHRASES AND PAGE NUMBERS

1. Author named in a signal phrase   126
2. Author named in parentheses   126
3. Author unknown   126
4. Page number unknown   126
5. One-page source   127

VARIATIONS ON THE GENERAL GUIDELINES

6. Two or three authors   127
7. Four or more authors   127
8. Organization as author   128
9. Authors with the same last name   128
10. Two or more works by the same author   128
11. Two or more works in one citation   128
12. Repeated citations from the same source 129
13. Encyclopedia or dictionary entry   129
14. Multivolume work   129
15. Entire work   129
16. Selection in an anthology   129
17. Government document   130
18. Historical document   130
19. Legal source   130
20. Visual such as a table, a chart, or another graphic 131
21. Personal communication and social media 131
22. Web source   131
23. Indirect source (source quoted in another source) 131

LITERARY WORKS AND SACRED TEXTS

24. Literary work without parts or line numbers 132
25. Verse play or poem   132
26. Novel with numbered divisions   133
27. Sacred text   133

to consult the source, the page number will take them straight to the passage that has been cited.

General guidelines for signal phrases and page numbers Items 1–5 explain how the MLA system usually works for all sources—in print, on the Web, in other media, and with or without authors and page numbers. Items 6–27 give variations on the basic guidelines.

■ **1. Author named in a signal phrase**   Ordinarily, introduce the material being cited with a signal phrase that includes the author's name.

According to Lorine Goodwin, a food historian, nineteenth-century reformers who sought to purify the food supply were called "fanatics" and "radicals" by critics who argued that consumers should be free to buy and eat what they want (77).

The signal phrase—*According to Lorine Goodwin*—names the author; the parenthetical citation gives the page on which the quoted words may be found.

When a quotation ends with a question mark or an exclamation point, handle the citation like this:

Burgess asks a critical question: "How can we think differently about food labeling?" (51).

■ **2. Author named in parentheses**   If you do not give the author's name in a signal phrase, put the last name in parentheses along with the page number (if the source has one). Use no punctuation between the name and the page number: (Moran 136).

According to a nationwide poll, 75% of Americans are opposed to laws that restrict or put limitations on access to unhealthy foods (Neergaard and Agiesta).

■ **3. Author unknown**   Either use the complete title in a signal phrase or use a short form of the title in parentheses. Titles of books and other long works are italicized; titles of articles and other short works are put in quotation marks (see also p. 168).

As a result, kids see about four thousand ads per year encouraging them to eat unhealthy food and drinks ("Facts on Junk Food").

NOTE: If the author is a corporation or a government agency, see items 8 and 17 on pages 128 and 130.

■ **4. Page number unknown**   Do not include the page number if a work lacks page numbers, as is the case with many Web sources. Do not use page numbers from a printout from a Web site. (When the pages of a Web source are stable, as in PDF files, supply a page number in your in-text citation.)

Michael Pollan points out that "cheap food" actually has "significant costs — to the environment, to public health, to the public purse, even to the culture."

If a source has numbered paragraphs or sections, use "par." (or "pars.") or "sec." (or "secs.") in the parentheses: (Smith, par. 4). Notice that a comma follows the author's name.

■ **5. One-page source** It is a good idea to include the page number for a one-page source because without it readers may not know where your citation ends or, worse, may not realize that you have provided a citation at all.

Sarah Conly uses John Stuart Mill's "harm principle" to argue that citizens need their government to intervene to prevent them from taking harmful actions — such as driving too fast or buying unhealthy foods — out of ignorance of the harm they can do (A23). But government intervention may overstep in the case of food choices.

Variations on the general guidelines This section describes the MLA guidelines for handling a variety of situations not covered in items 1–5.

■ **6. Two or three authors** Name the authors in a signal phrase, as in the following example, or include their last names in the parenthetical reference: (Gostin and Gostin 214).

As legal scholars Gostin and Gostin explain, "[I]nterventions that do not pose a truly significant burden on individual liberty" are justified if they "go a long way towards safeguarding the health and well-being of the populace" (214).

When you name three authors in the parentheses, separate the names with commas: (Alton, Davies, and Rice 56).

■ **7. Four or more authors** Name all authors or include only the first author's name followed by "et al." (Latin for "and others"). The format you use should match the format in your works cited entry (see item 3 on p. 138).

Only after results were reviewed by an independent panel did the researchers publish their findings (Blaine et al. 35).

■ **8. Organization as author**   For a government agency as author, see item 17 on p. 130.

The American Diabetes Association estimates that the cost of diagnosed diabetes in the United States in 2012 was $245 billion.

In the list of works cited, the American Diabetes Association is treated as the author and alphabetized under *A*. When you give the organization name in parentheses, abbreviate common words in the name: "Assn.," "Dept.," "Natl.," "Soc.," and so on.

The cost of diagnosed diabetes in the United States in 2012 was estimated at $245 billion (Amer. Diabetes Assn.).

■ **9. Authors with the same last name**   Include the author's first name in the signal phrase or first initial in parentheses.

One approach to the problem is to introduce nutrition literacy at the K-5 level in public schools (E. Chen 15).

■ **10. Two or more works by the same author**   Mention the title of the work in the signal phrase or include a short version of the title in the parentheses.

The American Diabetes Association tracks trends in diabetes across age groups. In 2012, more than 200,000 children and adolescents had diabetes ("Fast Facts"). Because of an expected dramatic increase in diabetes in young people over the next forty years, the association encourages "strategies for implementing childhood obesity prevention programs and primary prevention programs for youth at risk of developing type 2 diabetes" ("Number of Youth").

Titles of articles and other short works are placed in quotation marks; titles of books and other long works are italicized. (See also p. 168.)

■ **11. Two or more works in one citation**   List the authors (or titles) in alphabetical order and separate them with a semicolon.

The prevalence of early-onset Type 2 diabetes has been well documented (Finn 68; Sharma 2037; Whitaker 118).

It may be less distracting to use an information note for multiple citations (see 33c).

■ **12. Repeated citations from the same source** When you are writing about a single work, you may mention the author's name at the beginning of your paper and then include just the page numbers in your parenthetical citations. (See also 32a.)

In Susan Glaspell's short story "A Jury of Her Peers," two women accompany their husbands and a county attorney to an isolated house where a farmer named John Wright has been choked to death. The chief suspect is Wright's wife, Minnie, who is in jail awaiting trial. The sheriff's wife, Mrs. Peters, has come along to gather some items for Minnie, and Mrs. Hale has joined her. Initially, Mrs. Hale sympathizes with Minnie and objects to the male investigators "snoopin' round and criticizin'" her kitchen (249). Mrs. Peters shows respect for the law, saying that the men are doing "no more than their duty" (249).

■ **13. Encyclopedia or dictionary entry** When an encyclopedia or a dictionary entry does not have an author, it will be alphabetized in the list of works cited under the word or entry that you consulted (see item 28 on p. 149). Either in your text or in parentheses, mention the word or entry. No page number is required.

The word *crocodile* has a complex etymology ("Crocodile").

■ **14. Multivolume work**

In his studies of gifted children, Terman describes a pattern of accelerated language acquisition (2: 279).

■ **15. Entire work** Use the author's name in a signal phrase or in parentheses. There is no need to use a page number.

Pollan explores the issues surrounding food production and consumption from a political angle.

■ **16. Selection in an anthology** Put the name of the author of the selection (not the editor of the anthology) in the signal phrase or the parentheses.

In "Love Is a Fallacy," the narrator's logical teachings disintegrate when Polly declares that she should date Petey because "[h]e's got a raccoon coat" (Shulman 391).

In the list of works cited, the work is alphabetized under *Shulman*, the author of the story, not under the name of the editor of the anthology. (See item 35 on p. 152.)

■ **17. Government document** When a government agency is the author, you will alphabetize it in the list of works cited under the name of the government, such as United States or Great Britain (see item 72 on p. 164). For this reason, you must name the government as well as the agency in your in-text citation.

One government agency reports that seat belt use saved an average of more than fourteen thousand lives per year in the United States between 2000 and 2010 (United States, Dept. of Transportation, Natl. Highway Traffic Safety Administration 231).

■ **18. Historical document** For a historical document, such as the United States Constitution or the Canadian Charter of Rights and Freedoms, provide the document title, neither italicized nor in quotation marks, along with relevant article and section numbers. In parenthetical citations, use common abbreviations such as "art." and "sec." and abbreviations of well-known titles: (US Const., art. 1, sec. 2).

While the United States Constitution provides for the formation of new states (art. 4, sec. 3), it does not explicitly allow or prohibit the secession of states.

Cite other historical documents as you would any other work, by the first element in the works cited entry (see item 74 on p. 165).

■ **19. Legal source** For a legislative act (law) or court case, name the act or case either in a signal phrase or in parentheses. Italicize the names of cases but not the names of acts. (See also items 75 and 76 on p. 165.)

The Jones Act of 1917 granted US citizenship to Puerto Ricans.

In 1857, Chief Justice Roger B. Taney declared in *Dred Scott v. Sandford* that blacks, whether enslaved or free, could not be citizens of the United States.

■ **20. Visual such as a table, a chart, or another graphic**
To cite a visual that has a figure number in the source, use the
abbreviation "fig." and the number in place of a page number in your parenthetical citation: (Manning, fig. 4). If you
refer to the figure in your text, spell out the word "figure."

To cite a visual that does not have a figure number
in a print source, use the visual's title or a description in
your text and cite the author and page number as for any
other source.

For a visual not in a print source, identify the visual
in your text and then in parentheses use the first element
in the works cited entry: the artist's or photographer's
name or the title of the work. (See items 65–70 on
pp. 163–64.)

Photographs such as *Woman Aircraft Worker* (Bransby) and *Women
Welders* (Parks) demonstrate the US government's attempt to
document the contributions of women during World War II.

■ **21. Personal communication and social media**   Cite
personal letters, personal interviews, e-mail messages, and
social media posts by the name listed in the works cited
entry, as you would for any other source. Identify the type
of source in your text if you feel it is necessary for clarity.
(See items 27, 29c, and 77–81 in section 33b.)

■ **22. Web source**   Your in-text citation for a source from
the Web should follow the same guidelines as for other
sources. If the source lacks page numbers but has numbered paragraphs, sections, or divisions, use those numbers
with the appropriate abbreviation in your parenthetical
citation: "par.," "sec.," "ch.," "pt." Do not add such numbers if the source itself does not use them; simply give the
author or title in your in-text citation.

Julian Hawthorne points out profound differences between his
father and Ralph Waldo Emerson but concludes that "together
they met the needs of nearly all that is worthy in human nature"
(ch. 4).

■ **23. Indirect source (source quoted in another source)**
When a writer's or a speaker's quoted words appear in a
source written by someone else, begin the parenthetical
citation with the abbreviation "qtd. in." (See also item 12
on p. 142.)

Public health researcher Dan Beauchamp has said that "public health practices are 'communal in nature, and concerned with the well-being of the community as a whole and not just the well-being of any particular person'" (qtd. in Gostin and Gostin 217).

Literary works and sacred texts   Literary works and sacred texts are usually available in a variety of editions. Your list of works cited will specify which edition you are using. When possible, give enough information—such as book parts, play divisions, or line numbers—so that readers can locate the cited passage in any edition of the work.

■ **24. Literary work without parts or line numbers**   Most short stories and many novels and plays do not have parts or line numbers. In such cases, simply cite the page number.

At the end of Kate Chopin's "The Story of an Hour," Mrs. Mallard drops dead upon learning that her husband is alive. In the final irony of the story, doctors report that she died of a "joy that kills" (25).

■ **25. Verse play or poem**   For verse plays, give act, scene, and line numbers that can be located in any edition of the work. Use arabic numerals and separate the numbers with periods.

In Shakespeare's *King Lear*, Gloucester, blinded for suspected treason, learns a profound lesson from his tragic experience: "A man may see how this world goes / with no eyes" (4.2.148-49).

For a poem, cite the part, stanza, and line numbers, if it has them, separated with periods.

The Green Knight claims to approach King Arthur's court "because the praise of you, prince, is puffed so high, / And your manor and your men are considered so magnificent" (1.12.258-59).

For a poem that is not divided into numbered parts or stanzas, use line numbers. For a first reference, use the word "lines": (lines 5-8). Thereafter use just the numbers: (12-13). (See also 32a.)

■ **26. Novel with numbered divisions**   When a novel has numbered divisions, put the page number first, followed by a semicolon, and then the book, part, or chapter in which the passage may be found. Use abbreviations such as "bk.," "pt.," and "ch."

One of Kingsolver's narrators, teenager Rachel, complains that being forced to live in the Congo with her missionary family is "a sheer tapestry of justice" because her chances of finding a boyfriend are "dull and void" (117; bk. 2, ch. 10).

■ **27. Sacred text**   When citing a sacred text such as the Bible or the Qur'an, name the edition you are using in your works cited entry (see item 39 on p. 153). In your parenthetical citation, give the book, chapter, and verse (or their equivalent), separated with periods. Common abbreviations for books of the Bible are acceptable.

Consider the words of Solomon: "If your enemy is hungry, give him bread to eat; and if he is thirsty, give him water to drink" (*Oxford Annotated Bible*, Prov. 25.21).

   The title of a sacred work is italicized when it refers to a specific edition of the work, as in the preceding example. If you refer to the book in a general sense in your text, neither italicize the title nor put it in quotation marks.

The Bible and the Qur'an provide allegories that help readers understand how to lead a moral life.

33b MLA list of works cited

The elements you will need for the works cited list will differ slightly for some sources, but the main principles apply to all sources: You should identify an author, a creator, or a producer whenever possible; give a title; provide the date on which the source was produced; and indicate the medium of delivery. Some sources will require page numbers; some will require a sponsoring person or organization; and some will require other identifying information.

▶   Directory to MLA works cited models, **page 134**

▶   General guidelines for the works cited list, **page 136**

Directory to MLA works cited models

GENERAL GUIDELINES FOR LISTING AUTHORS

1.	Single author	137
2.	Two or three authors	137
3.	Four or more authors	138
4.	Organization or company as author	138
5.	No author listed	138
6.	Two or more works by the same author	139
7.	Two or more works by the same group of authors	139
8.	Editor or translator	139
9.	Author with editor or translator	141
10.	Graphic narrative or other illustrated work	141
11.	Author using a pseudonym (pen name) or screen name	141
12.	Author quoted by another author (indirect source)	142

ARTICLES AND OTHER SHORT WORKS

13.	Basic format for an article or other short work	142
14.	Article in a journal	143
15.	Article in a magazine	143
16.	Article in a newspaper	145
17.	Abstract or executive summary	147
18.	Article with a title in its title	147
19.	Editorial	148
20.	Unsigned article	148
21.	Letter to the editor	148
22.	Comment on an online article	148
23.	Paper or presentation at a conference	148
24.	Book review	149
25.	Film review or other review	149
26.	Performance review	149
27.	Interview	149
28.	Article in a reference work (encyclopedia, dictionary, wiki)	149
29.	Letter	149

BOOKS AND OTHER LONG WORKS

30.	Basic format for a book	150
31.	Parts of a book	150
32.	Book with a title in its title	152
33.	Book in a language other than English	152
34.	Entire anthology or collection	152
35.	One selection from an anthology or a collection	152
36.	Two or more selections from an anthology or a collection	152
37.	Edition other than the first	153
38.	Multivolume work	153
39.	Sacred text	153
40.	Book in a series	153

BOOKS AND OTHER LONG WORKS (*CONTINUED*)

41.	Republished book	156
42.	Publisher's imprint	156
43.	Pamphlet, brochure, or newsletter	156
44.	Dissertation	156
45.	Proceedings of a conference	156
46.	Manuscript	156

WEB SITES AND PARTS OF WEB SITES

47.	An entire Web site	157
48.	Short work from a Web site	158
49.	Long work from a Web site	158
50.	Entire blog	158
51.	Blog post or comment	158
52.	Academic course or department home page	158

AUDIO, VISUAL, AND MULTIMEDIA SOURCES

53.	Podcast	160
54.	Film (DVD, BD, or other format)	160
55.	Supplementary material accompanying a film	160
56.	Video or audio from the Web	161
57.	Video game	161
58.	Computer software or app	161
59.	Television or radio episode or program	161
60.	Transcript	162
61.	Performance	162
62.	Lecture or public address	162
63.	Musical score	162
64.	Sound recording	163
65.	Work of art	163
66.	Photograph	163
67.	Cartoon	163
68.	Advertisement	163
69.	Visual such as a table, a chart, or other graphic	164
70.	Map	164
71.	Digital file	164

GOVERNMENT AND LEGAL DOCUMENTS

72.	Government document	164
73.	Testimony before a legislative body	165
74.	Historical document	165
75.	Legislative act (law)	165
76.	Court case	165

PERSONAL COMMUNICATION AND SOCIAL MEDIA

77.	E-mail message	165
78.	Text message	165
79.	Posting to an online discussion list	166
80.	Facebook post or comment	166
81.	Twitter post (tweet)	166

General guidelines for the works cited list

In the list of works cited, include only sources that you have quoted, summarized, or paraphrased in your paper.

Authors and titles

- Arrange the list alphabetically by authors' last names or by titles for works with no authors.

- For the first author, place the last name first, a comma, and the first name. For subsequent authors, put the names in normal order (first name followed by last name).

- In titles of works, capitalize all words except articles (*a*, *an*, *the*), prepositions (*at*, *from*, *between*, and so on), coordinating conjunctions (*and*, *but*, *or*, *nor*, *for*, *so*, *yet*), and the *to* in infinitives — unless the word is first or last in the title or subtitle.

- Use quotation marks for titles of articles and other short works.

- Italicize titles of books and other long works.

Place of publication and publisher

- For sources that require a place of publication, give the city of publication without a state or country name.

- Shorten publishers' names ("Wiley" for "John Wiley and Sons," for instance). For university publishers, use "U" and "P" for "University" and "Press": UP of Florida.

- List a sponsor or a publisher for most sources from the Web.

- If a source has no sponsor or publisher, use "N.p." (for "No publisher").

- For a work found in a database, give the title of the database but not a sponsor.

Dates

- For a print source, give the most recent date on the title page or the copyright page.

- For a Web source, use the copyright date or the most recent update.

- For books and most journals, use the year of publication.

- For monthly magazines, use the month and year. Abbreviate all months except May, June, and July.

- For weekly magazines and newspapers, give the day, month, and year, with no commas (18 Feb. 2013). Abbreviate all months except May, June, and July.

- If there is no date of publication or update, use "n.d." (for "no date").
- For sources found on the Web or in a database, give your date of access.

Page numbers

- For most articles and other short works, give page numbers when available.
- If page numbers are not available, use "n. pag." (for "no pagination").
- Do not use the page numbers from a printout of a source.
- If an article does not appear on consecutive pages, give the number of the first page followed by a plus sign: 35+.

Medium

- Include the medium in which a work was published, produced, or delivered.
- Typical designations for the medium are "Print," "Web," "Television," "Film," "DVD," "Photograph," "Lecture," and "MP3 file."

URLs

- MLA does not require a URL in citations for online sources.
- If your instructor requires a URL, see the note at the end of item 47.

General guidelines for listing authors   The formatting of authors' names in items 1–12 applies to all sources—books, articles, Web sites—in print, on the Web, or in other media. For more models of specific source types, see items 13–81.

■ 1. Single author

author: last name first ⌐ title (book) ⌐ city of publication publisher

Bowker, Gordon. *James Joyce: A New Biography*. New York: Farrar,

date medium

2012. Print.

■ 2. Two or three authors

first author: last name first   second author: in normal order   title (book)

Gourevitch, Philip, and Errol Morris. *Standard Operating Procedure*.

city of publication publisher date medium

New York: Penguin, 2008. Print.

first author: other authors:
last name first   in normal order   title (newspaper article)

Farmer, John, John Azzarello, and Miles Kara. "Real Heroes, Fake Stories."

                date
newspaper title   of publication   page   medium

New York Times 14 Sept. 2008: WK10. Print.

■ **3. Four or more authors** Name all the authors or name the first author followed by "et al." (Latin for "and others"). In an in-text citation, use the same form for the authors' names as you use in the works cited entry. See item 7 on page 127.

first author: other authors:
last name first   in normal order

Leech, Geoffrey, Marianne Hundt, Christian Mair, and Nicholas Smith.

                                 city of
              title (book)   publication

Change in Contemporary English: A Grammatical Study. Cambridge:

   publisher   year   medium

Cambridge UP, 2009. Print.

■ **4. Organization or company as author**

author: organization
name, not abbreviated   title (book)

National Geographic. *National Geographic Visual Atlas of the World*.

    city of   publisher, with common
  publication   abbreviations   date   medium

Washington: Natl. Geographic Soc., 2008. Print.

Your in-text citation also should treat the organization as the author (see item 8 on p. 128).

■ **5. No author listed**

a. Article or other short work

                                       newspaper title
      article title   label   (city in brackets)

"Policing Ohio's Online Courses." Editorial. *Plain Dealer* [Cleveland]

      date   page(s)   medium

9 Oct. 2012: A5. Print.

b. Television program

                  title of
     episode title   TV show   producer   network

"Fast Times at West Philly High." *Frontline*. Prod. Debbie Morton. PBS.

    local   date of
station, city   broadcast   medium

KTWU, Topeka, 4 Dec. 2012. Television.

c. Book, entire Web site, or other long work

title (Web site)

Women of Protest: Photographs from the Records of the National Woman's Party.

sponsor | no date | medium | date of access

Lib. of Cong., n.d. Web. 29 Sept. 2012.

NOTE: The author's name may appear at the end of the page, in tiny print, or on another page of the site, such as the home page. Or an organization or a government may be the author (see items 4 and 72).

■ **6. Two or more works by the same author**   First alphabetize the works by title. Use the author's name for the first entry; for subsequent entries, use three hyphens and a period. The three hyphens must stand for exactly the same name as in the first entry.

García, Cristina. *Dreams of Significant Girls*. New York: Simon, 2011. Print.

---. *The Lady Matador's Hotel*. New York: Scribner, 2010. Print.

■ **7. Two or more works by the same group of authors**   To list multiple works by the same group of two or more authors, alphabetize the works by title. Use all authors' names for the first entry; begin subsequent entries with three hyphens and a period. The three hyphens must stand for all the authors' names.

Agha, Hussein, and Robert Malley. "The Arab Counterrevolution." *New York Review of Books*. NYREV, 29 Sept. 2011. Web. 12 Dec. 2012.

---. "This Is Not a Revolution." *New York Review of Books*. NYREV, 8 Nov. 2012. Web. 12 Dec. 2012.

■ **8. Editor or translator**   Begin with the editor's or translator's name. For one editor, use "ed." after the name; for more than one, use "eds." Use "trans." for one or more translators.

first editor: last name first | other editor(s): in normal order | title (book)

Jones, Russell M., and John H. Swanson, eds. *Dear Helen: Wartime Letters*

city of publication | publisher

from a Londoner to Her American Pen Pal. Columbia: U of Missouri P,

year | medium

2009. Print.

How to answer the basic question "Who is the author?"

PROBLEM: Sometimes when you need to cite a source, it's not clear who the author is. This is especially true for sources on the Web or other nonprint sources, which may have been created by one person and uploaded by a different person or an organization. Whom do you cite as the author in such a case? How do you determine who *is* the author?

EXAMPLE: The video "Surfing the Web on the Job" (see below) was uploaded to YouTube by CBSNewsOnline. Is the person or organization who uploads the video the author of the video? Not necessarily.

Surfing the Web on The Job

CBSNewsOnline · 42,491 videos

▶ **Subscribe** 〈 85,736 〉

Uploaded on Nov 12, 2009
As the Internet continues to emerge as a critical facet of everyday life, CBS News' Daniel Sieberg reports that companies are cracking down on employees' personal Web use.

STRATEGY: After you view or listen to the source a few times, ask yourself whether you can tell who is chiefly responsible for creating the content in the source. It might be an organization. It might be an identifiable individual. This video consists entirely of reporting by Daniel Sieberg, so in this case the author is Sieberg.

CITATION: To cite the source, you would use the basic MLA guidelines for a video found on the Web (item 56).

> author:
> last name first / title of video / Web site title / sponsor
>
> Sieberg, Daniel. "Surfing the Web on the Job." *YouTube*. YouTube,
>
> update date / medium / date of access
>
> 19 Nov. 2009. Web. 26 Nov. 2009.

If you want to include the person or organization who uploaded the video, you can add it as supplementary information at the end.

> author:
> last name first / title of video / Web site title / sponsor
>
> Sieberg, Daniel. "Surfing the Web on the Job." *YouTube*. YouTube,
>
> update date / medium / date of access / supplementary information
>
> 19 Nov. 2009. Web. 26 Nov. 2009. Uploaded by CBSNewsOnline.

■ **9. Author with editor or translator** Begin with the name
of the author. Place the editor's or translator's name after
the title. "Ed." or "Trans." means "Edited by" or "Translated by," so it is the same for one or more editors or
translators.

author: translator:
last name first   title (book)   in normal order

Scirocco, Alfonso. *Garibaldi: Citizen of the World*. Trans. Allan Cameron.

city of
publication   publisher   year medium

Princeton: Princeton UP, 2007. Print.

■ **10. Graphic narrative or other illustrated work** If a
work has both an author and an illustrator, the order in
your citation will depend on which of those persons you
emphasize in your paper.

a. Author first Begin with the author, followed by the title
and the illustrator. Use "Illus." (meaning "Illustrated by")
before the illustrator's name.

Moore, Alan. *V for Vendetta*. Illus. David Lloyd. New York: Vertigo-DC

    Comics, 2008. Print.

b. Illustrator first Begin with the illustrator, followed by the
title and the author. Use "illus." (meaning "illustrator")
after the illustrator's name; use "By" before the author's
name.

Weaver, Dustin, illus. *The Tenth Circle*. By Jodi Picoult. New York:

    Washington Square, 2006. Print.

c. Author and illustrator the same person Cite the work as
you would any other work with one author (not using the
label "illus." or "by").

Smith, Lane. *Abe Lincoln's Dream*. New York: Roaring Brook, 2012.

    Print.

■ **11. Author using a pseudonym (pen name) or screen
name** Begin with the author's name as it appears in the
source (the pseudonym). Give the author's real name,
if available, in brackets. (See also items 80 and 81 on
p. 166.)

Grammar Girl [Mignon Fogarty]. "When Are Double Words OK?"
   Grammar Girl: Quick and Dirty Tips for Better Writing.
   Macmillan, 28 Sept. 2012. Web. 10 Nov. 2012.

Pauline. Comment. "Is This the End?" By James Atlas. *New York
   Times*. New York Times, 25 Nov. 2012. Web. 29 Nov. 2012.

■ **12. Author quoted by another author (indirect source)**   If
one of your sources uses a quotation from another source
and you'd like to use the quotation, provide a works cited
entry for the source in which you found the quotation.
In your in-text citation, indicate that the quoted words
appear in the source (see item 23 on p. 131).

WORKS CITED ENTRY

Belmaker, Genevieve. "Five Ways Journalists Can Use Social Media
   for On-the-Ground Reporting in the Middle East." *Poynter*.
   Poynter Inst., 20 Nov. 2012. Web. 24 Nov. 2012.

IN-TEXT CITATION

Peter Townson points out that social media in the Middle East are
"kind of the preferred way for people to get news, because they
know there's no self-censorship involved" (qtd. in Belmaker).

Articles and other short works

   ▶ Citation at a glance: Article in a journal, **page 144**
   ▶ Citation at a glance: Article from a database, **page 146**

■ **13. Basic format for an article or other short work**

a. Print

author:
last name first   article title

Ferris, William R. "Southern Literature: A Blending of Oral, Visual, and

         journal volume,
         title   issue   year   page(s) medium

   Musical Voices." *Daedalus* 141.1 (2012): 139-53. Print.

b. Web

author:
last name first   title of short work

Sonderman, Jeff. "Survey: Public Prefers News from Professional Journalists."

title of
Web site   sponsor   update   medium   date of
                           date   access

   Poynter. Poynter Inst., 29 Aug. 2012. Web. 31 Oct. 2012.

c. Database

author:
last name first   article title   journal title

Emanuel, Lynn Collins. "The Noirs: Collecting the Evidence." *American*

            volume,   database
            issue   year   page(s)   title   medium

   Poetry Review 41.6 (2012): 6. *General OneFile*. Web.

       date of
       access

     14 Dec. 2012.

■ 14. Article in a journal

a. Print

author: last
name first   article title

Fuqua, Amy. "'The Furrow of His Brow': Providence and Pragmatism in Toni

                       volume,
              journal title   issue   year   page(s) medium

   Morrison's *Paradise*." *Midwest Quarterly* 54.1 (2012): 38-52. Print.

b. Online journal

       author:
       last name first   article title

Cáceres, Sigfrido Burgos. "Towards Concert in Africa: Seeking Progress and Power

                              volume,
                   journal title   issue   year

   through Cohesion and Unity." *African Studies Quarterly* 12.4 (2011):

                   date of
   page(s) medium   access

   59-73. Web. 31 Oct. 2012.

c. Database

      author:
      last name first   article title

Maier, Jessica. "A 'True Likeness': The Renaissance City Portrait."

            volume,   database
       journal title   issue   year   page(s)   title   medium

   Renaissance Quarterly 65.3 (2012): 711-52. *JSTOR*. Web.

       date of
       access

   30 Aug. 2012.

■ 15. Article in a magazine

a. Print (monthly)

      author:
      last name first   article title   magazine title   date   page(s)

Bryan, Christy. "Ivory Worship." *National Geographic* Oct. 2012: 28-61.

      medium

     Print.

Citation at a glance

Article in a journal MLA

To cite an article in a print journal in MLA style, include the following elements:

1. Author(s) of article
2. Title and subtitle of article
3. Title of journal
4. Volume and issue numbers (if any)
5. Year of publication
6. Page number(s) of article
7. Medium

JOURNAL TABLE OF CONTENTS

RHETORIC REVIEW 3
Volume 31, Number 4, 2012
4 — 5

Articles

Brian Gogan
Exchange in On the Exchange: A Baudrillardian Perspective
on Isocrates' *Antidosis*   353

1 **Joseph Turner**
2 *Sir Gawain and the Green Knight* and the History
of Medieval Rhetoric   371 6

Erin T. Chandler
The Present Time of Things Past: Julian of Norwich's Appropriation
of St. Augustine's Generative Theory of Memory   389

Jacob Dickerson
Metonymy and Indexicality: People and Place in the Five Points 405

FIRST PAGE OF ARTICLE

Rhetoric Review, Vol. 31, No. 4, 371–388, 2012
Copyright © Taylor & Francis Group, LLC
ISSN: 0735-0198 print / 1532-7981 online
DOI: 10.1080/07350198.2012.711196

Routledge
Taylor & Francis Group

1 JOSEPH TURNER

University of Delaware

2 ***Sir Gawain and the Green Knight* and the History
of Medieval Rhetoric**

*During the Middle Ages, rhetoric and literature were thoroughly intertwined,
whereas current notions of disciplinarity, in which literature and rhetoric
are constructed as separate traditions, muddy our understanding of medieval*

WORKS CITED ENTRY FOR AN ARTICLE IN A PRINT JOURNAL

1   2

Turner, Joseph. "*Sir Gawain and the Green Knight* and the History of

     3   4   5   6   7

Medieval Rhetoric." *Rhetoric Review* 31.4 (2012): 371-88. Print.

For more on citing articles in MLA style, see items 13–16.

■ 15. Article in a magazine (*cont.*)

b. Print (weekly)

author:
last name first　　　article title　　　magazine title　date　page(s) medium

Vick, Karl. "The Stateless Statesman." *Time* 15 Oct. 2012: 32-37. Print.

c. Web

author:
last name first　　　article title　　　Web site title

Leonard, Andrew. "The Surveillance State High School." *Salon*.

　　　sponsor　　date　medium　date of access

　　Salon Media Group, 27 Nov. 2012. Web. 4 Dec. 2012.

d. Database

author:
last name first　　　article title　　　magazine title　date

Rosenbaum, Ron. "The Last Renaissance Man." *Smithsonian* Nov. 2012:

　page(s)　database title　medium　date of access

　39-44. *OmniFile Full Text Select*. Web. 12 Jan. 2013.

■ 16. Article in a newspaper
If the city of publication is not obvious from the title of the newspaper, include the city in brackets after the newspaper title (see item 5a).

a. Print
If sections are numbered, include the section number between the date and the page number: 14 Apr. 2012, sec. 2: 21.

author:
last name first　　　　article title

Sherry, Allison. "Volunteers' Personal Touch Turns High-Tech Data

　　newspaper title　date　page(s) medium

　into Votes." *Denver Post* 30 Oct. 2012: 1A+. Print.

b. Web

author:
last name first　　　　article title

Amos, Adria. "STEM Teacher Uses 'Flip' Method to Put Classroom Focus on

　　Web site title　　　sponsor

　Students, Not Educator." *Knoxnews.com*. Knoxville News Sentinel,

　date　medium　date of access

　1 Oct. 2012. Web. 29 Oct. 2012.

Citation at a glance

Article from a database MLA

To cite an article from a database in MLA style, include the following elements:

1. Author(s) of article
2. Title and subtitle of article
3. Title of journal, magazine, or newspaper
4. Volume and issue numbers (for journal)
5. Date or year of publication
6. Page numbers of article ("n. pag." if none)
7. Name of database
8. Medium
9. Date of access

DATABASE RECORD

Searching: **OmniFile Full Text Select (H.W. Wilson)** ⟨**7**⟩

FROM CENSORS TO CRITICS: REPRESENTING "THE PEOPLE". ⟨**2**⟩

Authors: Weinberger, Stephen[1]

Source: Film & History (03603695); Fall2012, Vol. 42 Issue 2, p5-22, 18p

Document Type: Article

Subjects: United States; Motion pictures — Censorship — Law & legislation; Motion pictures — Social aspects; Motion pictures — History — 1900-1929; Motion pictures — History — 1930-1939; Right & left (Political science); Liberalism; Motion picture industry — United States — History; Conservatism — United States — History — 20th century

Abstract: The article presents an examination of the history of the U.S. motion picture industry during the 1920s and 1930s, focusing on the powers and actions of political censors and their opposition by liberal filmmakers. Discussion is offered exploring both the attitudes of filmmakers concerning their self-perception as spokesmen for the greater populace who had the authority to depict controversial material and those of conservative censors who sought to protect society from the same content. The history of film censorship boards and the industry's various reactions to them is then described in depth.

Author Affiliations: [1]Dickinson College

ISSN: 03603695

Accession Number: 84519245

Database: OmniFile Full Text Select (H.W. Wilson)

---

1 **Authors:** Weinberger, Stephen[1]

3 **Source:** Film & History (03603695); Fall2012, Vol. 42 Issue 2, p5-22, 18p
 ⟨**5**⟩ ⟨**4**⟩ ⟨**6**⟩

Reprinted by permission of EBSCO Publishing.

WORKS CITED ENTRY FOR AN ARTICLE FROM A DATABASE

⟨1⟩ ⟨2⟩
Weinberger, Stephen. "From Censors to Critics: Representing 'the

⟨3⟩ ⟨4⟩ ⟨5⟩ ⟨6⟩ ⟨7⟩
People.'" *Film & History* 42.2 (2012): 5-22. *OmniFile Full Text*

⟨8⟩ ⟨9⟩
Select. Web. 12 Jan. 2013.

For more on citing articles from a database in MLA style, see items 13–16.

■ **16. Article in a newspaper (cont.)**

c. E-reader

article title / newspaper title / date / page(s)

"Church Votes No on Female Bishops." *Boston Globe* 21 Nov. 2012: A3.

medium

E-reader.

d. Database

article title / label / newspaper title / date / page(s)

"The Road toward Peace." Editorial. *New York Times* 15 Feb. 1945: 18.

database title / medium

ProQuest Historical Newspapers: The New York Times. Web.

date of access

18 June 2013.

■ **17. Abstract or executive summary**

a. Abstract of an article

Bottomore, Stephen. "The Romance of the Cinematograph." Abstract. *Film History* 24.3 (2012): 341-44. *General OneFile*. Web. 25 Oct. 2012.

b. Abstract of a dissertation

Chen, Shu-Ling. "Mothers and Daughters in Morrison, Tan, Marshall, and Kincaid." Diss. U of Washington, 2000. *DAI* 61.6 (2000): AAT9975963. *ProQuest Dissertations and Theses*. Web. 22 Feb. 2012.

c. Executive summary

Pintak, Lawrence. *The Murrow Rural Information Initiative: Final Report*. Executive summary. Pullman: Murrow Coll. of Communication, Washington State U, 25 May 2012. PDF file.

■ **18. Article with a title in its title** Use single quotation marks around a title of a short work or a quoted term that appears in an article title. Italicize a title or term normally italicized.

Silber, Nina. "From 'Great Emancipator' to 'Vampire Hunter': The Many Stovepipe Hats of Cinematic Lincoln." *Cognoscenti*. WBUR, 22 Nov. 2012. Web. 13 Dec. 2012.

◼ 19. Editorial

"New State for the US?" Editorial. *Columbus Dispatch*. Dispatch Printing,
24 Nov. 2012. Web. 27 Nov. 2012.

◼ 20. Unsigned article

"Public Health Response to a Changing Climate." *Centers for Disease
Control and Prevention*. Centers for Disease Control and Prevention,
1 Oct. 2012. Web. 31 Oct. 2012.

◼ 21. Letter to the editor

Fahey, John A. "Recalling the Cuban Missile Crisis." Letter.
Washington Post 28 Oct. 2012: A16. *LexisNexis Library Express*.
Web. 15 Dec. 2012.

◼ 22. Comment on an online article   If the writer of the comment uses a screen name, see item 11.

author:
screen name   label   article title

pablosharkman. Comment. "'We Are All Implicated': Wendell Berry Laments

author of article

a Disconnection from Community and the Land." By Scott Carlson.

Web site title   sponsor

Chronicle of Higher Education. Chronicle of Higher Educ.,

date of
update date medium access

23 Apr. 2012. Web. 30 Oct. 2012.

◼ 23. Paper or presentation at a conference   See item 35; see also item 45 for proceedings of a conference. If you viewed the presentation live, cite it as a lecture or public address (see item 62).

first author:
last name first   other contributors: in normal order

Zuckerman, Ethan, with Tim Berners-Lee, Esther Dyson, Jaron Lanier, and

presentation title

Kaitlin Thaney. "Big Data, Big Challenges, and Big Opportunities."

label   conference title

Presentation at Wired for Change: The Power and the Pitfalls of Big Data.

conference   date of
sponsor   location   date   medium   access

Ford Foundation, New York. 15 Oct. 2012. Web. 30 Oct. 2012.

■ 24. Book review

Telander, Alex C. "In an MMO Far Far Away." Rev. of *Omnitopia Dawn*, by Diane Duane. *San Francisco Book Review*. 1776 Productions, 17 Jan. 2012. Web. 8 Aug. 2012.

■ 25. Film review or other review

Lane, Anthony. "Film within a Film." Rev. of *Argo*, dir. Ben Affleck, and *Sinister*, dir. Scott Derrickson. *New Yorker* 15 Oct. 2012: 98-99. Print.

■ 26. Performance review

Matson, Andrew. Rev. of *Until the Quiet Comes*, by Flying Lotus. *Seattle Times*. Seattle Times, 31 Oct. 2012. Web. 10 Nov. 2012.

■ 27. Interview See also item 60 for citing transcripts of interviews.

Kapoor, Anil. "Anil Kapoor on Q." Interview by Jian Ghomeshi. *Q*. CBC Radio, n.d. Web. 29 Oct. 2012.

Buffett, Warren, and Carol Loomis. Interview by Charlie Rose. *Charlie Rose*. PBS. WGBH, Boston, 26 Nov. 2012. Television.

Akufo, Dautey. Personal interview. 11 Apr. 2012.

■ 28. Article in a reference work (encyclopedia, dictionary, wiki) Page numbers are not necessary because the entries in the source are arranged alphabetically.

a. Print

Posner, Rebecca. "Romance Languages." *The Encyclopaedia Britannica: Macropaedia*. 15th ed. 1987. Print.

"Sonata." *The American Heritage Dictionary of the English Language*. 5th ed. 2011. Print.

b. Web

Durante, Amy M. "Finn Mac Cumhail." *Encyclopedia Mythica*. Encyclopedia Mythica, 17 Apr. 2011. Web. 20 Nov. 2012.

■ 29. Letter

a. Print

Wharton, Edith. Letter to Henry James. 28 Feb. 1915. *Henry James and Edith Wharton: Letters, 1900-1915*. Ed. Lyall H. Powers. New York: Scribner's, 1990. 323-26. Print.

■ **29. Letter (*cont.*)**

b. Web

Oblinger, Maggie. Letter to Charlie Thomas. 31 Mar. 1895. Nebraska State
Hist. Soc. *Prairie Settlement: Nebraska Photographs and Family
Letters, 1862-1912*. Web. 3 Sept. 2012.

c. Personal   For the medium, use "MS" for "manuscript," or
a handwritten letter; "TS" for "typescript," or a typed letter.

Primak, Shoshana. Letter to the author. 6 May 2012. TS.

Books and other long works

▶ Citation at a glance: Book, **page 151**

■ **30. Basic format for a book**

a. Print

author: last
name first   book title   city   publisher date medium
Wolfe, Tom. *Back to Blood*. New York: Little, 2012. Print.

b. E-book

author: last
name first book title   translators: in normal order
Tolstoy, Leo. *War and Peace*. Trans. Richard Pevear and Larissa Volokhonsky.

city   publisher date medium
New York: Knopf, 2007. Nook file.

c. Web

Saalman, Lora, ed. and trans. *The China-India Nuclear Crossroads*.
Washington: Carnegie Endowment for Intl. Peace, 2012.
Scribd. Web. 27 Nov. 2012.

■ **31. Parts of a book**

a. Foreword, introduction, preface, or afterword

author of foreword:
last name first book part   book title
Bennett, Hal Zina. Foreword. *Shimmering Images: A Handy Little Guide to*

author of book:
in normal order   city   imprint-publisher
Writing Memoir. By Lisa Dale Norton. New York: Griffin-St. Martin's,

date   page(s) medium
2008. xiii-xvi. Print.

Ozick, Cynthia. "Portrait of the Essay as a Warm Body." Introduction.
The Best American Essays 1998. Ed. Ozick. Boston: Houghton,
1998. xv-xxi. Print.

Citation at a glance

Book MLA

To cite a print book in MLA style, include the following elements:

1 Author(s)
2 Title and subtitle
3 City of publication
4 Publisher
5 Date of publication (latest date)
6 Medium

TITLE PAGE

FROM COPYRIGHT PAGE

THE LADY AND THE PEACOCK: *The Life of Aung San Suu Kyi*

Copyright © Peter Popham, 2011, 2012 **5**
Pages xii–xiv and 436 are a continuation of this copyright page.

Reprinted by permission of The Experiment, LLC.

WORKS CITED ENTRY FOR A PRINT BOOK

1 2
Popham, Peter. *The Lady and the Peacock: The Life of Aung San Suu*
3 4 5 6
Kyi. New York: Experiment, 2012. Print.

For more on citing books in MLA style, see items 30–42.

■ 31. Parts of a book (*cont.*)

b. Chapter in a book

Adams, Henry. "Diplomacy." *The Education of Henry Adams*. Boston:
    Houghton, 1918. N. pag. *Bartleby.com: Great Books Online*.
    Web. 8 Dec. 2012.

■ 32. Book with a title in its title

Masur, Louis P. *Runaway Dream:* Born to Run *and Bruce Springsteen's*
    American Vision. New York: Bloomsbury, 2009. Print.

Millás, Juan José. *"Personality Disorders" and Other Stories*. Trans.
    Gregory B. Kaplan. New York: MLA, 2007. Print.

■ 33. Book in a language other than English Capitalize the
original title according to the conventions of the book's
language.

Vargas Llosa, Mario. *El sueño del celta* [*The Dream of the Celt*]. Madrid:
    Alfaguara, 2010. Print.

■ 34. Entire anthology or collection The abbreviation
"eds." is for multiple editors. If the book has only one editor, use the singular "ed."

first editor: other editor(s):   title of
last name first   in normal order   anthology

Belasco, Susan, and Linck Johnson, eds. *The Bedford Anthology of American*

           volume   city   publisher   date   medium

     Literature. Vol. 2. Boston: Bedford, 2008. Print.

■ 35. One selection from an anthology or a collection
   ▶   Citation at a glance: Selection from an anthology or a
        collection, **page 154**

author of   title of
selection   selection   title of anthology

Lorde, Audre. "Black Mother Woman." *The Bedford Anthology of American*

                 editor(s) of anthology   volume   city

     Literature. Ed. Susan Belasco and Linck Johnson. Vol. 2. Boston:

publisher   date   page(s)   medium

     Bedford, 2008. 1419. Print.

■ 36. Two or more selections from an anthology or a
collection Provide an entry for the entire anthology (see
item 34) and a shortened entry for each selection. Use the
medium only for the complete anthology.

first editor   other editor(s)   title of anthology

Belasco, Susan, and Linck Johnson, eds. *The Bedford Anthology of American*

volume city publisher date medium

Literature. Vol. 2. Boston: Bedford, 2008. Print.

author of   title of   editor(s)
selection   selection   of anthology   page(s)

Lorde, Audre. "Black Mother Woman." Belasco and Johnson 1419.

title of   editor(s)
author of selection   selection   of anthology   page(s)

Silko, Leslie Marmon. "Yellow Woman." Belasco and Johnson 1475-81.

■ **37. Edition other than the first** Give the name of the translator or editor, if any, before the edition number (see also item 9).

Eagleton, Terry. *Literary Theory: An Introduction*. 3rd ed. Minneapolis:
    U of Minnesota P, 2008.

■ **38. Multivolume work** See item 14 on page 129 for an in-text citation of a multivolume work.

author: last   book   editor(s):   total
name first   title   in normal order   volumes   city   publisher

Stark, Freya. *Letters*. Ed. Lucy Moorehead. 8 vols. Salisbury: Compton,

inclusive
dates   medium

1974-82. Print.

■ **39. Sacred text** Give the title of the edition (taken from the title page), italicized. Add the name of the version, if there is one, after the medium.

The Oxford Annotated Bible with the Apocrypha. Ed. Herbert G. May
    and Bruce M. Metzger. New York: Oxford UP, 1965. Print. Rev.
    Standard Vers.

The Qur'an: Translation. Trans. Abdullah Yusuf Ali. Elmhurst:
    Tahrike, 2000. Print.

■ **40. Book in a series** After the medium, give the series name and series number, if any.

Denham, A. E., ed. *Plato on Art and Beauty*. New York: Palgrave, 2012.
    Print. Philosophers in Depth.

Citation at a glance
Selection from an anthology or a collection MLA

To cite a selection from an anthology in MLA style, include the following elements:

1 Author(s) of selection
2 Title and subtitle of selection
3 Title and subtitle of anthology
4 Editor(s) of anthology
5 City of publication
6 Publisher
7 Date of publication
8 Page numbers of selection
9 Medium

TITLE PAGE OF ANTHOLOGY

THE UNFINISHED
REVOLUTION

VOICES FROM THE GLOBAL FIGHT
FOR WOMEN'S RIGHTS

4 EDITED BY MINKY WORDEN

6 Seven Stories Press
5 NEW YORK

7
Seven Stories Press
NEW YORK

FROM COPYRIGHT PAGE

7
Copyright © 2012 by Minky Worden
Individual chapters © 2012 by each author

FIRST PAGE OF SELECTION

CHAPTER 3

2 **Technology's Quiet Revolution for Women**

1 Isobel Coleman

On the eve of Egypt's January 2011 revolution, I happened to be in Cairo, having dinner with Gamila Ismail, a longtime Egyptian political activist who had spent decades opposing the Mubarak regime. "What will happen tomorrow?" I asked her, referring to the public demonstration planned for the next day in Tahrir Square. "It will be the huge," she insisted, monitoring Twitter and Facebook feeds on her cell phone. Gamila and a young assistant had spent weeks helping to organize the demonstration through social media. "We think hundreds of thousands of people could join the protest. This could finally be our moment for real change." Indeed.

Much has been made of the role of social media in the Arab uprisings, in particular how it has given voice to youth and women in unprecedented ways. But social media is just the latest in a long line of technologies that have been driving profound changes in civil society for centuries. From the first notions of community developed

Isobel Coleman, a senior fellow at the Council on Foreign Relations, is the Director of the Council's Civil Society, Markets, and Democracy Initiative and CFR's Women and Foreign Policy Program. She is the author of Paradise Beneath Her Feet: How Women Are Transforming the Middle East (Random House, 2010) and a contributing author to Restoring the Balance: A Middle East Strategy for the Next President (Brookings Institution Press, 2008). She has also served as a track leader for the Girls and Women Action Area at the Clinton Global Initiative. In 2011, Newsweek named her as one of "150 Women Who Shake the World."

41 | 8

WORKS CITED ENTRY FOR A SELECTION FROM AN ANTHOLOGY

1   2

Coleman, Isobel. "Technology's Quiet Revolution for Women." *The*

3

Unfinished Revolution: Voices from the Global Fight for Women's

4   5   6   7

Rights. Ed. Minky Worden. New York: Seven Stories, 2012.

8   9

41-49. Print.

For more on citing selections from anthologies in MLA style, see items 34–36.

■ **41. Republished book**   After the title of the book, give the original year of publication, followed by the current publication information.

Trilling, Lionel. *The Liberal Imagination*. 1950. Introd. Louis Menand.
New York: New York Rev. of Books, 2008. Print.

■ **42. Publisher's imprint**   Give the name of the imprint (a division of a publishing company), a hyphen, and the name of the publisher.

Mantel, Hilary. *Bring Up the Bodies*. New York: Macrae-Holt, 2012.
Print.

■ **43. Pamphlet, brochure, or newsletter**
The Legendary Sleepy Hollow Cemetery. Concord: Friends of Sleepy
Hollow Cemetery, 2008. Print.

■ **44. Dissertation**

a. Published

Damberg, Cheryl L. *Healthcare Reform: Distributional Consequences
of an Employer Mandate for Workers in Small Firms*. Diss. Rand
Graduate School, 1995. Santa Monica: Rand, 1996. Print.

b. Unpublished

Jackson, Shelley. "Writing Whiteness: Contemporary Southern Literature
in Black and White." Diss. U of Maryland, 2000. Print.

■ **45. Proceedings of a conference**

Sowards, Stacey K., Kyle Alvarado, Diana Arrieta, and Jacob Barde,
eds. *Across Borders and Environments: Communication and
Environmental Justice in International Contexts*. Proc. of Eleventh
Biennial Conf. on Communication and the Environment, 25-28
June 2011, U of Texas at El Paso. Cincinnati: Intl. Environmental
Communication Assn., 2012. PDF file.

■ **46. Manuscript**

Arendt, Hannah. *Between Past and Future*. N.d. 1st draft. Hannah
Arendt Papers. MS Div., Lib. of Cong. *Manuscript Division, Library
of Congress*. Web. 24 Aug. 2012.

Web sites and parts of Web sites

■ 47. An entire Web site

a. Web site with author or editor

author or editor: title of
last name first   Web site   sponsor

Railton, Stephen. *Mark Twain in His Times*. Stephen Railton and U of Virginia Lib.,

    update
    date medium   date of
             access

    2012. Web. 27 Nov. 2012.

Halsall, Paul, ed. *Internet Modern History Sourcebook*. Fordham U,

    4 Nov. 2011. Web. 19 Sept. 2012.

b. Web site with organization as author

                       title of
government   department   Web site   sponsor

United States. Dept. of Agriculture. *USDA*. US Dept. of Agriculture,

    update
    date   medium   date of
                   access

    31 Oct. 2012. Web. 30 Nov. 2012.

c. Web site with no author If the site also has no title, begin with a label such as "Home page."

Jacob Leisler Papers Project. Dept. of History, New York U, n.d. Web.

    24 Aug. 2012.

d. Web site with no title Use a label or a description in place of a title.

Gray, Bethany. Home page. Iowa State U, 2012. Web. 22 Sept.

    2012.

NOTE: If your instructor requires a URL for Web sources, include the URL, enclosed in angle brackets, at the end of the entry.

Railton, Stephen. *Mark Twain in His Times*. Stephen Railton and U

    of Virginia Lib., 2012. Web. 27 Nov. 2012. <http://twain.lib

    .virginia.edu/>.

■ 48. Short work from a Web site

> ► Citation at a glance: Short work from a Web site, **page 159**

author: last name first | title of short work | title of Web site

Gallagher, Sean. "The Last Nomads of the Tibetan Plateau." *Pulitzer Center on*

sponsor | update date | medium | date of access

    Crisis Reporting. Pulitzer Center, 25 Oct. 2012. Web. 30 Oct. 2012.

■ 49. Long work from a Web site

author: last name first | title of long work | title of Web site | sponsor

Milton, John. *Paradise Lost: Book I. Poetry Foundation*. Poetry Foundation,

update date | medium | date of access

    2012. Web. 14 Dec. 2012.

■ 50. Entire blog   Cite as an entire Web site (item 47).

Kiuchi, Tatsuro. *Tatsuro Kiuchi: News & Blog*. N.p., 19 Oct. 2012. Web.

    29 Oct. 2012.

■ 51. Blog post or comment   Cite a blog post or comment as a short work from a Web site (item 48). If the post or comment has no title, use the label "Blog post" or "Blog comment." (See item 11 for the use of screen names.)

author: last name first | title of blog post | title of blog | sponsor

Eakin, Emily. "*Cloud Atlas*'s Theory of Everything." *NYR Blog*. NYREV,

update date | medium | date of access

    2 Nov. 2012. Web. 3 Dec. 2012.

author: screen name | label | title of blog post

mitchellfreedman. Blog comment. "*Cloud Atlas*'s Theory of Everything," by

author of blog post | title of blog | sponsor | date | medium | date of access

    Emily Eakin. *NYR Blog*. NYREV, 3 Nov. 2012. Web. 3 Dec. 2012.

■ 52. Academic course or department home page

Masiello, Regina. "355:101: Expository Writing." *Rutgers School of Arts*

    and Sciences. Writing Program, Rutgers U, 2012. Web.

    19 Aug. 2012.

Comparative Media Studies. Dept. home page. *Massachusetts Institute*

    of Technology. MIT, n.d. Web. 6 Oct. 2012.

Citation at a glance
Short work from a Web site MLA

To cite a short work from a Web site in MLA style, include the following elements:

1 Author(s) of short work (if any)
2 Title and subtitle of short work
3 Title and subtitle of Web site
4 Sponsor of Web site ("N.p." if none)
5 Latest update date ("n.d." if none)
6 Medium
7 Date of access

INTERNAL PAGE FROM WEB SITE

Courtesy of the Trustees of Amherst College. Reproduced by permission.

FOOTER ON PAGE

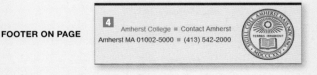

WORKS CITED ENTRY FOR A SHORT WORK FROM A WEB SITE

>   2   3   4
>
> "Losing a Country, Finding a Home." *Amherst College*. Amherst Coll.,
>
>   5   6   7
>
> n.d. Web. 12 Jan. 2013.

For more on citing sources from Web sites in MLA style, see items 48 and 49.

Audio, visual, and multimedia sources

■ 53. Podcast

a. Web

author:
last name first · podcast title · Web site title · sponsor

Tanner, Laura. "Virtual Reality in 9/11 Fiction." *Literature Lab*. Dept. of

no date · medium · date of access

English, Brandeis U, n.d. Web. 30 Oct. 2012.

b. Downloaded   Give the file type (such as "MP3 file" or "MOV file") as the medium.

author:
last name first · podcast title · Web site title · sponsor

Tanner, Laura. "Virtual Reality in 9/11 Fiction." *Literature Lab*. Dept. of English,

no date · medium

Brandeis U, n.d. MP3 file.

■ 54. Film (DVD, BD, or other format)   Generally, begin the entry with the title, followed by the director and lead performers, as in the first example. If your paper emphasizes one or more people involved with the film, you may begin with those names, as in the second example.

Typical designations for medium are "Film" (if viewed in a theater or streamed through a service such as Netflix); "DVD"; "BD" (for Blu-ray Disc); "Web" (if viewed on a Web site). If you aren't sure of the medium, use "Film."

film title · director · major performers

Argo. Dir. Ben Affleck. Perf. Affleck, Bryan Cranston, and Alan Arkin.

distributor · release date · medium

Warner Bros., 2012. Film.

director:
last name first · film title · major performers

Forster, Marc, dir. *Finding Neverland*. Perf. Johnny Depp, Kate Winslet,

distributor · release date

Julie Christie, Radha Mitchell, and Dustin Hoffman. Miramax, 2004.

medium

DVD.

■ 55. Supplementary material accompanying a film   Begin with the title of the supplementary material and the names of any contributors. Add information about the film, as in item 54.

"Sweeney's London." Prod. Eric Young. *Sweeney Todd: The Demon Barber of Fleet Street*. Dir. Tim Burton. DreamWorks, 2007. DVD. Disc 2.

■ **56. Video or audio from the Web**   Cite as a short work from a Web site (item 48).

```
        author:                        Web site              update
      last name first   title of video   title   sponsor     date   medium
Lewis, Paul. "Citizen Journalism." YouTube. YouTube, 14 May 2011. Web.

           date of
           access
      24 Sept. 2012.
```

Burstein, Julie. "Four Lessons in Creativity." *TED: Ideas Worth Spreading*. TED Conf., Mar. 2012. Web. 18 Aug. 2012.

■ **57. Video game**   Begin with the developer or author (if any); the title; the version ("Vers."), if there is one; the distributor and date of publication; and the platform or medium. If the game can be played on the Web, add information as for a work from a Web site (item 48).

Firaxis Games. *Sid Meier's Civilization Revolution*. Take-Two Interactive, 2008. Xbox 360. *Edgeworld*. Atom Entertainment, 1 May 2012. Web. 15 June 2012.

■ **58. Computer software or app**   Cite as a video game (item 57).

Words with Friends. Vers. 5.84. Zynga, 2013. iOS 4.3.

■ **59. Television or radio episode or program**

a. Broadcast

```
                                                         narrator
         title of episode              program title   (or host or speaker)
"Federal Role in Support of Autism." Washington Journal. Narr. Robb Harleston.

            broadcast
  network     date      medium
  C-SPAN. 1 Dec. 2012. Television.
```

b. Web

```
                                               narrator (or host
    title of episode        program title       or speaker)    network
"Back-to-School Cure." Currently Concordia. Narr. Melissa Mulligan. CJLO,

      date        Web site              date
   of posting      title    medium    of access
   22 Sept. 2012. CJLO.com. Web. 23 Sept. 2012.
```

■ 59. Television or radio episode or program (*cont.*)

c. Podcast

podcast title   episode number (if any)   narrator (or host or sponsor)   Web site title

"NIH Research Radio." Episode 0170. Narr. Joe Balintfy. *NIH Radio*.

sponsor   date of posting   medium

Natl. Inst. of Health, 19 Oct. 2012. MP3 file.

■ 60. Transcript

Cullen, Heidi. "Weather Warnings for a 'Climate Changed Planet.'"
Interview by Terry Gross. *Fresh Air*. Natl. Public Radio, 25 July
2011. *LexisNexis Library Express*. Web. 5 Apr. 2012. Transcript.

"Missing Athletes Join a Long List of Olympic Defectors." Narr.
Melissa Block. *All Things Considered*. Natl. Public Radio, 9 Aug.
2012. Web. 28 Aug. 2012. Transcript.

■ 61. Performance

Wetu in the City: An Urban Black Indian Tale. By Mwalim [Morgan
James Peters]. Dir. Naheem Garcia. Hibernian Hall, Boston.
16 Nov. 2012. Performance.

Symphony no. 4 in G. By Gustav Mahler. Cond. Mark Wigglesworth. Perf.
Juliane Banse and Boston Symphony Orch. Symphony Hall, Boston.
17 Apr. 2009. Performance.

■ 62. Lecture or public address

Berry, Wendell E. "It All Turns on Affection." Natl. Endowment for
the Humanities. John F. Kennedy Center for the Performing
Arts, Washington. 23 Apr. 2012. Lecture.

Clinton, Hillary Rodham. "Remarks on 'Creating an AIDS-Free
Generation.'" *US Department of State: Diplomacy in Action*. US
Dept. of State, 8 Nov. 2011. Web. 29 Oct. 2012.

■ 63. Musical score

Beethoven, Ludwig van. Symphony no. 5 in C Minor, op. 67. 1807.
Center for Computer Assisted Research in the Humanities. CCARH,
Stanford U, 2000. Web. 23 Aug. 2012.

■ 64. Sound recording

a. CD

Blige, Mary J. "Don't Mind." *Life II: The Journey Continues (Act 1)*.
     Geffen, 2011. CD.

b. Downloaded

Blige, Mary J. "Don't Mind." *Life II: The Journey Continues (Act 1)*.
     Geffen, 2011. MP3 file.

■ 65. Work of art

a. Original

Constable, John. *Dedham Vale*. 1802. Oil on canvas. Victoria and
     Albert Museum, London.

b. Web

Hessing, Valjean. *Caddo Myth*. 1976. Joslyn Art Museum, Omaha.
     Joslyn Art Museum. Web. 19 Apr. 2012.

c. Digital file

Diebenkorn, Richard. *Ocean Park No. 38*. 1971. Phillips Collection,
     Washington. JPEG file.

■ 66. Photograph

a. Original

Feinstein, Harold. *Hangin' Out, Sharing a Public Bench, NYC*. 1948.
     Photograph. Panopticon Gallery, Boston.

b. Web

McCurry, Steve. *A World of Prayer*. *Magnum Photos*. Magnum Photos,
     29 Oct. 2012. Web. 31 Oct. 2012.

c. Digital file

Lucy Branham in Occoquan Prison Dress. 1919. Lib. of Cong.
     JPEG file.

■ 67. Cartoon

Zyglis, Adam. "Delta and Denial." Cartoon. *Buffalo News*. Buffalo
     News, 11 Jan. 2013. Web. 21 Jan. 2013.

■ 68. Advertisement

UnitedHealthcare. Advertisement. *Smithsonian* Dec. 2012: 27. Print.

■ **69. Visual such as a table, a chart, or another graphic**

"Canada's Energy Flow 2007." Chart. *Economist*. Economist Newspaper,
26 Oct. 2012. Web. 30 Oct. 2012.

"CDC Climate Ready States and Cities Initiative." Graphic. *Centers for
Disease Control and Prevention*. Centers for Disease Control and
Prevention, 1 Oct. 2012. Web. 31 Oct. 2012.

■ **70. Map**

"Population Origin Groups in Rural Texas." Map. *Perry-Castañeda Library
Map Collection*. U of Texas at Austin, 1976. Web. 17 Mar. 2012.

■ **71. Digital file**   A digital file is any document or image
that exists in digital form, independent of a Web site. Begin
with information required for the source (such as a photograph, a report, or a sound recording). For the medium, give
the type of file: "JPEG file," "PDF file," "MP3 file," and so on.

photographer	photograph title	date of composition	location of photograph

Hine, Lewis W. *Girl in Cherryville Mill*. 1908. Prints and Photographs Div., Lib.

	medium

 of Cong. JPEG file.

"Back to School." *This American Life*. Narr. Ira Glass. Episode 474.
Chicago Public Media, 14 Sept. 2012. MP3 file.

National Institute of Mental Health. *What Rescue Workers Can Do*.
Washington: US Dept. of Health and Human Services, 2006. PDF file.

Government and legal documents

■ **72. Government document**

government	department	agency (or agencies)

United States. Dept. of Agriculture. Food and Nutrition Service. Child

	title (long work)

 Nutrition Programs. *Eligibility Manual for School Meals: Determining and*

	Web site title	sponsor

 Verifying Eligibility. *National School Lunch Program*. US Dept. of

update date	medium	date of access

 Agriculture, Aug. 2012. Web. 30 Oct. 2012.

Canada. Minister of Indian Affairs and Northern Dev. *Gathering
Strength: Canada's Aboriginal Action Plan*. Ottawa: Minister of
Public Works and Govt. Services Can., 2000. Print.

■ 73. Testimony before a legislative body

Carson, Johnnie. "Assessing US Policy on Peacekeeping Operations
in Africa." Testimony before the US House Foreign Affairs
Committee, Subcommittee on Africa, Global Health, and Human
Rights. *US Department of State: Diplomacy in Action*. US Dept. of
State, 13 Sept. 2012. Web. 29 Sept. 2012.

■ 74. Historical document   The titles of most historical documents, such as the US Constitution and the Canadian Charter of Rights and Freedoms, are neither italicized nor put in quotation marks.

Jefferson, Thomas. First Inaugural Address. 1801. *The American Reader*.
Ed. Diane Ravitch. New York: Harper, 1990. 42-44. Print.

Constitution of the United States. 1787. *The Charters of Freedom*. US Natl.
Archives and Records Administration, n.d. Web. 19 Jan. 2013.

■ 75. Legislative act (law)   Begin with the name of the act, followed by its Public Law number; its Statutes at Large volume and page numbers; its date of enactment; and the medium.

Electronic Freedom of Information Act Amendments of 1996. Pub. L.
104-231. 110 Stat. 3048. 2 Oct. 1996. Print.

■ 76. Court case   Name the first plaintiff and the first defendant. Then give the volume, name, and page number of the law report; the court name; the year of the decision; and publication information. Do not italicize the name of the case. (In the text of the paper, the name of the case is italicized; see item 19 on p. 130.)

Utah v. Evans. 536 US 452. Supreme Court of the US. 2002. *Supreme
Court Collection*. Legal Information Inst., Cornell U Law School,
n.d. Web. 30 Apr. 2012.

Personal communication and social media

■ 77. E-mail message

Lowe, Walter. "Review Questions." Message to the author. 15 Mar. 2013.
E-mail.

■ 78. Text message

Wiley, Joanna. Message to the author. 29 Nov. 2012. Text message.

■ **79. Posting to an online discussion list**

Baker, Frank. "A New Twist on a Classic." *Developing Digital Literacies*.
    NCTE, 30 Nov. 2012. Web. 10 Jan. 2013.

■ **80. Facebook post or comment** For the use of screen names, see item 11 on page 141. If the post has no title, use the label "Post" in place of a title.

Bedford/St. Martin's. "Liz Losh Discusses Teaching about Interactive
    Media with Comics: http://ow.ly/imucP." *Facebook*. Facebook,
    5 Mar. 2013. Web. 26 Mar. 2013.

Erin Houlihan. Post. *Facebook*. Facebook, 23 Nov. 2012. Web. 26 Nov. 2012.

■ **81. Twitter post (tweet)** Give the text of the entire tweet in quotation marks, using the writer's capitalization and punctuation. Follow the text with the date and time noted on the tweet. Use "Tweet" as the medium. For the use of screen names, see item 11 on page 141.

Curiosity Rover. "The journey of 352,000,000 miles begins with a
    single launch. One year ago today, I left Earth for Mars http://
    twitpic.com/bgq1vn." 26 Nov. 2012, 10:10 a.m. Tweet.

33c MLA information notes (optional)

Researchers who use the MLA system of parenthetical documentation may also use information notes for one of two purposes:

1. to provide additional material that is important but might interrupt the flow of the paper
2. to refer to several sources that support a single point or to provide comments on sources

Information notes may be either footnotes or endnotes. Footnotes appear at the foot of the page; endnotes appear on a separate page at the end of the paper, before the list of works cited. For either style, the notes are numbered consecutively throughout the paper. The text of the paper contains a raised arabic numeral that corresponds to the number of the note.

TEXT

In the past several years, employees have filed a number of lawsuits against employers because of online monitoring practices.[1]

NOTE

1. For a discussion of federal law applicable to electronic surveillance in the workplace, see Kesan 293.

34 MLA manuscript format; sample pages

The following guidelines are consistent with advice given in the *MLA Handbook for Writers of Research Papers*, 7th ed. (New York: MLA, 2009), and with typical requirements for student papers. For pages from sample MLA papers, see pages 170–73.

34a MLA manuscript format

Formatting the paper   Papers written in MLA style should be formatted as follows.

Font   If your instructor does not require a specific font, choose one that is standard and easy to read (such as Times New Roman).

Title and identification   MLA does not require a title page. On the first page of your paper, place your name, your instructor's name, the course title, and the date on separate lines against the left margin. Then center your title. (See pp. 170 and 172 for sample first pages.)

If your instructor requires a title page, ask for formatting guidelines. A format similar to the one on page 222 may be acceptable.

Page numbers (running head)   Put the page number preceded by your last name in the upper right corner of each page, one-half inch below the top edge. Use arabic numerals (1, 2, 3, and so on).

Margins, line spacing, and paragraph indents   Leave margins of one inch on all sides of the page. Left-align the text.

Double-space throughout the paper. Do not add extra space above or below the title of the paper or between paragraphs.

Indent the first line of each paragraph one-half inch from the left margin.

Capitalization, italics, and quotation marks   In titles of works, capitalize all words except articles (*a*, *an*, *the*), prepositions (*to*, *from*, *between*, and so on), coordinating conjunctions (*and*, *but*, *or*, *nor*, *for*, *so*, *yet*), and the *to* in infinitives—unless the word is first or last in the title or subtitle.

In the text of an MLA paper, when a complete sentence follows a colon, lowercase the first word following the colon unless the sentence is a quotation or a well-known expression or principle.

Italicize the titles of books, journals, magazines, and other long works, such as Web sites. Use quotation marks around the titles of articles, short stories, poems, and other short works.

Long quotations   When a quotation is longer than four typed lines of prose or three lines of poetry, set it off from the text by indenting the entire quotation one inch from the left margin. Double-space the indented quotation and do not add extra space above or below it.

Do not use quotation marks when a quotation has been set off from the text by indenting. See pages 170 and 172 for examples.

URLs   When you need to break a URL at the end of a line in the text of your paper, break it only after a slash or a double slash and do not insert a hyphen. For MLA rules on dividing URLs in your list of works cited, see page 169.

Headings   MLA neither encourages nor discourages the use of headings and provides no guidelines for their use. If you would like to insert headings in a long essay or research paper, check first with your instructor.

Visuals   MLA classifies visuals as tables and figures (figures include graphs, charts, maps, photographs, and drawings). Label each table with an arabic numeral ("Table 1," "Table 2," and so on) and provide a clear caption that identifies the subject. Capitalize the caption as you would a title (see 22c); do not italicize the label and caption or place them in quotation marks. Place the label and caption on separate lines above the table, flush with the left margin.

For a table that you have borrowed or adapted, give the source below the table in a note like the following:

Source: Boris Groysberg and Michael Slind; "Leadership Is a Conversation"; *Harvard Business Review* June 2012: 83; print.

For each figure, place the figure number (u...
abbreviation "Fig.") and a caption below the figur...
left. Capitalize the caption as you would a sentence; i...
source information following the caption. (When referring
to the figure in your paper, use the abbreviation "fig." in
parenthetical citations; otherwise spell out the word.)

Place visuals in the text, as close as possible to the sentences that relate to them, unless your instructor prefers
that visuals appear in an appendix.

Preparing the list of works cited Begin the list on a
new page at the end of the paper. Center the title "Works
Cited" about one inch from the top of the page. Double-
space throughout. See pages 171 and 173 for sample lists
of works cited.

Alphabetizing the list Alphabetize by the last names of the
authors (or editors); if a work has no author or editor, alphabetize by the first word of the title other than *A*, *An*, or *The*.

If your list includes two or more works by the same
author, see items 6 and 7 on page 139.

Indenting Do not indent the first line of each works cited
entry, but indent any additional lines one-half inch.

URLs If you need to include a URL in a works cited entry
and it must be divided across lines, break the URL only after
a slash or a double slash. Do not insert a hyphen at the end
of the line. Insert angle brackets around the URL. (See the
note following item 47 on p. 157.) If your word processing
program automatically turns URLs into links (by underlining
them and changing the color), turn off this feature.

34b Sample pages from MLA papers

Following are excerpts from two MLA papers: a research
paper written for a composition course and an analysis of
a short story written for a literature class.

hackerhandbooks.com/pocket
e MLA papers > Sample student writing
> Harba, "What's for Dinner? Personal Choices vs. Public
Health" (research)
> Larson, "The Transformation of Mrs. Peters: An Analysis of
'A Jury of Her Peers'" (literary analysis)

Sample MLA page: Research paper

Harba 1

Sophie Harba

Engl 1101

Professor Baros-Moon

30 April 2013

1   What's for Dinner? Personal Choices vs. Public Health

     Should the government enact laws to regulate healthy eating

2 choices? Many Americans would answer an emphatic "No," arguing

that what and how much we eat should be left to individual choice

rather than unreasonable laws. Others might argue that it would be

unreasonable for the government not to enact legislation, given the rise

of chronic diseases that result from harmful diets. In this debate, both

the definition of reasonable regulations and the role of government

3 to legislate food choices are at stake. In the name of public health

and safety, state governments have the responsibility to shape health

policies and to regulate healthy eating choices, especially since doing

4 so offers a potentially large social benefit for a relatively small cost.

     Debates surrounding the government's role in regulating food

have a long history in the United States. According to Lorine Goodwin,

5 a food historian, nineteenth-century reformers who sought to purify the

6 food supply were called "fanatics" and "radicals" by critics who argued

that consumers should be free to buy and eat what they want (77).

7 Thanks to regulations, though, such as the 1906 federal Pure Food and

Drug Act, food, beverages, and medicine are largely free from toxins.

In addition, to prevent contamination and the spread of disease, meat

and dairy products are now inspected by government agents to ensure

that they meet health requirements. Such regulations can be considered

8 reasonable because they protect us from harm with little, if any,

noticeable consumer cost.

---

1 Title, centered. **2** Opening research question engages readers.
3 Writer highlights the research conversation. **4** Thesis answers
the research question and presents Harba's main point. **5** Signal
phrase names the author. **6** Historical background provides
context for debate. **7** Parenthetical citation includes a page
number. **8** Harba explains her use of a key term, *reasonable*.

(Annotations indicate MLA-style formatting and effective writing.)

Sample MLA list of works cited

Works Cited **1**

Conly, Sarah. "Three Cheers for the Nanny State." *New York Times*
    25 Mar. 2013: A23.

"The Facts on Junk Food Marketing and Kids." *Prevention Institute*.
    Prevention Inst., n.d. Web. 21 Apr. 2013. **2**

Goodwin, Lorine Swainston. *The Pure Food, Drink, and Drug* **3**
    Crusaders, 1879-1914. Jefferson: McFarland, 2006. Print.

Gostin, L. O., and K. G. Gostin. "A Broader Liberty: J. S. Mill, **4**
    Paternalism, and the Public's Health." *Public Health* 123.3
    (2009): 214-21. *Academic Search Premier*. Web. 17 Apr. 2013.

Mello, Michelle M., David M. Studdert, and Troyen A. Brennan.
    "Obesity—The New Frontier of Public Health Law." *New*
    England Journal of Medicine 354.24 (2006): 2601-10.
    Expanded Academic ASAP. Web. 22 Apr. 2013.

Neergaard, Lauran, and Jennifer Agiesta. "Obesity's a Crisis but **5**
    We Want Our Junk Food, Poll Shows." *Huffington Post*.
    TheHuffingtonPost.com, 4 Jan. 2013. Web. 20 Apr. 2013.

Nestle, Marion. *Food Politics: How the Food Industry Influences* **6**
    Nutrition and Health. Berkeley: U of California P, 2013. Print.

Pollan, Michael. "The Food Movement, Rising." *New York Review* **7**
    of Books. NYREV, 10 June 2010. Web. 19 Apr. 2013.

Resnik, David. "Trans Fat Bans and Human Freedom." *American* **8**
    Journal of Bioethics 10.3 (2010): 27-32. *Academic Search*
    Premier. Web. 17 Apr. 2013.

United States. Dept. of Agriculture and Dept. of Health and Human **9**
    Services. *Dietary Guidelines for Americans, 2010*. Dept. of
    Agriculture and Dept. of Health and Human Services, 2010.
    Web. 17 Apr. 2013.

1 Heading, centered. **2** Abbreviation "n.d." for online source with no update date. **3** Authors' names inverted; works alphabetized by last names. **4** First line of entry at left margin; extra lines indented ½". **5** Short work from Web site. **6** Double-spacing throughout. **7** Article from online periodical. **8** Article from a database. **9** Government agency as author.

Sample MLA page: Literary analysis

Dan Larson

Professor Duncan

English 102

19 April 2013

1

The Transformation of Mrs. Peters:

An Analysis of "A Jury of Her Peers"

In Susan Glaspell's 1917 short story "A Jury of Her Peers," two

women accompany their husbands and a county attorney to an isolated

house where a farmer named John Wright has been choked to death.

The chief suspect is Wright's wife, Minnie, who is in jail awaiting trial.

The sheriff's wife, Mrs. Peters, has come along to gather some items for

Minnie, and Mrs. Hale has joined her. Initially, Mrs. Hale sympathizes

with Minnie and objects to the male investigators "snoopin' round and

criticizin'" her kitchen (249). But Mrs. Peters shows respect for the law,

2 saying that the men are doing "no more than their duty" (249). By

the end of the story, however, Mrs. Peters has joined Mrs. Hale in

3 lying to the men and committing a crime—hiding key evidence. What

causes this dramatic change?

One critic, Leonard Mustazza, argues that Mrs. Hale recruits

Mrs. Peters "as a fellow 'juror' in the case, moving the sheriff's wife . . .

towards identification with the accused wom[a]n" (494). However,

4 Mrs. Peters also reaches insights on her own. Her observations in the

kitchen lead her to understand Minnie's plight:

> The sheriff's wife had looked from the stove to the
>
> **5** sink—to the pail of water which had been carried in from
>
> outside. . . . That look of seeing into things, of seeing
>
> through a thing to something else, was in the eyes of the
>
> sheriff's wife now. (251-52)

1 Title, centered. **2** Quotation from literary work followed by
page number. **3** Writer's research question. **4** Debatable thesis.
5 Long quotation indented 1"; page numbers in parentheses after
final period.

(Annotations indicate MLA-style formatting and effective writing.)

Sample MLA list of works cited

Works Cited

Ben-Zvi, Linda. "'Murder, She Wrote': The Genesis of Susan [1]
    Glaspell's *Trifles*." *Theatre Journal* 44.2 (1992): 141-62.
    Rpt. in *Susan Glaspell: Essays on Her Theater and Fiction*.
    Ed. Ben-Zvi. Ann Arbor: U of Michigan P, 1995. 19-48.
    Print.

Glaspell, Susan. "A Jury of Her Peers." *Literature and Its Writers:*
    An Introduction to Fiction, Poetry, and Drama. Ed. Ann
    Charters and Samuel Charters. 6th ed. Boston: Bedford,
    2013. 243-58. Print.

Hedges, Elaine. "Small Things Reconsidered: 'A Jury of Her [2]
    Peers.'" *Women's Studies* 12.1 (1986): 89-110. Rpt. in
    Susan Glaspell: Essays on Her Theater and Fiction. Ed. Linda
    Ben-Zvi. Ann Arbor: U of Michigan P, 1995. 49-69. Print.

Mustazza, Leonard. "Generic Translation and Thematic Shift in [3]
    Susan Glaspell's *Trifles* and 'A Jury of Her Peers.'" *Studies*
    in Short Fiction 26.4 (1989): 489-96. Print.

[1] List alphabetized by last names. [2] Article reprinted in
anthology. [3] Article in journal.

APA Papers

35 Supporting a thesis 175

36 Avoiding plagiarism 177

37 Integrating sources 180

38 APA documentation style 184

Directory to APA in-text citation models 185

Directory to APA reference list models 192

39 APA manuscript format 217

SAMPLE PAGES 222

Most instructors in the social sciences and some instructors in other disciplines will ask you to document your sources with the American Psychological Association (APA) system of in-text citations and references described in section 38. You face three main challenges when writing an APA-style paper that draws on sources: (1) supporting a thesis, (2) citing your sources and avoiding plagiarism, and (3) integrating quotations and other source material.

35 Supporting a thesis

Most research assignments ask you to form a thesis and to support that thesis with well-organized evidence. A thesis, which usually appears at the end of the introduction, is a one-sentence (or occasionally a two-sentence) statement of your central idea. In a paper reviewing the literature on a topic, the thesis analyzes the often competing conclusions drawn by a variety of researchers.

35a Forming a working thesis

Once you have read a variety of sources and considered your issue from different perspectives, you are ready to form a working thesis. Your thesis should express your informed, reasoned judgment, not your opinion. Here are some examples.

RESEARCH QUESTION

Is medication the right treatment for the escalating problem of childhood obesity?

POSSIBLE THESIS

Understanding the limitations of medical treatments for children highlights the complexity of the childhood obesity problem in the United States and underscores the need for physicians, advocacy groups, and policymakers to search for other solutions.

RESEARCH QUESTION

How can a business improve employee motivation?

POSSIBLE THESIS

Setting clear expectations, sharing information in a timely fashion, and publicly offering appreciation to specific employees can help align individual motivation with corporate goals.

RESEARCH QUESTION

Why are boys diagnosed with ADHD more often than girls?

POSSIBLE THESIS

Recent studies have suggested that ADHD is diagnosed more often in boys than in girls because of personality differences between boys and girls as well as gender bias in referring adults, but an overlooked cause is that ADHD often coexists with other behavior disorders that exaggerate or mask gender differences.

Each of these thesis statements expresses a view on a debatable issue — an issue about which informed people might disagree. The writers will need to persuade readers to take their positions seriously.

35b Organizing your ideas

APA encourages the use of headings to help readers follow the organization of a paper. For an original research report, the major headings often follow a standard model: Method, Results, Discussion. For a review of the literature, headings will vary, depending on the topic. For examples of headings in APA papers, see pages 224 and 228.

35c Using sources to inform and support your argument

Sources can play several different roles as you develop your points.

Providing background information or context You can use facts and statistics to support generalizations or to establish the importance of your topic.

Explaining terms or concepts Explain words, phrases, or ideas that might be unfamiliar to your readers. Quoting or paraphrasing a source can help you define terms and concepts in accessible language.

Supporting your claims   Back up your assertions with facts, examples, and other evidence from your research.

Lending authority to your argument   Expert opinion can give weight to your argument. But don't rely on experts to make your argument for you. Construct your argument in your own words and cite authorities in the field to support your position.

Anticipating and countering other interpretations   Do not ignore sources that seem contrary to your position or that offer interpretations different from your own. Instead, use them to give voice to opposing ideas and interpretations before you counter them.

36   Avoiding plagiarism

In a research paper, you draw on the work of other writers, and you must document their contributions by citing your sources. When you acknowledge your sources, you avoid plagiarism, a serious academic offense.

Three different acts are considered plagiarism: (1) failing to cite quotations and borrowed ideas, (2) failing to enclose borrowed language in quotation marks, and (3) failing to put summaries and paraphrases in your own words.

36a   Citing quotations and borrowed ideas

When you cite sources, you give credit to writers from whom you've borrowed words and ideas. You also let your readers know where your information comes from, so that they can evaluate the original source.

You must cite anything you borrow from a source, including direct quotations; statistics and other specific facts; visuals such as cartoons, graphs, and diagrams; and any ideas you present in a summary or a paraphrase.

The only exception is common knowledge—information that your readers may know or could easily locate in general sources. For example, most general encyclopedias will tell readers that Sigmund Freud wrote *The*

hackerhandbooks.com/pocket
🅴 APA papers > Exercises: 36–1 to 36–5
☑ APA papers > LearningCurve: Working with sources (APA)

Interpretation of Dreams and that chimpanzees can learn American Sign Language. When you have seen certain information repeatedly in your reading, you don't need to cite it. However, when information has appeared in only a few sources, when it is highly specific (as with statistics), or when it is controversial, you should cite the source.

APA recommends an author-date style of citations. Here, briefly, is how the author-date system usually works. See section 38 for a detailed discussion of variations.

1. The source is introduced by a signal phrase that includes the last name of the author followed by the date of publication in parentheses.
2. The material being cited is followed by a page number in parentheses.
3. At the end of the paper, an alphabetized list of references gives publication information for the source.

IN-TEXT CITATION

As researchers Yanovski and Yanovski (2002) have explained, obesity was once considered "either a moral failing or evidence of underlying psychopathology" (p. 592).

ENTRY IN THE LIST OF REFERENCES

Yanovski, S. Z., & Yanovski, J. A. (2002). Drug therapy: Obesity. *The New England Journal of Medicine, 346*, 591-602.

36b Enclosing borrowed language in quotation marks

To show that you are using a source's exact phrases or sentences, you must enclose them in quotation marks. To omit the quotation marks is to claim—falsely—that the language is your own. Such an omission is plagiarism even if you have cited the source.

ORIGINAL SOURCE

In an effort to seek the causes of this disturbing trend, experts have pointed to a range of important potential contributors to the rise in childhood obesity that are unrelated to media.

—Henry J. Kaiser Family Foundation, "The Role of Media in Childhood Obesity" (2004), p. 1

PLAGIARISM

According to the Henry J. Kaiser Family Foundation (2004), experts have pointed to a range of important potential contributors to the rise in childhood obesity that are unrelated to media (p. 1).

BORROWED LANGUAGE IN QUOTATION MARKS

According to the Henry J. Kaiser Family Foundation (2004), "experts have pointed to a range of important potential contributors to the rise in childhood obesity that are unrelated to media" (p. 1).

NOTE: When quoted sentences are set off from the text by indenting, quotation marks are not used (see pp. 181–82).

36c Putting summaries and paraphrases in your own words

A summary condenses information; a paraphrase conveys information in about the same number of words as in the original source. When you summarize or paraphrase, you must name the source and restate the source's meaning in your own words. You commit plagiarism if you half-copy, or patchwrite, the author's sentences, either by mixing the author's phrases with your own without using quotation marks or by plugging your own synonyms into the author's sentence structure. The following paraphrases are plagiarized—even though the source is cited—because their language and structure are too close to those of the source.

ORIGINAL SOURCE

> In an effort to seek the causes of this disturbing trend, experts have pointed to a range of important potential contributors to the rise in childhood obesity that are unrelated to media.
>
> —Henry J. Kaiser Family Foundation, "The Role of Media in Childhood Obesity" (2004), p. 1

PLAGIARISM: UNACCEPTABLE BORROWING OF PHRASES

According to the Henry J. Kaiser Family Foundation (2004), experts have indicated a range of significant potential contributors to the rise in childhood obesity that are not linked to media (p. 1).

PLAGIARISM: UNACCEPTABLE BORROWING OF STRUCTURE

According to the Henry J. Kaiser Family Foundation (2004), experts have identified a variety of significant factors causing a rise in childhood obesity, factors that are not linked to media (p. 1).

To avoid plagiarizing an author's language, don't look at the source while you are summarizing or paraphrasing. After you've restated the author's ideas in your own words, return to the source and check that you haven't used the author's language or sentence structure or misrepresented the author's ideas.

ACCEPTABLE PARAPHRASE

A report by the Henry J. Kaiser Family Foundation (2004) described sources other than media for the childhood obesity crisis (p. 1).

37 Integrating sources

Quotations, summaries, paraphrases, and facts will help you develop your argument, but they cannot speak for you. You can use several strategies to integrate information from sources into your paper while maintaining your own voice.

37a Using quotations appropriately

Limiting your use of quotations In your writing, keep the emphasis on your own words. Do not quote excessively. It is not always necessary to quote full sentences from a source. Often you can integrate words or phrases from a source into your own sentence structure.

As researchers continue to face a number of unknowns about obesity, it may be helpful to envision treating the disorder, as Yanovski and Yanovski (2002) suggested, "in the same manner as any other chronic disease" (p. 592).

Using the ellipsis mark To condense a quoted passage, you can use the ellipsis mark (three periods, with spaces

hackerhandbooks.com/pocket
APA papers > Exercises: 37–1 to 37–4
APA papers > LearningCurve: Working with sources (APA)

between) to indicate that you have omitted words. What remains must be grammatically complete.

Roman (2003) reported that "social factors are nearly as significant as individual metabolism in the formation of . . . dietary habits of adolescents" (p. 345).

The writer has omitted the words *both healthy and unhealthy* from the source.

When you want to omit a full sentence or more, use a period before the three ellipsis dots.

According to Sothern and Gordon (2003), "Environmental factors may contribute as much as 80% to the causes of childhood obesity. . . . Research suggests that obese children demonstrate decreased levels of physical activity and increased psychosocial problems" (p. 104).

Ordinarily, do not use an ellipsis mark at the beginning or at the end of a quotation. Readers will understand that you have taken the quoted material from a longer passage. The only exception occurs when you feel it is necessary, for clarity, to indicate that your quotation begins or ends in the middle of a sentence.

Make sure that omissions and ellipsis marks do not distort the meaning of your source.

Using brackets   Brackets allow you to insert your own words into quoted material to clarify a confusing reference or to make the quoted words fit grammatically into the context of your writing.

The cost of treating obesity currently totals $117 billion per year—a price, according to the surgeon general, "second only to the cost of [treating] tobacco use" (Carmona, 2004).

To indicate an error such as a misspelling in a quotation, insert [*sic*], italicized and with brackets around it, right after the error.

Setting off long quotations   When you quote forty or more words, set off the quotation by indenting it one-half inch from the left margin. Use the normal right margin and double-space the quotation.

Long quotations should be introduced by an informative sentence, usually followed by a colon. Quotation marks are unnecessary because the indented format tells readers that the passage is taken from the source.

Yanovski and Yanovski (2002) have traced the history of treatments for obesity:

> For many years, obesity was approached as if it were either a moral failing or evidence of underlying psychopathology. With the advent of behavioral treatments for obesity in the 1960s, hope arose that modification of maladaptive eating and exercise habits would lead to sustained weight loss, and that time-limited programs would produce permanent changes in weight. (p. 592)

At the end of the indented quotation, the parenthetical citation goes outside the final punctuation mark.

37b Using signal phrases to integrate sources

Whenever you include a direct quotation, a paraphrase, or a summary in your paper, prepare readers for it with a *signal phrase*. A signal phrase usually names the author of the source, gives the publication date in parentheses, and often provides some context. It is generally acceptable in APA style to call authors by their last name only, even on first mention. If your paper refers to two authors with the same last name, use their initials as well.

See the chart on page 183 for a list of verbs commonly used in signal phrases.

Marking boundaries Avoid dropping quotations into your text without warning. Provide clear signal phrases, including at least the author's name and the date of publication. Signal phrases mark the boundaries between source material and your own words and ideas.

DROPPED QUOTATION

Obesity was once considered in a very different light. "For many years, obesity was approached as if it were either a moral failing or evidence of underlying psychopathology" (Yanovski & Yanovski, 2002, p. 592).

QUOTATION WITH SIGNAL PHRASE

As researchers Yanovski and Yanovski (2002) have explained, obesity was once considered "either a moral failing or evidence of underlying psychopathology" (p. 592).

Using signal phrases in APA papers

To avoid monotony, try to vary both the language and the placement of your signal phrases.

Model signal phrases

In the words of Carmona (2004), "..."

As Yanovski and Yanovski (2002) have noted, "..."

Hoppin and Taveras (2004), medical researchers, pointed out that "..."

"...," claimed Critser (2003).

"...," wrote Duenwald (2004), "..."

Researchers McDuffie et al. (2003) have offered a compelling argument for this view: "..."

Hilts (2002) answered these objections with the following analysis: "..."

Verbs in signal phrases

Are you providing background, explaining a concept, supporting a claim, lending authority, or refuting a belief? Choose a verb that is appropriate for the way you are using the source.

admitted	contended	reasoned
agreed	declared	refuted
argued	denied	rejected
asserted	emphasized	reported
believed	insisted	responded
claimed	noted	suggested
compared	observed	thought
confirmed	pointed out	wrote

NOTE: In APA style, use the past tense or present perfect tense to introduce quotations and other source material: *Davis (2005) noted* or *Davis (2005) has noted*. Use the present tense only to discuss the application or effect of your own results (*the data suggest*) or knowledge that has been clearly established (*researchers agree*).

Putting source material in context Provide context for any source material that appears in your paper. A signal phrase can help you connect your own ideas with those of another writer by clarifying how the source will contribute to your paper. It's a good idea to embed source material, especially long quotations, between sentences of your own that interpret the source and link the source to your argument.

QUOTATION WITH EFFECTIVE CONTEXT

A report by the Henry J. Kaiser Family Foundation (2004) outlined trends that may have contributed to the childhood obesity crisis, including food advertising for children as well as

> a reduction in physical education classes . . . , an increase
> in the availability of sodas and snacks in public schools,
> the growth in the number of fast-food outlets . . . , and
> the increasing number of highly processed high-calorie and
> high-fat grocery products. (p. 1)

Addressing each of these areas requires more than a doctor armed with a prescription pad; it requires a broad mobilization not just of doctors and concerned parents but of educators, food industry executives, advertisers, and media representatives.

NOTE: When you bring other sources into a conversation about your research topic, you are synthesizing sources. For more on synthesis, see 31c.

Integrating statistics and other facts When you are citing a statistic or another specific fact, a signal phrase is often not necessary. In most cases, readers will understand that the citation refers to the statistic or fact (not the whole paragraph).

In purely financial terms, the drugs cost more than $3 a day on average (Duenwald, 2004).

There is nothing wrong, however, with using a signal phrase.

Duenwald (2004) pointed out that in purely financial terms, the drugs cost more than $3 a day on average.

38 APA documentation style

In most social science classes, you will be asked to use the APA system for documenting sources, which is set forth in the *Publication Manual of the American Psychological Association*, 6th ed. (Washington, DC: APA, 2010).

Directory to APA in-text citation models

1.	Basic format for a quotation	185
2.	Basic format for a summary or a paraphrase	186
3.	Work with two authors	186
4.	Work with three to five authors	187
5.	Work with six or more authors	187
6.	Work with unknown author	187
7.	Organization as author	187
8.	Authors with the same last name	188
9.	Two or more works by the same author in the same year	188
10.	Two or more works in the same parentheses	188
11.	Multiple citations to the same work in one paragraph	188
12.	Web source	189
13.	An entire Web site	190
14.	Multivolume work	190
15.	Personal communication	190
16.	Course materials	190
17.	Part of a source (chapter, figure)	190
18.	Indirect source	191
19.	Sacred or classical text	191

38a APA in-text citations

APA's in-text citations provide the author's last name and the year of publication, usually before the cited material, and a page number in parentheses directly after the cited material. In the following models, the elements of the in-text citation are highlighted.

NOTE: APA style requires the use of the past tense or the present perfect tense in signal phrases introducing cited material: *Smith (2012) reported, Smith (2012) has argued.* See also page 183.

■ **1. Basic format for a quotation** Ordinarily, introduce the quotation with a signal phrase that includes the author's last name followed by the year of publication in parentheses. Put the page number (preceded by "p.") in parentheses after the quotation. For sources from the Web without page numbers, see item 12a on page 189.

Critser (2003) noted that many health care providers still "remain either in ignorance or outright denial about the health danger to the poor and the young" (p. 5).

If the author is not named in the signal phrase, place the author's name, the year, and the page number in parentheses after the quotation: (Critser, 2003, p. 5). (See items 6 and 12 for citing sources that lack authors; item 12 also explains how to handle sources without dates or page numbers.)

NOTE: Do not include a month in an in-text citation, even if the entry in the reference list includes the month.

■ **2. Basic format for a summary or a paraphrase**   As for a quotation (see item 1), include the author's last name and the year either in a signal phrase introducing the material or in parentheses following it. Use a page number, if one is available, following the cited material. For sources from the Web without page numbers, see item 12a on page 189.

Yanovski and Yanovski (2002) explained that sibutramine suppresses appetite by blocking the reuptake of the neurotransmitters serotonin and norepinephrine in the brain (p. 594).

Sibutramine suppresses appetite by blocking the reuptake of the neurotransmitters serotonin and norepinephrine in the brain (Yanovski & Yanovski, 2002, p. 594).

■ **3. Work with two authors**   Name both authors in the signal phrase or in parentheses each time you cite the work. In the parentheses, use "&" between the authors' names; in the signal phrase, use "and."

According to Sothern and Gordon (2003), "Environmental factors may contribute as much as 80% to the causes of childhood obesity" (p. 104).

Obese children often engage in limited physical activity (Sothern & Gordon, 2003, p. 104).

■ **4. Work with three to five authors**   Identify all authors in the signal phrase or in parentheses the first time you cite the source.

In 2003, Berkowitz, Wadden, Tershakovec, and Cronquist concluded, "Sibutramine . . . must be carefully monitored in adolescents, as in adults, to control increases in [blood pressure] and pulse rate" (p. 1811).

In subsequent citations, use the first author's name followed by "et al." in either the signal phrase or the parentheses.

As Berkowitz et al. (2003) advised, "Until more extensive safety and efficacy data are available, . . . weight-loss medications should be used only on an experimental basis for adolescents" (p. 1811).

■ **5. Work with six or more authors**   Use the first author's name followed by "et al." in the signal phrase or in parentheses.

McDuffie et al. (2002) found that orlistat, combined with behavioral therapy, produced an average weight loss of 4.4 kg, or 9.7 pounds (p. 646).

■ **6. Work with unknown author**   If the author is unknown, mention the work's title in the signal phrase or give the first word or two of the title in parentheses. Titles of short works such as articles are put in quotation marks; titles of long works such as books and reports are italicized.

Children struggling to control their weight must also struggle with the pressures of television advertising that, on the one hand, encourages the consumption of junk food and, on the other, celebrates thin celebrities ("Television," 2002).

NOTE: In the rare case when "Anonymous" is specified as the author, treat it as if it were a real name: (Anonymous, 2001). In the list of references, also use the name Anonymous as author.

■ **7. Organization as author**   Name the organization in the signal phrase or in the parentheses the first time you cite the source.

Obesity puts children at risk for a number of medical complications, including Type 2 diabetes, hypertension, sleep apnea, and orthopedic problems (Henry J. Kaiser Family Foundation, 2004, p. 1).

If the organization has a familiar abbreviation, you may include it in brackets the first time you cite the source and use the abbreviation alone in later citations.

FIRST CITATION	(Centers for Disease Control and Prevention [CDC], 2012)
LATER CITATIONS	(CDC, 2012)

■ **8. Authors with the same last name** If your reference list includes two or more authors with the same last name, use initials with the last names in your in-text citations.

Research by E. Smith (1989) revealed that. . . .

One 2012 study contradicted . . . (R. Smith, p. 234).

■ **9. Two or more works by the same author in the same year** In the reference list, you will use lowercase letters ("a," "b," and so on) with the year to order the entries. (See item 8 on p. 197.) Use those same letters with the year in the in-text citation.

Research by Durgin (2003b) has yielded new findings about the role of counseling in treating childhood obesity.

■ **10. Two or more works in the same parentheses** Put the works in parentheses in the same order that they appear in the reference list, separated with semicolons.

Researchers have indicated that studies of pharmacological treatments for childhood obesity are inconclusive (Berkowitz et al., 2003; McDuffie et al., 2002).

■ **11. Multiple citations to the same work in one paragraph** If you give the author's name in the text of your paper (not in parentheses) and you mention that source again in the text of the same paragraph, give only the author's name, not the date, in the later citation. If any subsequent reference in the same paragraph is in parentheses, include both the author and the date in the parentheses.

Principal Jean Patrice said, "You have to be able to reach students where they are instead of making them come to you. If you don't, you'll lose them" (personal communication, April 10, 2006). Patrice expressed her desire to see all students get something out of their educational experience. This feeling is common among members of Waverly's faculty. With such a positive view of student potential, it is no wonder that 97% of Waverly High School graduates go on to a four-year university (Patrice, 2006).

12. Web source Cite sources from the Web as you would cite any other source, giving the author and the year when they are available.

Atkinson (2001) found that children who spent at least four hours a day watching TV were less likely to engage in adequate physical activity during the week.

Usually a page number is not available; occasionally a Web source will lack an author or a date (see 12a, 12b, and 12c).

a. No page numbers If the source has numbered paragraphs, use the paragraph number preceded by the abbreviation "para.": (Hall, 2012, para. 5). If the source has no numbered paragraphs but contains headings, cite the appropriate heading in parentheses; you may also indicate which paragraph under the heading you are referring to, even if the paragraphs are not numbered.

Hoppin and Taveras (2004) pointed out that several other medications were classified by the Drug Enforcement Administration as having the "potential for abuse" (Weight-Loss Drugs section, para. 6).

NOTE: Some PDF documents have stable page numbers; when that is the case, you can give the page number in the parenthetical citation.

b. Unknown author Mention the title of the source in a signal phrase or give the first word or two of the title in parentheses (see also item 6). (If an organization serves as the author, see item 7.)

The body's basal metabolic rate, or BMR, is a measure of its at-rest energy requirement ("Exercise," 2003).

c. Unknown date Use the abbreviation "n.d." (for "no date").

Attempts to establish a definitive link between television programming and children's eating habits have been problematic (Magnus, n.d.).

■ **13. An entire Web site** If you are citing an entire Web site, not an internal page or a section, give the URL in the text of your paper but do not include it in the reference list.

The U.S. Center for Nutrition Policy and Promotion website (http://www.cnpp.usda.gov/) provides useful information about diet and nutrition for children and adults.

■ **14. Multivolume work** Add the volume number in parentheses with the page number.

Banford (2009) has demonstrated stable weight loss over time from a combination of psychological counseling, exercise, and nutritional planning (Volume 2, p. 135).

■ **15. Personal communication** Interviews that you conduct, memos, letters, e-mail messages, social media posts, and similar communications should be cited in the text only, not in the reference list. (Use the first initial with the last name in parentheses.)

One of Atkinson's colleagues, who has studied the effect of the media on children's eating habits, has suggested that advertisers need to design ads responsibly for their younger viewers (F. Johnson, personal communication, October 20, 2013).

■ **16. Course materials** Cite lecture notes from your instructor or your own class notes as personal communication (see item 15). If your instructor distributes or posts material that contains publication information, cite as you would the appropriate source. See also item 65 on page 216.

■ **17. Part of a source (chapter, figure)** To cite a specific part of a source, such as a whole chapter or a figure or table, identify the element in parentheses. Don't abbreviate terms such as "Figure," "Chapter," and "Section"; "page" is always abbreviated "p." (or "pp." for more than one page).

> The data support the finding that weight loss stabilizes with consistent therapy and ongoing monitoring (Hanniman, 2010, Figure 8-3, p. 345).

■ **18. Indirect source**   When a writer's or a speaker's quoted words appear in a source written by someone else, begin the parenthetical citation with the words "as cited in." In the following example, Critser is the author of the source given in the reference list; that source contains a quotation by Satcher.

> Former surgeon general Dr. David Satcher described "a nation of young people seriously at risk of starting out obese and dooming themselves to the difficult task of overcoming a tough illness" (as cited in Critser, 2003, p. 4).

■ **19. Sacred or classical text**   Identify the text, the version or edition, and the chapter, verse, or line. It is not necessary to include the source in the reference list.

> Peace activists have long cited the biblical prophet's vision of a world without war: "And they shall beat their swords into plowshares, and their spears into pruning hooks" (Isaiah 2:4, Revised Standard Version).

38b APA list of references

The information you will need for the reference list at the end of your paper will differ slightly for some sources, but the main principles apply to all sources: You should identify an author, a creator, or a producer whenever possible; give a title; and provide the date on which the source was produced. Some sources will require page numbers; some will require a publisher; and some will require retrieval information.

▶   General guidelines for the reference list, **page 194**

Directory to APA reference list models

GENERAL GUIDELINES FOR LISTING AUTHORS

1. Single author   195
2. Two to seven authors   195
3. Eight or more authors   196
4. Organization as author   196
5. Unknown author   196
6. Author using a pseudonym (pen name) or screen name   196
7. Two or more works by the same author   197
8. Two or more works by the same author in the same year   197
9. Editor   197
10. Author and editor   197
11. Translator   198
12. Editor and translator   198

ARTICLES AND OTHER SHORT WORKS

13. Article in a journal   198
14. Article in a magazine   199
15. Article in a newspaper   203
16. Abstract   203
17. Supplemental material   203
18. Article with a title in its title   204
19. Letter to the editor   204
20. Editorial or other unsigned article   204
21. Newsletter article   204
22. Review   204
23. Published interview   204
24. Article in a reference work (encyclopedia, dictionary, wiki)   205
25. Comment on an online article   205
26. Testimony before a legislative body   205
27. Paper presented at a meeting or symposium (unpublished)   205
28. Poster session at a conference   205

BOOKS AND OTHER LONG WORKS

29. Basic format for a book   205
30. Edition other than the first   207
31. Selection in an anthology or a collection   207
32. Multivolume work   208
33. Introduction, preface, foreword, or afterword   208
34. Dictionary or other reference work   208

BOOKS AND OTHER LONG WORKS (*CONTINUED*)

35.	Republished book	208
36.	Book with a title in its title	208
37.	Book in a language other than English	208
38.	Dissertation	209
39.	Conference proceedings	209
40.	Government document	209
41.	Report from a private organization	209
42.	Legal source	210
43.	Sacred or classical text	210

WEB SITES AND PARTS OF WEB SITES

44.	Entire Web site	210
45.	Document from a Web site	210
46.	Section in a Web document	211
47.	Blog post	211
48.	Blog comment	211

AUDIO, VISUAL, AND MULTIMEDIA SOURCES

49.	Podcast	211
50.	Video or audio on the Web	211
51.	Transcript of an audio or a video file	213
52.	Film (DVD, BD, or other format)	213
53.	Television or radio program	213
54.	Music recording	214
55.	Lecture, speech, or address	214
56.	Data set or graphic representation of data (graph, chart, table)	214
57.	Mobile application software (app)	214
58.	Video game	215
59.	Map	215
60.	Advertisement	215
61.	Work of art or photograph	215
62.	Brochure or fact sheet	215
63.	Press release	216
64.	Presentation slides	216
65.	Lecture notes or other course materials	216

PERSONAL COMMUNICATION AND SOCIAL MEDIA

66.	E-mail	216
67.	Online posting	216
68.	Twitter post (tweet)	216
69.	Facebook post	217

General guidelines for the reference list

In the list of references, include only sources that you have quoted, summarized, or paraphrased in your paper.

Authors and dates

- Alphabetize entries by authors' last names; if a work has no author, alphabetize it by its title.

- For all authors' names, put the last name first, followed by a comma; use initials for the first and middle names.

- With two or more authors, use an ampersand (&) before the last author's name. Separate the names with commas. Include names for the first seven authors; if there are eight or more authors, give the first six authors, three ellipsis dots, and the last author.

- If the author is a company or an organization, give the name in normal order.

- Put the date of publication in parentheses immediately after the first element of the citation.

- For books, give the year of publication. For magazines, newspapers, and newsletters, give the year and month or the year, month, and day. For Web sources, give the date of posting, if available. Use the season if a publication gives only a season, not a month.

Titles

- Italicize the titles and subtitles of books, journals, and other long works.

- Use no italics or quotation marks for the titles of articles.

- For books and articles, capitalize only the first word of the title and subtitle and all proper nouns.

- For the titles of journals, magazines, and newspapers, capitalize all words of four letters or more (and all nouns, pronouns, verbs, adjectives, and adverbs of any length).

Place of publication and publisher

- Take the information about a book from its title page and copyright page. If more than one place of publication is listed, use only the first.

- Give the city and state for all US cities. Use postal abbreviations for all states.

- Give the city and country for all non-US cities; include the province for Canadian cities. Do not abbreviate the country and province.

- Do not give a state if the publisher's name includes it (Ann Arbor: University of Michigan Press, for example).

- In publishers' names, omit terms such as "Company" (or "Co.") and "Inc." but keep "Books" and "Press." Omit first names or initials (Norton, not W. W. Norton).
- If the publisher is the same as the author, use the word "Author" in the publisher position.

Volume, issue, and page numbers

- For a journal or a magazine, give only the volume number if the publication is paginated continuously through each volume; give the volume and issue numbers if each issue begins on page 1.
- Italicize the volume number and put the issue number, not italicized, in parentheses.
- When an article appears on consecutive pages, provide the range of pages. When an article does not appear on consecutive pages, give all page numbers: A1, A17.
- For daily and weekly newspapers, use "p." or "pp." before page numbers (if any). For journals and magazines, do not use "p." or "pp."

URLs, DOIs, and other retrieval information

- For articles and books from the Web, use the DOI (digital object identifier) if the source has one, and do not give a URL. If a source does not have a DOI, give the URL.
- Use a retrieval date for a Web source only if the content is likely to change. Most of the examples in 38b do not show a retrieval date because the content of the sources is stable. If you are unsure about whether to use a date, include it or consult your instructor.

General guidelines for listing authors The formatting of authors' names in items 1–12 applies to all sources in print and on the Web—books, articles, Web sites, and so on. For more models of specific source types, see items 13–69.

■ **1. Single author**

author: last name + initial(s) | year (book) | title (book)

Rosenberg, T. (2011). *Join the club: How peer pressure can transform the world.*

place of publication | publisher

New York, NY: Norton.

■ **2. Two to seven authors** List up to seven authors by last names followed by initials. Use an ampersand (&) before the name of the last author. (See items 3–5 on pp. 186–87 for citing works with multiple authors in the text of your paper.)

all authors:
last name + initial(s)

Ludwig, J., Duncan, G. J., Gennetian, L. A., Katz, L. F., Kessler, R. C., Kling,

year
(journal)   title (article)

J. R., & Sanbonmatsu, L. (2012). Neighborhood effects on the long-

journal
title   volume   page(s)

term well-being of low-income adults. *Science, 337,* 1505-1510.

DOI

doi:10.1126/science.1224648

■ **3. Eight or more authors** List the first six authors followed by three ellipsis dots and the last author's name.

Tøttrup, A. P., Klaassen, R. H. G., Kristensen, M. W., Strandberg, R.,
Vardanis, Y., Lindström, Å., . . . Thorup, K. (2012). Drought in
Africa caused delayed arrival of European songbirds. *Science,*
338, 1307. doi:10.1126/science.1227548

■ **4. Organization as author**

author:
organization name   year   title (book)

American Psychiatric Association. (2013). *Diagnostic and statistical manual of*

organization
place   as author
edition   of publication   and publisher

mental disorders (5th ed.). Washington, DC: Author.

■ **5. Unknown author**

year + month + day
title (article)   (weekly publication)   journal title

The rise of the sharing economy. (2013, March 9). *The Economist,*

volume,
issue   page(s)

406(8826), 14.

place of
title (book)   year   publication   publisher

New concise world atlas. (2010). New York, NY: Oxford University Press.

■ **6. Author using a pseudonym (pen name) or screen name** Use the author's real name, if known, and give the pseudonym or screen name in brackets exactly as it appears in the source. If only the screen name is known, begin with that name and do not use brackets. (See also items 47 and 68 on citing screen names in social media.)

screen name — littlebigman.
year + month + day (daily publication) — (2012, December 13).
title of original article — Re: Who's watching? Privacy concerns persist as smart meters roll out
label — [Comment].
title of publication — *National Geographic Daily News*.
URL for Web publication — Retrieved from http://news.nationalgeographic.com/

■ **7. Two or more works by the same author** Use the author's name for all entries. List the entries by year, the earliest first.

Heinrich, B. (2009). *Summer world: A season of bounty*. New York, NY: Ecco.

Heinrich, B. (2012). *Life everlasting: The animal way of death*. New York, NY: Houghton Mifflin Harcourt.

■ **8. Two or more works by the same author in the same year** List the works alphabetically by title. In the parentheses, following the year add "a," "b," and so on. Use these same letters when giving the year in the in-text citation. (See also pp. 220–21 and item 9 on p. 188.)

Bower, B. (2012a, December 15). Families in flux. *Science News, 182*(12), 16.

Bower, B. (2012b, November 3). Human-Neandertal mating gets a new date. *Science News, 182*(9), 8.

■ **9. Editor** Use the abbreviation "Ed." for one editor, "Eds." for more than one editor.

all editors: last name + initial(s) — Carr, S. C., MacLachlan, M., & Furnham, A. (Eds.).
year — (2012).
title (book) — *Humanitarian work psychology*.
place of publication — New York, NY:
publisher — Palgrave.

■ **10. Author and editor** Begin with the name of the author, followed by the name of the editor and the abbreviation "Ed." For an author with two or more editors, use the abbreviation "Ed." after each editor's name: Gray, W., & Jones, P. (Ed.), & Smith, A. (Ed.).

author — James, W.,
editor — & Pelikan, J. (Ed.).
year — (2009).
title (book) — *The varieties of religious experience*.
place of publication — New York, NY:
publisher — Library of America.
original publication information — (Original work published 1902)

■ **11. Translator** Begin with the name of the author. After the title, in parentheses place the name of the translator and the abbreviation "Trans." (for "Translator"). Add the original date of publication at the end of the entry.

Scheffer, P. (2011). *Immigrant nations* (L. Waters, Trans.). Cambridge, England:

Polity Press. (Original work published 2007)

author · year · title (book) · translator · place of publication · publisher · original publication information

■ **12. Editor and translator** If the editor and translator are the same person, the same name appears in both the editor position and the translator position.

Girard, R., & Williams, J. G. (Ed.). (2012). *Resurrection from the
  underground* (J. G. Williams, Trans.). East Lansing: Michigan
  State University Press. (Original work published 1996)

Articles and other short works

  ▶ Citation at a glance: Article in a journal or magazine, **page 200**
  ▶ Citation at a glance: Article from a database, **page 202**

■ **13. Article in a journal** If an article from the Web or a database has no DOI, include the URL for the journal's home page.

a. Print

Bippus, A. M., Dunbar, N. E., & Liu, S.-J. (2012). Humorous responses to

  interpersonal complaints: Effects of humor style and nonverbal expression.

  The Journal of Psychology, 146, 437-453.

all authors: last name + initial(s) · year · article title · journal title · volume · page(s)

b. Web

Vargas, N., & Schafer, M. H. (2013). Diversity in action: Interpersonal networks

  and the distribution of advice. *Social Science Research, 42*(1), 46-58.

  doi:10.1016/j.ssresearch.2012.08.013

all authors: last name + initial(s) · year · article title · journal title · volume, issue · page(s) · DOI

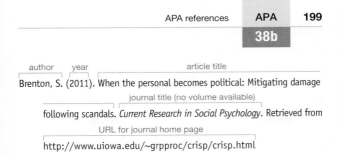

author   year   article title
Brenton, S. (2011). When the personal becomes political: Mitigating damage

                     journal title (no volume available)

     following scandals. *Current Research in Social Psychology*. Retrieved from

            URL for journal home page

     http://www.uiowa.edu/~grpproc/crisp/crisp.html

c. Database

        year
author   (journal)   article title
Sohn, K. (2012). The social class origins of U.S. teachers, 1860-1920.

                volume,
     journal title   issue   page(s)   DOI
     Journal of Social History, 45(4), 908-935. doi:10.1093/jsh/shr121

■ **14. Article in a magazine**   If an article from the Web or
a database has no DOI, include the URL for the journal's
home page.

a. Print

         year + month
author   (monthly magazine)   article title   magazine title
Comstock, J. (2012, December). The underrated sense. *Psychology Today,*

    volume,
    issue   page(s)
    45(6), 46-47.

b. Web

       date of posting
author   (when available)   article title   magazine title
Burns, J. (2012, December 3). The measure of all things. *The American Prospect.*

        URL for home page
    Retrieved from http://prospect.org/

c. Database

      year + month   volume,
author   (monthly magazine)   article title   magazine title   issue   page(s)
Tucker, A. (2012, November). Primal instinct. *Smithsonian, 43*(7), 54-63.

        URL for magazine home page
    Retrieved from http://www.smithsonianmag.com/

Citation at a glance

Article in a journal or magazine `APA`

To cite an article in a print journal or magazine in APA style, include the following elements:

1 Author(s)
2 Year of publication for journal; complete date for magazine
3 Title and subtitle of article
4 Name of journal or magazine
5 Volume number; issue number, if required (see p. 195)
6 Page number(s) of article

JOURNAL TABLE OF CONTENTS

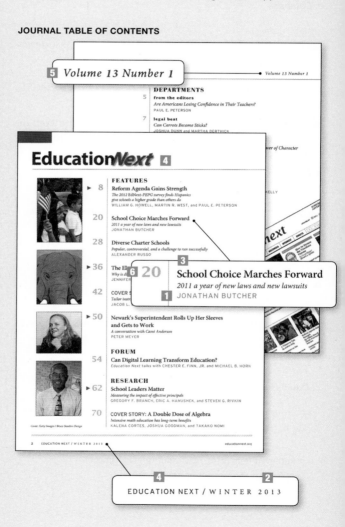

FIRST PAGE OF ARTICLE

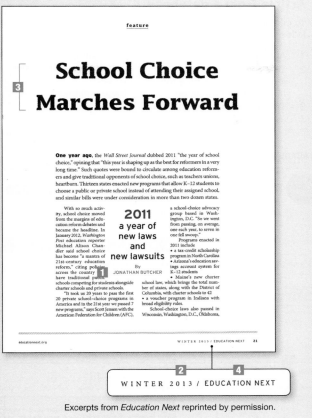

feature

School Choice Marches Forward

3

One year ago, the *Wall Street Journal* dubbed 2011 "the year of school choice," opining that "this is shaping up as the best for reformers in a very long time." Such quotes were bound to circulate among education reformers and give traditional opponents of school choice, such as teachers unions, heartburn. Thirteen states enacted new programs that allow K–12 students to choose a public or private school instead of attending their assigned school, and similar bills were under consideration in more than two dozen states.

With so much activity, school choice moved from the margins of education reform debates and became the headline. In January 2012, *Washington Post* education reporter Michael Alison Chandler said school choice has become "a mantra of 21st-century education reform," citing policies across the country **1** have traditional public schools competing for students alongside charter schools and private schools.

"It took us 20 years to pass the first 20 private school-choice programs in America and in the 21st year we passed 7 new programs," says Scott Jensen with the American Federation for Children (AFC),

2011 a year of new laws and new lawsuits
By JONATHAN BUTCHER

a school-choice advocacy group based in Washington, D.C. "So we went from passing, on average, one each year, to seven in one fell swoop."

Programs enacted in 2011 include

- a tax-credit scholarship program in North Carolina
- Arizona's education savings account system for K–12 students
- Maine's new charter school law, which brings the total number of states, along with the District of Columbia, with charter schools to 42
- a voucher program in Indiana with broad eligibility rules.

School-choice laws also passed in Wisconsin, Washington, D.C., Oklahoma,

educationnext.org

WINTER 2013 / EDUCATION NEXT   21

2   **4**

WINTER 2013 / EDUCATION NEXT

Excerpts from *Education Next* reprinted by permission.

REFERENCE LIST ENTRY FOR AN ARTICLE IN A PRINT JOURNAL OR MAGAZINE

1   2   3   4

Butcher, J. (2013). School choice marches forward. *Education Next,*

5   6

13(1), 20-27.

For more on citing articles in APA style, see items 13–15.

Citation at a glance
Article from a database APA

To cite an article from a database in APA style, include the following elements:

1. Author(s)
2. Year of publication for journal; complete date for magazine or newspaper
3. Title and subtitle of article
4. Name of periodical
5. Volume number; issue number, if required (see p. 195)
6. Page number(s)
7. DOI (digital object identifier)
8. URL for periodical's home page (if there is no DOI)

DATABASE RECORD

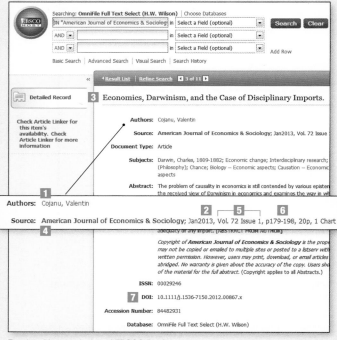

REFERENCE LIST ENTRY FOR AN ARTICLE FROM A DATABASE

  1   2   3

Cojanu, V. (2013). Economics, Darwinism, and the case of

                                4

disciplinary imports. *American Journal of Economics & Sociology*,

5   6   7

72, 179-198. doi:10.1111/j.1536-7150.2012.00867.x

For more on citing articles from a database in APA style, see items 13–15.

■ 15. Article in a newspaper

a. Print

author   year + month + day   article title

Swarns, R. L. (2012, December 9). A family, for a few days a year. *The*

newspaper title   page(s)

New York Times, pp. 1, 20.

b. Web

author: last
name + initial(s)   year + month + day   article title

Villanueva-Whitman, E. (2012, November 27). Working to stimulate

newspaper title

memory function. *Des Moines Register*. Retrieved from http://www

URL for
home page

.desmoinesregister.com/

■ 16. Abstract

a. Abstract of a journal article

Morales, J., Calvo, A., & Bialystok, E. (2013). Working memory
     development in monolingual and bilingual children [Abstract].
     Journal of Experimental Child Psychology, 114, 187-202.
     Retrieved from http://www.sciencedirect.com/

b. Abstract of a paper

Denham, B. (2012). Diffusing deviant behavior: A communication
     perspective on the construction of moral panics [Abstract]. Paper
     presented at the AEJMC 2012 Conference, Chicago, IL. Retrieved
     from http://www.aejmc.org/home/2012/04/ctm-2012-abstracts/

■ 17. Supplemental material
If an article on the Web contains supplemental material that is not part of the main article, cite the material as you would an article and add the label "Supplemental material" in brackets following the title.

Reis, S., Grennfelt, P., Klimont, Z., Amann, M., ApSimon, H., Hettelingh,
     J.-P., . . . Williams, M. (2012). From acid rain to climate change
     [Supplemental material]. *Science 338*(6111), 1153-1154.
     doi:10.1126/science.1226514

■ **18. Article with a title in its title**   If an article title contains another article title or a term usually placed in quotation marks, use quotation marks around the internal title or the term.

Easterling, D., & Millesen, J. L. (2012, Summer). Diversifying
civic leadership: What it takes to move from "new faces"
to adaptive problem solving. *National Civic Review*, 20-27.
doi:10.1002/ncr.21073

■ **19. Letter to the editor**   If the letter has no title, use the bracketed words as the title, as in the following example.

Lim, C. (2012, November-December). [Letter to the editor]. *Sierra*.
Retrieved from http://www.sierraclub.org/sierra/

■ **20. Editorial or other unsigned article**

The business case for transit dollars [Editorial]. (2012, December 9).
Star Tribune. Retrieved from http://www.startribune.com/

■ **21. Newsletter article**

Scrivener, L. (n.d.). Why is the minimum wage issue important for
food justice advocates? *Food Workers — Food Justice, 15*.
Retrieved from http://www.thedatabank.com/dpg/199
/pm.asp?nav=1&ID=41429

■ **22. Review**   In brackets, give the type of work reviewed, the title, and the author for a book or the year for a film. If the review has no author or title, use the material in brackets as the title.

Aviram, R. B. (2012). [Review of the book *What do I say? The therapist's guide
to answering client questions*, by L. N. Edelstein & C. A. Waehler].
Psychotherapy, 49(4), 570-571. doi:10.1037/a0029815

Bradley, A., & Olufs, E. (2012). Family dynamics and school violence
[Review of the motion picture *We need to talk about Kevin*, 2011].
PsycCRITIQUES, 57(49). doi:10.1037/a0030982

■ **23. Published interview**

Githongo, J. (2012, November 20). A conversation with John Githongo
[Interview by Baobab]. *The Economist*. Retrieved from http://
www.economist.com/

■ 24. Article in a reference work (encyclopedia, dictionary, wiki)

a. Print

Konijn, E. A. (2008). Affects and media exposure. In W. Donsbach
(Ed.), *The international encyclopedia of communication* (Vol. 1,
pp. 123-129). Malden, MA: Blackwell.

b. Web

Ethnomethodology. (2006). In *STS wiki*. Retrieved December 15, 2012,
from http://www.stswiki.org/index.php?title=Ethnomethodology

■ 25. Comment on an online article   If both the writer's real name and screen name are given, put the real name first, followed by the screen name in brackets.

Danboy125. (2012, November 9). Re: No flowers on the psych ward
[Comment]. *The Atlantic*. Retrieved from http://www.theatlantic.com/

■ 26. Testimony before a legislative body

Carmona, R. H. (2004, March 2). *The growing epidemic of childhood
obesity*. Testimony before the Subcommittee on Competition,
Foreign Commerce, and Infrastructure of the U.S. Senate
Committee on Commerce, Science, and Transportation. Retrieved
from http://www.hhs.gov/asl/testify/t040302.html

■ 27. Paper presented at a meeting or symposium (unpublished)

Karimi, S., Key, G., & Tat, D. (2011, April 22). *Complex predicates in
focus*. Paper presented at the West Coast Conference on Formal
Linguistics, Tucson, AZ.

■ 28. Poster session at a conference

Lacara, N. (2011, April 24). *Predicate which appositives*. Poster session presented at the West Coast Conference on Formal Linguistics, Tucson, AZ.

Books and other long works

▶ Citation at a glance: Book, **page 206**

■ 29. Basic format for a book

a. Print

author(s):
last name
+ initial(s)   year   book title

Child, B. J. (2012). *Holding our world together: Ojibwe women and the*

                                    place of
                                    publication   publisher

survival of community. New York, NY: Viking.

Citation at a glance
Book APA

To cite a print book in APA style, include the following elements:

1 Author(s)
2 Year of publication
3 Title and subtitle
4 Place of publication
5 Publisher

TITLE PAGE

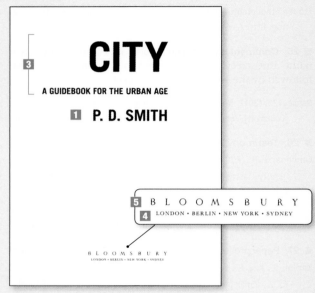

3

CITY

A GUIDEBOOK FOR THE URBAN AGE

1 P. D. SMITH

5 B L O O M S B U R Y
4 LONDON · BERLIN · NEW YORK · SYDNEY

BLOOMSBURY
LONDON · BERLIN · NEW YORK · SYDNEY

FROM COPYRIGHT PAGE

First published in Great Britain and the USA in 2012 **2**

Bloomsbury Publishing Plc, 50 Bedford Square, London WC1B 3DP
Bloomsbury USA, 175 Fifth Avenue, New York, NY 10010

Copyright © 2012 by P. D. Smith

REFERENCE LIST ENTRY FOR A PRINT BOOK

   1   2   3   4

Smith, P. D. (2012). *City: A guidebook for the urban age*. London,

        5

England: Bloomsbury.

For more on citing books in APA style, see items 29–37.

■ **29. Basic format for a book (*cont.*)**

b. Web (or online library)   Give the URL for the home page of the Web site or the online library.

| author(s) | year | book title |

Amponsah, N. A., & Falola, T. (2012). *Women's roles in sub-Saharan Africa.*

URL

Retrieved from http://books.google.com/

c. E-book   Give the version in brackets after the title ("Kindle version," "Nook version," and so on). Include the DOI or, if a DOI is not available, the URL for the home page of the site from which you downloaded the book.

Wolf, D. A., & Folbre, N. (Eds.). (2012). *Universal coverage of long-term care in the United States* [Adobe Digital Editions version]. Retrieved from https://www.russellsage.org/

d. Database   Give the URL for the database.

Beasley, M. H. (2012). *Women of the Washington press: Politics, prejudice, and persistence.* Retrieved from http://muse.jhu.edu/

■ **30. Edition other than the first**

Harvey, P. (2013). *An introduction to Buddhism: Teachings, history, and practices* (2nd ed.). Cambridge, England: Cambridge University Press.

■ **31. Selection in an anthology or a collection**

a. Entire anthology

| editor(s) | year |

Warren, A. E. A., Lerner, R. M., & Phelps, E. (Eds.). (2011). *Thriving and*

title of anthology

spirituality among youth: Research perspectives and future possibilities.

place of
publication   publisher

Hoboken, NJ: Wiley.

b. Selection in an anthology

author of
selection   year   title of selection

Lazar, S. W. (2012). Neural correlates of positive youth development.

editors of anthology

In A. E. A. Warren, R. M. Lerner, & E. Phelps (Eds.), *Thriving and*

title of anthology

spirituality among youth: Research perspectives and future possibilities

page numbers   place of
of selection   publication   publisher

(pp. 77-90). Hoboken, NJ: Wiley.

■ 32. Multivolume work

a. All volumes

Khalakdina, M. (2008-2011). *Human development in the Indian context: A socio-cultural focus* (Vols. 1-2). New Delhi, India: Sage.

b. One volume, with title

Jensen, R. E. (Ed.). (2012). *Voices of the American West: Vol. 1. The Indian interviews of Eli S. Ricker, 1903-1919*. Lincoln: University of Nebraska Press.

■ 33. Introduction, preface, foreword, or afterword

Zachary, L. J. (2012). Foreword. In L. A. Daloz, *Mentor: Guiding the journey of adult learners* (pp. v-vii). San Francisco, CA: Jossey-Bass.

■ 34. Dictionary or other reference work

Leong, F. T. L. (Ed.). (2008). *Encyclopedia of counseling* (Vols. 1-4). Thousand Oaks, CA: Sage.

Nichols, J. D., & Nyholm, E. (2012). *A concise dictionary of Minnesota Ojibwe*. Minneapolis: University of Minnesota Press.

■ 35. Republished book

Mailer, N. (2008). *Miami and the siege of Chicago: An informal history of the Republican and Democratic conventions of 1968*. New York, NY: New York Review Books. (Original work published 1968)

■ 36. Book with a title in its title   If the book title contains another book title or an article title, do not italicize the internal title and do not put quotation marks around it.

Marcus, L. (Ed.). (1999). *Sigmund Freud's* The interpretation of dreams*: New interdisciplinary essays*. Manchester, England: Manchester University Press.

■ 37. Book in a language other than English   Place the English translation, not italicized, in brackets.

Carminati, G. G., & Méndez, A. (2012). *Étapes de vie, étapes de soins* [Stages of life, stages of care]. Chêne-Bourg, Switzerland: Médecine & Hygiène.

■ 38. Dissertation

a. Published

Hymel, K. M. (2009). *Essays in urban economics* (Doctoral dissertation). Available from ProQuest Dissertations and Theses database. (AAT 3355930)

b. Unpublished

Mitchell, R. D. (2007). *The Wesleyan Quadrilateral: Relocating the conversation* (Unpublished doctoral dissertation). Claremont School of Theology, Claremont, CA.

■ 39. Conference proceedings

Yu, F.-Y., Hirashima, T., Supnithi, T., & Biswas, G. (2011). *Proceedings of the 19th International Conference on Computers in Education: ICCE 2011*. Retrieved from http://www.apsce.net:8080 /icce2011/program/proceedings/

■ 40. Government document   If the document has a number, place the number in parentheses after the title.

U.S. Transportation Department, Pipeline and Hazardous Materials Safety Administration. (2012). *Emergency response guidebook 2012*. Washington, DC: Author.

U.S. Census Bureau, Bureau of Economic Analysis. (2012, December). *U.S. international trade in goods and services, October 2012* (Report No. CB12-232, BEA12-55, FT-900 [12-10]). Retrieved from http://www .census.gov/foreign-trade/Press-Release/2012pr/10/

■ 41. Report from a private organization   If the publisher and the author are the same for a print source, see item 4 on page 196.

Ford Foundation. (2012, November). *Eastern Africa*. Retrieved from http://www.fordfoundation.org/pdfs/library/Eastern-Africa -brochure-2012.pdf

Atwood, B., Beam, M., Hindman, D. B., Hindman, E. B., Pintak, L., & Shors, B. (2012, May 25). *The Murrow Rural Information Initiative: Final report*. Pullman: Murrow College of Communication, Washington State University.

■ **42. Legal source** The title of a court case is italicized in an in-text citation, but it is not italicized in the reference list.

Sweatt v. Painter, 339 U.S. 629 (1950). Retrieved from Cornell
University Law School, Legal Information Institute
website: http://www.law.cornell.edu/supct/html/historics
/USSC_CR_0339_0629_ZS.html

■ **43. Sacred or classical text** It is not necessary to list sacred works such as the Bible or the Qur'an or classical Greek and Roman works (such as the *Odyssey*) in your reference list. See item 19 on page 191 for how to cite these sources in the text of your paper.

Web sites and parts of Web sites

▶ Citation at a glance: Section in a Web document, **page 212**

NOTE: In an APA paper or an APA reference list entry, the word "website" is spelled all lowercase, as one word.

■ **44. Entire Web site** Do not include an entire Web site in the reference list. Give the URL in parentheses when you mention it in the text of your paper. (See item 13 on p. 190.)

■ **45. Document from a Web site** If the publisher is known and is not named as the author, include the publisher in your retrieval statement.

Wagner, D. A., Murphy, K. M., & De Korne, H. (2012, December).
*Learning first: A research agenda for improving learning in
low-income countries*. Retrieved from Brookings Institution
website: http://www.brookings.edu/research/papers/2012/12
/learning-first-wagner-murphy-de-korne

Gerber, A. S., & Green, D. P. (2012). *Field experiments: Design, analysis,
and interpretation*. Retrieved from Yale Institution for Social and
Policy Studies website: http://isps.yale.edu/research/data/d081#
.UUy2HFdPL5w

Centers for Disease Control and Prevention. (2012, December 10).
Concussion in winter sports. Retrieved from http://www.cdc.gov
/Features/HockeyConcussions/index.html

■ **46. Section in a Web document** Cite as a chapter in a book or a selection in an anthology (see item 31b).

Pew Research Center. (2012, December 12). About the 2012 Pew
    global attitudes survey. In *Social networking popular across*
    globe. Retrieved from http://www.pewglobal.org/2012/12/12
    /social-networking-popular-across-globe

Chang, W.-Y., & Milan, L. M. (2012, October). Relationship between
    degree field and emigration. In *International mobility and*
    employment characteristics among recent recipients of U.S.
    doctorates. Retrieved from National Science Foundation website:
    http://www.nsf.gov/statistics/infbrief/nsf13300

■ **47. Blog post** If both the writer's real name and screen name are given, put the real name first, followed by the screen name in brackets. End with the URL for the post.

Kerssen, T. (2012, October 5). Hunger is political: Food Sovereignty
    Prize honors social movements [Blog post]. Retrieved from
    http://www.foodfirst.org/en/node/4020

■ **48. Blog comment**

Studebakerhawk_14611. (2012, December 5). Re: A people's history of
    MOOCs [Blog comment]. Retrieved from http://www.insidehighered
    .com/blogs/library-babel-fish/people's-history-moocs

Audio, visual, and multimedia sources

■ **49. Podcast**

Schulz, K. (2011, March). *Kathryn Schulz: On being wrong* [Video
    podcast]. Retrieved from TED on http://itunes.apple.com/

Taylor, A., & Parfitt, G. (2011, January 13). *Physical activity and*
    mental health: What's the evidence? [Audio podcast]. Retrieved
    from Open University on http://itunes.apple.com/

■ **50. Video or audio on the Web**

Kurzen, B. (2012, April 5). *Going beyond Muslim-Christian conflict in*
    Nigeria [Video file]. Retrieved from http://www.youtube.com
    /watch?v=JD8MIJOA050

Citation at a glance
Section in a Web document APA

To cite a section in a Web document in APA style, include the following elements:

1. Author(s)
2. Date of publication or most recent update ("n.d." if there is no date)
3. Title of section
4. Title of document
5. URL of section

WEB DOCUMENT CONTENTS PAGE

ON-SCREEN VIEW OF DOCUMENT

5 ⊙ http://www.health.state.mn.us/divs/chs/annsum/10annsum/Fertility2010.pdf

Courtesy of the Minnesota Department of Health. Reproduced by permission.

Minnesota Department of Health. (n.d.). Fertility. In *2010*

Minnesota health statistics annual summary. Retrieved from

5

http://www.health.state.mn.us/divs/chs/annsum/10annsum

/Fertility2010.pdf

For more on citing documents from Web sites in APA style, see items 45 and 46.

50. Video or audio on the Web (*cont.*)

Bever, T., Piattelli-Palmarini, M., Hammond, M., Barss, A., & Bergesen, A. (2012, February 2). *A basic introduction to Chomsky's linguistics* [Audio file]. Retrieved from University of Arizona, College of Social & Behavioral Sciences, Department of Linguistics website: http://linguistics.arizona.edu/node/711

51. Transcript of an audio or a video file

Malone, T. W. *Collective intelligence* [Transcript of video file]. Retrieved from http://edge.org/conversation/collective-intelligence

52. Film (DVD, BD, or other format)
In brackets following the title, add a description of the medium. Use "Motion picture" if you viewed the film in a theater; "Video file" if you downloaded the film from the Web or through a streaming service; "DVD" or "BD" if you viewed the film on DVD or Blu-ray Disc. For a motion picture or a DVD or BD, add the location where the film was made and the studio. If you retrieved the film from the Web or used a streaming service, give the URL for the home page.

Affleck, B. (Director). (2012). *Argo* [Motion picture]. Burbank, CA: Warner Bros.

Ross, G. (Director and Writer), & Collins, S. (Writer). (2012). *The hunger games* [Video file]. Retrieved from http://netflix.com/

53. Television or radio program

a. Series

Hager, M. (Executive producer), & Schieffer, B. (Moderator). (2012). *Face the nation* [Television series]. Washington, DC: CBS News.

b. Episode on the air

Harleston, R. (Host). (2012, December 1). Federal role in support
of autism [Television series episode]. In *Washington journal*.
Washington, DC: C-SPAN.

c. Episode on the Web

Morton, D. (Producer). (2012). Fast times at West Philly High
[Television series episode]. In M. Hager (Executive producer),
Frontline. Retrieved from http://www.wgbh.org/

■ 54. Music recording

Chibalonza, A. Jubilee. (2012). On *African voices* [CD]. Merenberg,
Germany: ZYX Music.

African voices [CD]. (2012). Merenberg, Germany: ZYX Music.

■ 55. Lecture, speech, or address

Verghese, A. (2012, December 6). *Colonialism and patterns of ethnic
conflict in contemporary India*. Address at the Freeman Spogli
Institute, Stanford University, Stanford, CA.

Donovan, S. (2012, June 12). *Assisted housing mobility in challenging
times* [Video file]. Address at the 5th National Conference on
Assisted Housing Mobility, Urban Institute, Washington, DC.

■ 56. Data set or graphic representation of data (graph, chart, table)
If the item is numbered in the source,
indicate the number in parentheses after the title. If the
graphic appears within a larger document, do not italicize
the title of the graphic.

U.S. Department of Agriculture, Economic Research Service. (2011).
Daily intake of nutrients by food source: 2005-08 [Data set].
Retrieved from http://www.ers.usda.gov/data-products
/food-consumption-and-nutrient-intakes.aspx

Gallup. (2012, December 5). *In U.S., more cite obesity as most urgent
health problem* [Graphs]. Retrieved from http://www.gallup.com
/poll/159083/cite-obesity-urgent-health-problem.aspx

■ 57. Mobile application software (app)
Begin with
the developer of the app, if known (as in the second
example).

MindNode Touch 2.3 [Mobile application software]. (2012). Retrieved
from http://itunes.apple.com/

Source Tree Solutions. mojoPortal [Mobile application software].
(2012). Retrieved from http://www.microsoft.com/web/gallery/

■ **58. Video game**   If the game can be played on the Web
or was downloaded from the Web, give the URL instead of
publication information.

Firaxis Games. (2010). Sid Meier's Civilization V [Video game]. New
York, NY: Take-Two Interactive. Xbox 360.

Atom Entertainment. (2012). Edgeworld [Video game]. Retrieved from
http://www.addictinggames.com/

■ **59. Map**

Ukraine [Map]. (2008). Retrieved from the University of Texas at
Austin Perry-Castañeda Library Map Collection website: http://
www.lib.utexas.edu/maps/cia08/ukraine_sm_2008.gif

Syrian uprising map [Map]. (2012, October). Retrieved from http://www
.polgeonow.com/2012/10/syria-uprising-map-october-2012-7.html

■ **60. Advertisement**

VMware [Advertisement]. (2012, September). *Harvard Business Review,
90*(9), 27.

■ **61. Work of art or photograph**

Olson, A. (2011). *Short story* [Painting]. Museum of Contemporary Art,
Chicago, IL.

Crowner, S. (2012). *Kurtyna fragments* [Painting]. Retrieved from http://
www.walkerart.org/

Weber, J. (1992). *Toward freedom* [Outdoor mural]. Sherman Oaks, CA.

■ **62. Brochure or fact sheet**

National Council of State Boards of Nursing. (2011). *A nurse's guide to
professional boundaries* [Brochure]. Retrieved from https://www
.ncsbn.org/

World Health Organization. (2012, September). *Road traffic injuries*
(No. 358) [Fact sheet]. Retrieved from http://www.who.int
/mediacentre/factsheets/fs358/en/index.html

■ 63. Press release

Urban Institute. (2012, October 11). Two studies address health
  policy on campaign trail [Press release]. Retrieved from http://
  www.urban.org/publications/901537.html

■ 64. Presentation slides

Boeninger, C. F. (2008, August). *Web 2.0 tools for reference and instructional
  services* [Presentation slides]. Retrieved from http://libraryvoice.com
  /archives/2008/08/04/opal-20-conference-presentation-slides

■ 65. Lecture notes or other course materials   Cite materials that your instructor has posted on the Web as you would a Web document or a section in a Web document (see item 45 or 46). If the materials are handouts or printouts, cite whatever information is available in the source. Cite the instructor's personal notes or material that is not posted (such as slides) as personal communication in the text of your paper (see items 15 and 16 on p. 190).

Blum, R. (2011). Neurodevelopment in the first decade of life
  [Lecture notes and audio file]. In R. Blum & L. M. Blum, *Child
  health and development*. Retrieved from http://ocw.jhsph.edu
  /index.cfm/go/viewCourse/course/childhealth/coursePage
  /lectureNotes/

Personal communication and social media

■ 66. E-mail   E-mail messages, letters, and other personal communication are not included in the list of references. (See item 15 on p. 190 for citing these sources in the text of your paper.)

■ 67. Online posting   If an online posting is not archived, cite it as a personal communication in the text of your paper and do not include it in the list of references. If the posting is archived, give the URL and the name of the discussion list if it is not part of the URL.

McKinney, J. (2006, December 19). Adult education-healthcare
  partnerships [Electronic mailing list message]. Retrieved from
  http://www.nifl.gov/pipermail/healthliteracy/2006/000524.html

■ 68. Twitter post (tweet)   If both the writer's real name and screen name are given, put the real name first,

followed by the screen name in brackets. If only the screen name is known, do not put it in brackets. Include the entire text of the tweet as the title; end with the URL.

CQ Researcher. (2012, December 5). Up to 80 percent of the 600,000 processed foods sold in America have sugar added to their recipes. See http://bit.ly/UmfA4L [Tweet]. Retrieved from https://twitter.com/cqresearcher/status/276449095521038336

■ **69. Facebook post** If both the writer's real name and screen name are given, put the real name first, followed by the screen name in brackets. If only the screen name is known, do not put it in brackets. Give a few words of the post as a title. Include the URL for the poster's Facebook page. If you are citing a personal Facebook page that will not be accessible to your readers, cite it as personal communication in your text, not in the reference list (see item 15 on p. 190).

U.S. Department of Education. (2012, October 9). They are resilient [Facebook post]. Retrieved October 15, 2012, from http://www .facebook.com/ED.gov

39 APA manuscript format; sample pages

The guidelines in this section are consistent with advice given in the *Publication Manual of the American Psychological Association*, 6th ed. (Washington, DC: APA, 2010), and with typical requirements for undergraduate papers.

39a APA manuscript format

Formatting the paper The guidelines on pages 217–20 describe APA's recommendations for formatting the text of your paper. For guidelines on preparing the reference list, see pages 220–21.

Font If your instructor does not require a specific font, choose one that is standard and easy to read (such as Times New Roman).

Title page Begin at the top left, with the words "Running head," followed by a colon and the title of your paper (shortened to no more than fifty characters) in all capital letters. Put the page number 1 flush with the right margin.

About halfway down the page, on separate lines, center the full title of your paper, your name, and your school's name. At the bottom of the page, you may add the heading "Author Note," centered, followed by a brief paragraph that lists specific information about the course or department or provides acknowledgments or contact information. See pages 222 and 227 for sample title pages.

Page numbers and running head Number all pages with arabic numerals (1, 2, 3, and so on) in the upper right corner one-half inch from the top of the page. Flush with the left margin on the same line as the page number, type a running head consisting of the title of the paper (shortened to no more than fifty characters) in all capital letters. On the title page only, include the words "Running head" followed by a colon before the title. See pages 222–28.

Margins, line spacing, and paragraph indents Use margins of one inch on all sides of the page. Left-align the text.

Double-space throughout the paper. Indent the first line of each paragraph one-half inch.

Capitalization, italics, and quotation marks In headings and in titles of works in the text of the paper, capitalize all words of four letters or more (and all nouns, pronouns, verbs, adjectives, and adverbs of any length). Capitalize the first word following a colon if the word begins a complete sentence.

Italicize the titles of books, journals, magazines, and other long works, such as Web sites. Use quotation marks around the titles of articles, short stories, and other short works.

NOTE: APA has different requirements for titles in the reference list. See page 221.

Long quotations When a quotation is forty or more words, set it off from the text by indenting it one-half inch from the left margin. Double-space the quotation. Do not use quotation marks around it. (See pp. 181–82 for more information and an example.)

Footnotes If you insert a footnote number in the text of your paper, place the number, raised above the line (superscript), immediately following any mark of punctuation except a dash. At the bottom of the page, begin the note with a one-half-inch indent and the superscript number corresponding to the number in the text. Insert an extra double-spaced line between the last line of text on the page and the footnote. Double-space the footnote. (See p. 224 for an example.)

Abstract and keywords An abstract is a 150-to-250-word paragraph that provides readers with a quick overview of your essay.

If your instructor requires one, include an abstract on a new page after the title page. Center the word "Abstract" (in regular font, not boldface) one inch from the top of the page. Double-space the abstract and do not indent the first line.

A list of keywords follows the abstract; the keywords help readers search for a published paper on the Web or in a database. Leave one line of space after the abstract and begin the next line with the word "Keywords," italicized and indented one-half inch, followed by a colon. Then list important words related to your paper. (See p. 223 for an example.) Check with your instructor for requirements in your course.

Headings For most undergraduate papers, one level of heading is usually sufficient. (See pp. 224, 228, and 229.)

First-level headings are centered and boldface. In research papers and laboratory reports, the major headings are "Method," "Results," and "Discussion." In other types of papers, the major headings should be informative and concise, conveying the structure of the paper.

Second-level headings are flush left and boldface. Third-level headings are indented and boldface, followed by a period and the text on the same line.

First-Level Heading Centered

Second-Level Heading Flush Left

Third-level heading indented. Text immediately follows.

Visuals (tables and figures)   APA classifies visuals as tables and figures (figures include graphs, charts, drawings, and photographs).

Label each table with an arabic numeral (Table 1, Table 2, and so on) and provide a clear title. Place the label and the title on separate lines above the table, flush left and double-spaced. Type the table number in regular font; italicize the table title.

If you have used data from an outside source or have taken or adapted the table from a source, give the source information in a note below the table. Provide any explanatory footnotes below the source note. Double-space source notes and footnotes; do not indent the first line of each note. (See p. 225 for an example of a table.)

For each figure, place the figure number and a caption below the figure, flush left and double-spaced. Begin with the word "Figure" and an arabic numeral, both italicized, followed by a period. Place the caption, not italicized, on the same line. If you have taken or adapted the figure from an outside source, give the source information immediately following the caption. Use the term "From" or "Adapted from" before the source information.

Preparing the list of references   Begin your list of references on a new page at the end of the paper. Center the title "References" one inch from the top of the page. Double-space throughout. For a sample reference list, see page 226.

Indenting entries   Type the first line of each entry flush left and indent any additional lines one-half inch.

Alphabetizing the list   Alphabetize the reference list by the last names of the authors (or editors) or by the first word of an organization name (if the author is an organization). When a work has no author or editor, alphabetize by the first word of the title other than *A*, *An*, or *The*.

If your list includes two or more works by the same author, arrange the entries by year, the earliest first. If your list includes two or more works by the same author in the same year, arrange the works alphabetically by title. Add the letters "a," "b," and so on within the parentheses after the year. For journal articles, use only the year and the letter: (2012a). For articles in magazines and newspapers, use the full date and the letter in the reference list: (2012a, July 7); use only the year and the letter in the in-text citation.

Authors' names Invert all authors' names and use initials instead of first names. Separate the names with commas. For two to seven authors, use an ampersand (&) before the last author's name. For eight or more authors, give the first six authors, three ellipsis dots, and the last author (see item 3 on p. 196).

Titles of books and articles In the reference list, italicize the titles and subtitles of books. Do not italicize or use quotation marks around the titles of articles. For both books and articles, capitalize only the first word of the title and subtitle (and all proper nouns). Capitalize names of journals, magazines, and newspapers as you would capitalize them normally (see 22c).

Abbreviations for page numbers Abbreviations for "page" and "pages" ("p." and "pp.") are used before page numbers of newspaper articles and selections in anthologies (see item 15 on p. 203 and item 31 on p. 207). Do not use "p." or "pp." before page numbers of articles in journals and magazines (see items 13 and 14 on pp. 198 and 199).

Breaking a URL or DOI When a URL or a DOI (digital object identifier) must be divided, break it after a double slash or before any other mark of punctuation. Do not insert a hyphen; do not add a period at the end.

39b Sample APA pages

On the following pages are excerpts from a review of the literature written for a psychology class, a clinical practice paper written for a nursing class, and a business proposal written for a business class.

hackerhandbooks.com/pocket
🄴 APA papers > Sample student writing
  > Mirano, "Can Medication Cure Obesity in Children? A Review of the Literature" (literature review)
  > Riss, "Acute Lymphoblastic Leukemia and Hypertension in One Client" (nursing practice paper)
  > Ratajczak, "Proposal to Add a Wellness Program" (business proposal)

[1] Running head: CAN MEDICATION CURE OBESITY IN CHILDREN?   1 [2]

Can Medication Cure Obesity in Children?

A Review of the Literature

[3]   Luisa Mirano

Northwest-Shoals Community College

Author Note

[4]   This paper was prepared for Psychology 108, Section B, taught by
Professor Kang.

---

[1] Short title, no more than 50 characters, in all capital letters on
all pages; words "Running head" on title page only. [2] Arabic
page number on all pages. [3] Full title and writer's name and
affiliation, centered. [4] Author's note (optional) for extra
information.

(Annotations indicate APA-style formatting and effective writing.)

Sample APA abstract

                              Abstract   **2**

In recent years, policymakers and medical experts have expressed   **3**

alarm about the growing problem of childhood obesity in the United

States. While most agree that the issue deserves attention, consensus

dissolves around how to respond to the problem. This literature review

examines one approach to treating childhood obesity: medication. The

paper compares the effectiveness for adolescents of the only two drugs

approved by the Food and Drug Administration (FDA) for long-term

treatment of obesity, sibutramine and orlistat. This examination of

pharmacological treatments for obesity points out the limitations of

medication and suggests the need for a comprehensive solution that

combines medical, social, behavioral, and political approaches to this

complex problem.

                                                                   4

Keywords: obesity, childhood, adolescence, medication, public

policy

1 Short title, no more than 50 characters, flush left; page number flush right. **2** Abstract appears on separate page; heading centered and not boldface. **3** Abstract is a 150-to-250-word overview of paper. **4** Keywords (optional) help readers search for a published paper on the Web or in a database.

Sample APA page

[1]

Can Medication Cure Obesity in Children?

A Review of the Literature

[2] In March 2004, U.S. Surgeon General Richard Carmona called attention to a health problem in the United States that, until recently, has been overlooked: childhood obesity. Carmona said that the "astounding" 15% child obesity rate constitutes an "epidemic." Since the early 1980s, that rate has "doubled in children and tripled in adolescents." Now more than 9 million children are classified as obese.[1] This literature review considers whether the use of medication is a promising approach for solving the childhood obesity problem by responding to the following questions:

[3]
1. What are the implications of childhood obesity?
2. Is medication effective at treating childhood obesity?
3. Is medication safe for children?
4. Is medication the best solution?

[4] Understanding the limitations of medical treatments for children highlights the complexity of the childhood obesity problem in the United States and underscores the need for physicians, advocacy groups, and policymakers to search for other solutions.

[5]   **What Are the Implications of Childhood Obesity?**

Obesity can be a devastating problem from both an individual and a societal perspective. Obesity puts children at risk for a number of medical complications, including Type 2 diabetes, hypertension,

[6]   [1]Obesity is measured in terms of body-mass index (BMI): weight in kilograms divided by square of height in meters. An adolescent with a BMI in the 95th percentile for his or her age and gender is considered obese.

---

[1] Full title, centered and not boldface.   **[2]** Signal phrase introduces source.   **[3]** Questions provide organization and are repeated as main headings.   **[4]** Paper's thesis.   **[5]** First-level heading, centered and boldface.   **[6]** Footnote defines essential term without interrupting text.

Sample APA table

Table 1 **1**

Effectiveness of Sibutramine and Orlistat in Adolescents **2**

Medication	Subjects	Treatment[a]	Side effects	Average weight loss/gain
Sibutramine	Control	0-6 months: placebo 6-12 months: sibutramine	Months 6-12: increased blood pressure; increased pulse rate	After 6 months: loss of 3.2 kg (7 lb) After 12 months: loss of 4.5 kg (9.9 lb)
	Medicated	0-12 months: sibutramine	Increased blood pressure; increased pulse rate	After 6 months: loss of 7.8 kg (17.2 lb) After 12 months: loss of 7.0 kg (15.4 lb)
Orlistat	Control	0-12 months: placebo	None	Gain of 0.67 kg (1.5 lb)
	Medicated	0-12 months: orlistat	Oily spotting; flatulence; abdominal discomfort	Loss of 1.3 kg (2.9 lb)

3

Note. The data on sibutramine are adapted from "Behavior Therapy and Sibutramine for the Treatment of Adolescent Obesity," by R. I. Berkowitz, T. A. Wadden, A. M. Tershakovec, & J. L. Cronquist, 2003, *Journal of the American Medical Association, 289*, pp. 1807-1809. The data on orlistat are adapted from *Xenical (Orlistat) Capsules: Complete Product Information*, by Roche Laboratories, December 2003, retrieved from http://www.rocheusa.com /products/xenical/pi.pdf **4**

[a]The medication and/or placebo were combined with behavioral therapy in all groups over all time periods. **5**

1 Table summarizes findings from two sources. **2** Table number and title on separate lines; title italic. **3** Abbreviations and numerals used throughout table to save space. **4** Note gives sources of data used in table. Format of note differs from format of reference list. **5** Content note explains data common to all subjects.

CAN MEDICATION CURE OBESITY IN CHILDREN? 9

References

Berkowitz, R. I., Wadden, T. A., Tershakovec, A. M., & Cronquist, J. L. (2003). Behavior therapy and sibutramine for the treatment of adolescent obesity. *Journal of the American Medical Association, 289,* 1805-1812.

Carmona, R. H. (2004, March 2). *The growing epidemic of childhood obesity*. Testimony before the Subcommittee on Competition, Foreign Commerce, and Infrastructure of the U.S. Senate Committee on Commerce, Science, and Transportation. Retrieved from http://www.hhs.gov/asl/testify/t040302.html

Critser, G. (2003). *Fat land*. Boston, MA: Houghton Mifflin.

Duenwald, M. (2004, January 6). Slim pickings: Looking beyond ephedra. *The New York Times,* p. F1. Retrieved from http://nytimes.com/

Henry J. Kaiser Family Foundation. (2004, February). *The role of media in childhood obesity*. Retrieved from http://www.kff.org /entmedia/7030.cfm

Hilts, P. J. (2002, March 20). Petition asks for removal of diet drug from market. *The New York Times*, p. A26. Retrieved from http:// nytimes.com/

Hoppin, A. G., & Taveras, E. M. (2004, June 25). Assessment and management of childhood and adolescent obesity. *Clinical Update*. Retrieved from http://www.medscape.com/viewarticle /481633

McDuffie, J. R., Calis, K. A., Uwaifo, G. I., Sebring, N. G., Fallon, E. M., Hubbard, V. S., & Yanovski, J. A. (2002). Three-month tolerability of orlistat in adolescents with obesity-related comorbid conditions. *Obesity Research, 10,* 642-650.

1 List of references on new page; heading centered and not boldface. **2** List alphabetized by authors' last names (or by titles for works with no authors). **3** Authors' names inverted, with initials for first name(s). **4** First line of each entry flush left, subsequent lines indented ½". **5** Double-spaced throughout. **6** Work with up to seven authors: all authors' names listed, with ampersand (&) before last author's name.

Sample APA title page

1 Running head: ALL AND HTN IN ONE CLIENT   1 **2**

Acute Lymphoblastic Leukemia and Hypertension in One Client:

A Nursing Practice Paper

Julie Riss   **3**

George Mason University

Author Note   **4**

This paper was prepared for Nursing 451, taught by Professor Durham. The author wishes to thank the nursing staff of Milltown General Hospital for help in understanding client care and diagnosis.

1 Short title, no more than 50 characters, in all capital letters on all pages; words "Running head" on title page only. **2** Arabic page number on all pages. **3** Full title and writer's name and affiliation, centered. **4** Author's note (optional) for extra information.

(Annotations indicate APA-style formatting and effective writing.)

Sample APA page

1   Acute Lymphoblastic Leukemia and Hypertension in One Client:

A Nursing Practice Paper

2   **Historical and Physical Assessment**

3   **Physical History**

E.B. is a 16-year-old white male 5'10" tall weighing 190 lb. He
was admitted to the hospital on April 14, 2006, due to decreased
platelets and a need for a PRBC transfusion. He was diagnosed in

4   October 2005 with T-cell acute lymphoblastic leukemia (ALL), after
a 2-week period of decreased energy, decreased oral intake, easy
bruising, and petechia. The client had experienced a 20-lb weight loss
in the previous 6 months. At the time of diagnosis, his CBC showed a
WBC count of 32, an H & H of 13/38, and a platelet count of 34,000.
He began induction chemotherapy on October 12, 2005, receiving
vincristine, 6-mercaptopurine, doxorubicin, intrathecal methotrexate,
and then high-dose methotrexate per protocol. During his hospital stay
he required packed red cells and platelets on two different occasions.
He was diagnosed with hypertension (HTN) due to systolic blood
pressure readings consistently ranging between 130s and 150s and
was started on nifedipine. E.B. has a history of mild ADHD, migraines,
and deep vein thrombosis (DVT). He has tolerated the induction
and consolidation phases of chemotherapy well and is now in the
maintenance phase.

5   **Psychosocial History**

There is a possibility of a depressive episode a year previously
when he would not attend school. He got into serious trouble and was
sent to a shelter for 1 month. He currently lives with his mother, father,
and 14-year-old sister.

Family History

Paternal: prostate cancer and hypertension in grandfather

---

1 Full title, centered and not boldface. **2** First-level heading,
centered and boldface. **3** Second-level heading, flush left and
boldface. **4** Writer's summary of client's medical history.
5 Headings guide readers and define sections.

Sample proposal (memo), APA style

MEMORANDUM **1** **2**

To: Jay Crosson, Senior Vice President, Human Resources

From: Kelly Ratajczak, Intern, Purchasing Department

Subject: Proposal to Add a Wellness Program

Date: April 24, 2006

Health care costs are rising. In the long run, implementing a wellness   **3**
program in our corporate culture will decrease the company's health
care costs.

4

Research indicates that nearly 70% of health care costs are from   **5**
common illnesses related to high blood pressure, overweight, lack of
exercise, high cholesterol, stress, poor nutrition, and other preventable
health issues (Hall, 2006). Health care costs are a major expense
for most businesses, and they do not reflect costs due to the loss of
productivity or absenteeism. A wellness program would address most, if
not all, of these health care issues and related costs.

Benefits of Healthier Employees   **6**

Not only would a wellness program substantially reduce costs associated
with employee health care, but our company would prosper through
many other benefits. Businesses that have wellness programs show
a lower cost in production, fewer sick days, and healthier employees
("Workplace Health," 2006). Our healthier employees will help to cut
not only our production and absenteeism costs but also potential costs
such as higher turnover because of low employee morale.

Implementing the Program

Implementing a good wellness program means making small changes to
the work environment, starting with a series of information sessions.

---

1 Formatting consistent with typical style for business memo.
2 Title page counted in numbering, but no page number appears.
3 Clear point in first paragraph. **4** Paragraph separated by extra
line of space; first line of paragraph not indented. **5** Introduction
provides background information. **6** Headings, flush left and
boldface, define sections.

Chicago Papers

40 Supporting a thesis 231

41 Avoiding plagiarism 233

42 Integrating sources 236

43 *Chicago* documentation style 240

Directory to Chicago-style notes and bibliography entries 242

44 *Chicago* manuscript format 262

SAMPLE PAGES 266

Many history instructors and some humanities instructors require you to document sources with footnotes or endnotes based on the *Chicago Manual of Style* system explained in section 43. When you write a *Chicago*-style paper using sources, you face three main challenges in addition to documenting those sources: (1) supporting a thesis, (2) avoiding plagiarism, and (3) integrating quotations and other source material.

40   Supporting a thesis

Most research assignments ask you to form a thesis, or main idea, and to support that thesis with well-organized evidence.

40a   Forming a working thesis

A thesis is a one-sentence (or occasionally a two-sentence) statement of your central idea. Usually your thesis will appear at the end of the first paragraph (see the example on p. 267).

The thesis of your paper will be your reasoned and informed answer to the central research question you pose, as in the following examples.

RESEARCH QUESTION

To what extent was Confederate Major General Nathan Bedford Forrest responsible for the massacre of Union troops at Fort Pillow?

POSSIBLE THESIS

Although we will never know whether Nathan Bedford Forrest directly ordered the massacre of Union troops at Fort Pillow, evidence suggests that he was responsible for it.

RESEARCH QUESTION

How did the 365-day combat tour affect soldiers' experiences of the Vietnam War?

POSSIBLE THESIS

Letters and diaries written by combat soldiers in Vietnam reveal that when soldiers' tours of duty were shortened, their investment in the war shifted from fighting for victory to fighting for survival.

Each of these thesis statements expresses a view on a debatable issue—an issue about which intelligent, well-meaning people might disagree. The writer's job is to convince such readers that this view is worth taking seriously.

40b Organizing your ideas

The body of your paper will consist of evidence in support of your thesis. To get started, sketch an informal plan that organizes your evidence. The student who wrote about Fort Pillow used a simple list of questions as the blueprint for his paper. These questions became headings that help readers follow the writer's line of argument.

What happened at Fort Pillow?

Did Forrest order the massacre?

Can Forrest be held responsible for the massacre?

40c Using sources to inform and support your argument

Sources can play several different roles as you develop your points.

Providing background information or context You can use facts and statistics to support generalizations or to establish the importance of your topic.

Explaining terms or concepts Explain words, phrases, or ideas important to your topic that may be unfamiliar to readers. Quoting or paraphrasing a source can help you define terms and concepts in accessible language.

Supporting your claims Back up your assertions with facts, examples, and other evidence from your research.

Lending authority to your argument Expert opinion can give weight to your argument. But don't rely on experts to make your argument for you. Construct your argument in your own words and cite authorities in the field to support your position.

Anticipating and countering objections Do not ignore sources that seem contrary to your position or that offer arguments different from your own. Instead, use them to raise opposing ideas and interpretations before you counter them.

41 Avoiding plagiarism

In a research paper, you draw on the work of other writers, and you must document their contributions by citing your sources. When you acknowledge your sources, you avoid plagiarism, a serious academic offense.

Three different acts are considered plagiarism: (1) failing to cite quotations and borrowed ideas, (2) failing to enclose borrowed language in quotation marks, and (3) failing to put summaries and paraphrases in your own words.

41a Citing quotations and borrowed ideas

When you cite sources, you give credit to writers from whom you've borrowed words and ideas. You also let your readers know where your information comes from so that they can evaluate the original source.

You must cite anything you borrow from a source, including direct quotations; statistics and other specific facts; visuals such as cartoons, graphs, and diagrams; and any ideas you present in a summary or a paraphrase.

The only exception is common knowledge—information your readers could easily locate. For example, most encyclopedias will tell readers that the Korean War ended in 1953 and that President Theodore Roosevelt was the first American to receive a Nobel Prize. When you have seen certain general information repeatedly in your reading, you don't need to cite it. However, when information has appeared in only a few sources, when it is highly specific (as with statistics), or when it is controversial, you should cite it.

Chicago citations consist of superscript numbers in the text of the paper that refer readers to notes with corresponding numbers either at the foot of the page (footnotes) or at the end of the paper (endnotes).

TEXT

Governor John Andrew was not allowed to recruit black soldiers from out of state. "Ostensibly," writes Peter Burchard, "no recruiting was done outside Massachusetts, but it was an open secret that Andrew's agents were working far and wide."[1]

NOTE

1. Peter Burchard, *One Gallant Rush: Robert Gould Shaw and His Brave Black Regiment* (New York: St. Martin's, 1965), 85.

For detailed advice on using *Chicago* notes, see 43a. When you use footnotes or endnotes, you will usually need to provide a bibliography as well (see 43b).

41b Enclosing borrowed language in quotation marks

To show that you are using a source's exact phrases or sentences, you must enclose them in quotation marks. To omit the quotation marks is to claim—falsely—that the language is your own. Such an omission is plagiarism even if you have cited the source.

ORIGINAL SOURCE

> For many Southerners it was psychologically impossible to see a black man bearing arms as anything but an incipient slave uprising complete with arson, murder, pillage, and rapine.
> —Dudley Taylor Cornish, *The Sable Arm: Negro Troops in the Union Army, 1861–1865*, p. 158

PLAGIARISM

According to Civil War historian Dudley Taylor Cornish, for many Southerners it was psychologically impossible to see a black man bearing arms as anything but an incipient slave uprising complete with arson, murder, pillage, and rapine.[2]

BORROWED LANGUAGE IN QUOTATION MARKS

According to Civil War historian Dudley Taylor Cornish, "For many Southerners it was psychologically impossible to see a black man bearing arms as anything but an incipient slave uprising complete with arson, murder, pillage, and rapine."[2]

NOTE: When quoted sentences are set off from the text by indenting, quotation marks are not needed (see p. 237).

41c Putting summaries and paraphrases in your own words

A summary condenses information; a paraphrase conveys information in about the same number of words as in the original source. When you summarize or paraphrase, you must name the source and restate the source's meaning in your own words.

In the following example, the paraphrase is plagiarized—even though the source is cited—because too much of its language is borrowed from the source without quotation marks. The highlighted phrases have been copied exactly (without quotation marks). In addition, the writer has closely followed the sentence structure of the original source, merely making a few substitutions (such as *Fifty percent* for *Half* and *angered and perhaps frightened* for *enraged and perhaps terrified*).

ORIGINAL SOURCE

> Half of the force holding Fort Pillow were Negroes, former slaves now enrolled in the Union Army. Toward them Forrest's troops had the fierce, bitter animosity of men who had been educated to regard the colored race as inferior and who for the first time had encountered that race armed and fighting against white men. The sight enraged and perhaps terrified many of the Confederates and aroused in them the ugly spirit of a lynching mob.
>
> —Albert Castel, "The Fort Pillow Massacre," pp. 46–47

PLAGIARISM: UNACCEPTABLE BORROWING

Albert Castel suggests that much of the brutality at Fort Pillow can be traced to racial attitudes. Fifty percent of the troops holding Fort Pillow were Negroes, former slaves who had joined the Union Army. Toward them Forrest's soldiers displayed the savage hatred of men who had been taught the inferiority of blacks and who for the first time had confronted them armed and fighting against white men. The vision angered and perhaps frightened the Confederates and aroused in them the ugly spirit of a lynching mob.[3]

To avoid plagiarizing an author's language, don't look at the source while you are summarizing or paraphrasing. After you've restated the author's idea in your own words, return to the source and check that you haven't used the author's language or sentence structure or misrepresented the author's ideas.

ACCEPTABLE PARAPHRASE

Albert Castel suggests that much of the brutality at Fort Pillow can be traced to racial attitudes. Nearly half of the Union troops were blacks, men whom the Confederates had been raised to consider their inferiors. The shock and perhaps fear of facing armed ex-slaves in battle for the first time may well have unleashed the fury that led to the massacre.[3]

42 Integrating sources

Quotations, summaries, paraphrases, and facts will support your argument, but they cannot speak for you. You can use several strategies to integrate information from sources into your paper while maintaining your own voice.

42a Using quotations appropriately

Limiting your use of quotations In your writing, keep the emphasis on your own words. Do not quote excessively. It is not always necessary to quote full sentences from a source. Often you can integrate words or phrases from a source into your own sentence structure.

As Hurst has pointed out, until "an outcry erupted in the Northern press," even the Confederates did not deny that there had been a massacre at Fort Pillow.[4]

Union surgeon Dr. Charles Fitch testified that after he was in custody he "saw" Confederate soldiers "kill every negro that made his appearance dressed in Federal uniform."[5]

Using the ellipsis mark You can use the ellipsis mark (three periods, with spaces between) to condense a quoted passage and indicate that you have omitted words. What remains must be grammatically complete.

Union surgeon Fitch's testimony that all women and children had been evacuated from Fort Pillow before the attack conflicts with Forrest's report: "We captured . . . about 40 negro women and children."[6]

The writer has omitted several words not relevant to the issue at hand: *164 Federals, 75 negro troops, and.*

When you want to omit a full sentence or more, use a period before the three ellipsis dots. For an example, see the long quotation at the bottom of this page.

You do not need an ellipsis mark at the beginning or at the end of a quotation. Readers will understand that you have taken the quoted material from a longer passage.

Make sure omissions and ellipsis marks do not distort the meaning of your source.

Using brackets   Brackets allow you to insert your own words into quoted material to clarify a confusing reference or to make the quoted words fit grammatically into the context of your writing.

According to Albert Castel, "It can be reasonably argued that he [Forrest] was justified in believing that the approaching steamships intended to aid the garrison [at Fort Pillow]."[7]

NOTE: Use [*sic*], italicized and with brackets around it, to indicate that an error in a quoted sentence appears in the original source. (See the example below.)

Setting off long quotations   *Chicago* style allows you to set off a long quotation or run it into your text. For emphasis, you may want to set off a quotation of more than five typed lines; you should always set off quotations of ten lines or more. To set off a quotation, indent it one-half inch from the left margin and keep the standard right margin. Double-space the quotation.

Introduce long quotations with an informative sentence, usually ending in a colon. Because the indented format tells readers that the words are taken directly from the source, you don't need quotation marks.

In a letter home, Confederate officer Achilles V. Clark recounted what happened at Fort Pillow:

> Words cannot describe the scene. The poor deluded negroes would run up to our men fall upon their knees and with uplifted hands scream for mercy but they were ordered to their feet and then shot down. The whitte [*sic*] men fared but little better. . . . I with several others tried to stop the butchery and at one time had partially succeeded, but Gen. Forrest ordered them shot down like dogs, and the carnage continued.[8]

42b Using signal phrases to integrate sources

Whenever you include a direct quotation, a paraphrase, or a summary in your paper, prepare readers for it with a *signal phrase*. A signal phrase usually names the author of the source and often provides some context for the source material. The first time you mention an author, use the full name: *Shelby Foote argues....* When you refer to the author again, you may use the last name only: *Foote raises an important question.*

See the chart on page 239 for a list of verbs commonly used in signal phrases.

Marking boundaries   Avoid dropping quotations into your text without warning. Provide clear signal phrases, including at least the author's name. A signal phrase indicates the boundary between your words and the source's words.

DROPPED QUOTATION

Unionists claimed that their troops had abandoned their arms and were in full retreat. "The Confederates, however, all agreed that the Union troops retreated to the river with arms in their hands."⁹

QUOTATION WITH SIGNAL PHRASE

Unionists claimed that their troops had abandoned their arms and were in full retreat. "The Confederates, however," writes historian Albert Castel, "all agreed that the Union troops retreated to the river with arms in their hands."⁹

Introducing summaries and paraphrases   Introduce most summaries and paraphrases with a signal phrase that mentions the author and places the material in context. Readers will then understand where the summary or paraphrase begins.

The signal phrase (highlighted) in the following example shows that the whole paragraph, not just the last sentence, is based on the source.

According to Jack Hurst, official Confederate policy was that black soldiers were to be treated as runaway slaves; in addition, the Confederate Congress decreed that white Union officers commanding black troops be killed. Confederate Lieutenant General Kirby Smith went one step further, declaring that he would kill all captured black troops. Smith's policy never met with strong opposition from the Richmond government.¹⁰

Using signal phrases in *Chicago* papers

To avoid monotony, try to vary both the language and the placement of your signal phrases.

Model signal phrases

In the words of historian James M. McPherson, ". . ."[1]

As Dudley Taylor Cornish has argued, ". . ."[2]

In a letter to his wife, a Confederate soldier who witnessed the massacre wrote that ". . ."[3]

". . . ," claims Benjamin Quarles.[4]

". . . ," writes Albert Castel, ". . ."[5]

Shelby Foote offers an intriguing interpretation: ". . ."[6]

Verbs in signal phrases

Are you providing background, explaining a concept, supporting a claim, lending authority, or refuting a belief? Choose a verb that is appropriate for the way you are using the source.

admits	contends	reasons
agrees	declares	refutes
argues	denies	rejects
asserts	emphasizes	reports
believes	insists	responds
claims	notes	suggests
compares	observes	thinks
confirms	points out	writes

NOTE: In *Chicago* style, use the present tense or present perfect tense to introduce quotations or other material from nonfiction sources: *Foote points out* or *Foote has pointed out*. Use the past tense only if you include a date that specifies the time of the original author's writing.

Putting source material in context Provide context for any source material that appears in your paper. A signal phrase can help you connect your own ideas with those of another writer by clarifying how the source will contribute to your paper. It's a good idea to embed source material, especially long quotations, between sentences of your own that interpret the source and link the source to your argument.

QUOTATION WITH EFFECTIVE CONTEXT

In a respected biography of Nathan Bedford Forrest, Hurst suggests that the temperamental Forrest "may have ragingly ordered a massacre and even intended to carry it out—until he rode inside the fort and viewed the horrifying result" and ordered it stopped.[11] While this is an intriguing interpretation of events, even Hurst would probably admit that it is merely speculation.

NOTE: When you bring other sources into a conversation about your research topic, you are synthesizing sources. For more on synthesis, see 31c.

Integrating statistics and other facts When you cite a statistic or another specific fact, a signal phrase is often not necessary. In most cases, readers will understand that the citation refers to the statistic or fact (not the whole paragraph).

Of 295 white troops garrisoned at Fort Pillow, 168 were taken prisoner. Black troops fared worse, with only 58 of 262 captured and most of the rest presumably killed or wounded.[12]

There is nothing wrong, however, with using a signal phrase to introduce a statistic or other specific fact in your paper.

43 *Chicago* documentation style

In history and some other humanities courses, you may be asked to use the documentation system of *The Chicago Manual of Style*, 16th ed. (Chicago: University of Chicago Press, 2010). In *Chicago* style, superscript numbers (like this[1]) in the text of the paper refer readers to notes with corresponding numbers either at the foot of the page (footnotes) or at the end of the paper (endnotes). A bibliography is often required as well; it appears at the end of the paper and gives publication information for all the works cited in the notes.

TEXT

A Union soldier, Jacob Thompson, claimed to have seen Forrest order the killing, but when asked to describe the six-foot-two general, he called him "a little bit of a man."[12]

FOOTNOTE OR ENDNOTE

   12. Brian Steel Wills, *A Battle from the Start: The Life of Nathan Bedford Forrest* (New York: HarperCollins, 1992), 187.

BIBLIOGRAPHY ENTRY

Wills, Brian Steel. *A Battle from the Start: The Life of Nathan Bedford Forrest*. New York: HarperCollins, 1992.

43a First and later notes for a source

The first time you cite a source, the note should include publication information for that work as well as the page number for the passage you are citing.

   1. Peter Burchard, *One Gallant Rush: Robert Gould Shaw and His Brave Black Regiment* (New York: St. Martin's, 1965), 85.

For later references to a source you have already cited, you may simply give the author's last name, a short form of the title, and the page or pages cited. A short form of the title of a book or another long work is italicized; a short form of the title of an article or another short work is put in quotation marks.

   4. Burchard, *One Gallant Rush*, 31.

When you have two notes in a row from the same source, you may use "Ibid." (meaning "in the same place") and the page number for the second note. Use "Ibid." alone if the page number is the same.

   5. Jack Hurst, *Nathan Bedford Forrest: A Biography* (New York: Knopf, 1993), 8.

   6. Ibid., 174.

43b *Chicago*-style bibliography

A bibliography at the end of your paper lists the works you have cited in your notes; it may also include works you consulted but did not cite. See pages 264–65 for formatting; see page 269 for a sample bibliography.

Directory to *Chicago*-style notes and bibliography entries

GENERAL GUIDELINES FOR LISTING AUTHORS

1.	One author	243
2.	Two or three authors	244
3.	Four or more authors	244
4.	Organization as author	244
5.	Unknown author	244
6.	Multiple works by the same author	244
7.	Editor	244
8.	Editor with author	245
9.	Translator with author	245

BOOKS AND OTHER LONG WORKS

10.	Basic format for a book	245
11.	Edition other than the first	247
12.	Volume in a multivolume work	247
13.	Work in an anthology	247
14.	Introduction, preface, foreword, or afterword	247
15.	Republished book	247
16.	Book with a title in its title	247
17.	Work in a series	248
18.	Sacred text	248
19.	Government document	248
20.	Unpublished dissertation	248
21.	Published proceedings of a conference	248
22.	Source quoted in another source (a secondary source)	249

ARTICLES AND OTHER SHORT WORKS

23.	Article in a journal	249
24.	Article in a magazine	251
25.	Article in a newspaper	253
26.	Unsigned newspaper article	254
27.	Article with a title in its title	254
28.	Review	254
29.	Letter to the editor	254
30.	Article in a reference work (encyclopedia, dictionary, wiki)	255
31.	Letter in a published collection	255

WEB SOURCES

32.	An entire Web site	255
33.	Short work from a Web site	258
34.	Blog post	258
35.	Comment on a blog post	258

AUDIO, VISUAL, AND MULTIMEDIA SOURCES

36.   Podcast   258
37.   Online audio or video   259
38.   Published or broadcast interview   259
39.   Film (DVD, BD, or other format)   259
40.   Sound recording   259
41.   Musical score or composition   259
42.   Work of art   261
43.   Performance   261

PERSONAL COMMUNICATION AND SOCIAL MEDIA

44.   Personal communication   261
45.   Online posting or e-mail   261
46.   Facebook post   262
47.   Twitter post (tweet)   262

NOTE: If you include a bibliography, you may shorten all notes, including the first reference to a source (see p. 241). Check with your instructor, however, to see whether using an abbreviated note for a first reference to a source is acceptable.

43c Model notes and bibliography entries

The following models are consistent with guidelines in *The Chicago Manual of Style*, 16th ed. For each type of source, a model note appears first, followed by a model bibliography entry. The note shows the format you should use when citing a source for the first time. For subsequent citations of a source, use shortened notes (see p. 241).

Some sources from the Web, typically periodical articles, use a permanent locator called a digital object identifier (DOI). Use the DOI, when it is available, in place of a URL. (For guidelines about breaking a URL or DOI across lines, see p. 264.)

General guidelines for listing authors

1. One author

1. Salman Rushdie, *Joseph Anton: A Memoir* (New York: Random House, 2012), 135.

Rushdie, Salman. *Joseph Anton: A Memoir*. New York: Random House, 2012.

■ **2. Two or three authors**   Give all authors' names in both the note and the bibliography entry.

    2. Bill O'Reilly and Martin Dugard, *Killing Lincoln: The Shocking Assassination That Changed America Forever* (New York: Holt, 2012), 33.

O'Reilly, Bill, and Martin Dugard. *Killing Lincoln: The Shocking
    Assassination That Changed America Forever.* New York: Holt, 2012.

■ **3. Four or more authors**   In the note, give the first author's name followed by "et al." (Latin for "and others"); in the bibliography entry, list all authors' names.

    3. Lynn Hunt et al., *The Making of the West: Peoples and Cultures,* 4th ed. (Boston: Bedford/St. Martin's, 2012), 541.

Hunt, Lynn, Thomas R. Martin, Barbara H. Rosenwein, R. Po-chia
    Hsia, and Bonnie G. Smith. *The Making of the West: Peoples
    and Cultures.* 4th ed. Boston: Bedford/St. Martin's, 2012.

■ **4. Organization as author**

    4. Johnson Historical Society, *Images of America: Johnson* (Charleston, SC: Arcadia Publishing, 2011), 24.

Johnson Historical Society. *Images of America: Johnson.* Charleston,
    SC: Arcadia Publishing, 2011.

■ **5. Unknown author**

    5. *The Men's League Handbook on Women's Suffrage* (London, 1912), 23.

The Men's League Handbook on Women's Suffrage. London, 1912.

■ **6. Multiple works by the same author**   In the bibliography, arrange the entries alphabetically by title. Use six hyphens in place of the author's name in the second and subsequent entries.

Winchester, Simon. *The Alice behind Wonderland.* New York: Oxford
    University Press, 2011.

------. *Atlantic: Great Sea Battles, Heroic Discoveries, Titanic Storms, and
    a Vast Ocean of a Million Stories.* New York: HarperCollins, 2010.

■ **7. Editor**

    7. Teresa Carpenter, ed., *New York Diaries: 1609-2009* (New York: Modern Library, 2012), 316.

Carpenter, Teresa, ed. *New York Diaries: 1609-2009.* New York:
    Modern Library, 2012.

8. Editor with author

8. Susan Sontag, *As Consciousness Is Harnessed to Flesh: Journals and Notebooks, 1964-1980*, ed. David Rieff (New York: Farrar, Straus and Giroux, 2012), 265.

Sontag, Susan. *As Consciousness Is Harnessed to Flesh: Journals and Notebooks, 1964-1980*. Edited by David Rieff. New York: Farrar, Straus and Giroux, 2012.

9. Translator with author

9. Richard Bidlack and Nikita Lomagin, *The Leningrad Blockade, 1941-1944: A New Documentary from the Soviet Archives*, trans. Marian Schwartz (New Haven: Yale University Press, 2012), 26.

Bidlack, Richard, and Nikita Lomagin. *The Leningrad Blockade, 1941-1944: A New Documentary from the Soviet Archives*. Translated by Marian Schwartz. New Haven: Yale University Press, 2012.

Books and other long works

▶ Citation at a glance: Book, **page 246**

10. Basic format for a book

a. Print

10. Mary N. Woods, *Beyond the Architect's Eye: Photographs and the American Built Environment* (Philadelphia: University of Pennsylvania Press, 2009), 45.

Woods, Mary N. *Beyond the Architect's Eye: Photographs and the American Built Environment*. Philadelphia: University of Pennsylvania Press, 2009.

b. E-book

10. Drew Gilpin Faust, *This Republic of Suffering: Death and the American Civil War* (New York: Knopf, 2008), Nook edition, chap. 4.

Faust, Drew Gilpin. *This Republic of Suffering: Death and the American Civil War*. New York: Knopf, 2008. Nook edition.

c. Web (or online library)

10. Charles Hursthouse, *New Zealand, or Zealandia, the Britain of the South* (1857; HathiTrust Digital Library, n.d.), 2:356, http://hdl.handle.net/2027/uc1.b304920.

Hursthouse, Charles. *New Zealand, or Zealandia, the Britain of the South*. 2 vols. 1857. HathiTrust Digital Library, n.d. http://hdl.handle.net/2027/uc1.b304920.

Citation at a glance
Book *Chicago*

To cite a print book in *Chicago* style, include the following elements:

1. Author(s)
2. Title and subtitle
3. City of publication
4. Publisher
5. Year of publication
6. Page number(s) cited (for notes)

TITLE PAGE

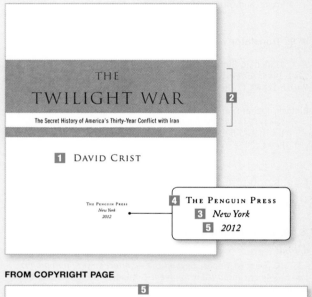

THE
TWILIGHT WAR **2**
The Secret History of America's Thirty-Year Conflict with Iran

1 DAVID CRIST

THE PENGUIN PRESS
New York
2012

4 THE PENGUIN PRESS
3 *New York*
5 *2012*

FROM COPYRIGHT PAGE

5

First published in 2012 by The Penguin Press,
a member of Penguin Group (USA) Inc.

The Penguin Press, New York, 2012.

NOTE

    1   2

1. David Crist, *The Twilight War: The Secret History of America's*

               3   4   5   6

Thirty-Year Conflict with Iran (New York: Penguin, 2012), 354.

BIBLIOGRAPHY

   1   2

Crist, David. *The Twilight War: The Secret History of America's Thirty-*

            3   4   5

Year Conflict with Iran. New York: Penguin, 2012.

For more on citing books in *Chicago* style, see items 10–18.

■ 11. Edition other than the first

11. Josephine Donovan, *Feminist Theory: The Intellectual Traditions*, 4th ed. (New York: Continuum, 2012), 86.

Donovan, Josephine. *Feminist Theory: The Intellectual Traditions*. 4th ed. New York: Continuum, 2012.

■ 12. Volume in a multivolume work

12. Robert A. Caro, *The Passage of Power*, vol. 4 of *The Years of Lyndon Johnson* (New York: Knopf, 2012), 198.

Caro, Robert A. *The Passage of Power*. Vol. 4 of *The Years of Lyndon Johnson*. New York: Knopf, 2012.

If the volumes do not have individual titles, give the volume and page number in the note (for example, 2:356) and the total number of volumes in the bibliography entry (see item 10c).

■ 13. Work in an anthology

13. Janet Walsh, "Unequal in Africa: How Property Rights Can Empower Women," in *The Unfinished Revolution: Voices from the Global Fight for Women's Rights*, ed. Minky Worden (New York: Seven Stories Press, 2012), 161.

Walsh, Janet. "Unequal in Africa: How Property Rights Can Empower Women." In *The Unfinished Revolution: Voices from the Global Fight for Women's Rights*, edited by Minky Worden, 159-66. New York: Seven Stories Press, 2012.

■ 14. Introduction, preface, foreword, or afterword

14. Alice Walker, afterword to *The Indispensable Zinn: The Essential Writings of the "People's Historian,"* by Howard Zinn (New York: Free Press, 2012), 373.

Walker, Alice. Afterword to *The Indispensable Zinn: The Essential Writings of the "People's Historian,"* by Howard Zinn, 371-76. New York: Free Press, 2012.

■ 15. Republished book

15. W. S. Blatchley, *A Nature Wooing at Ormond by the Sea* (1902; repr., Stockbridge, MA: Hard Press, 2012), 26.

Blatchley, W. S. *A Nature Wooing at Ormond by the Sea*. 1902. Reprint, Stockbridge, MA: Hard Press, 2012.

■ 16. Book with a title in its title   Use quotation marks around any title, whether a long or a short work, within an italicized title.

16. Claudia Durst Johnson, ed., *Race in Mark Twain's "Adventures of Huckleberry Finn"* (Detroit: Greenhaven Press, 2009).

Johnson, Claudia Durst, ed. *Race in Mark Twain's "Adventures of Huckleberry Finn."* Detroit: Greenhaven Press, 2009.

■ **17. Work in a series**   The series name follows the book title.

17. Lois E. Horton, *Harriet Tubman and the Fight for Freedom: A Brief History with Documents*, Bedford Series in History and Culture (Boston: Bedford/St. Martin's, 2013), 35.

Horton, Lois E. *Harriet Tubman and the Fight for Freedom: A Brief History with Documents*. Bedford Series in History and Culture. Boston: Bedford/St. Martin's, 2013.

■ **18. Sacred text**   Sacred texts are usually not included in the bibliography.

18. Matt. 20:4-9 (Revised Standard Version).

18. Qur'an 18:1-3.

■ **19. Government document**

19. United States Senate, Committee on Foreign Relations, *Implications of the Kyoto Protocol on Climate Change: Hearing before the Committee on Foreign Relations, United States Senate*, 105th Cong., 2nd sess. (Washington, DC: GPO, 1998).

United States Senate. Committee on Foreign Relations. *Implications of the Kyoto Protocol on Climate Change: Hearing before the Committee on Foreign Relations, United States Senate*, 105th Cong., 2nd sess. Washington, DC: GPO, 1998.

■ **20. Unpublished dissertation**

20. Stephanie Lynn Budin, "The Origins of Aphrodite" (PhD diss., University of Pennsylvania, 2000), 301-2, ProQuest (AAT 9976404).

Budin, Stephanie Lynn. "The Origins of Aphrodite." PhD diss., University of Pennsylvania, 2000. ProQuest (AAT 9976404).

For a published dissertation, cite as a book.

■ **21. Published proceedings of a conference**   Cite as a book, adding the location and dates of the conference after the title.

21. Stacey K. Sowards, Kyle Alvarado, Diana Arrieta, and Jacob Barde, eds., *Across Borders and Environments: Communication and Environmental Justice in International Contexts*, University of Texas at El Paso, June 25-28, 2011 (Cincinnati, OH: International Environmental Communication Association, 2012), 114.

Sowards, Stacey K., Kyle Alvarado, Diana Arrieta, and Jacob Barde, eds. *Across Borders and Environments: Communication and Environmental Justice in International Contexts*. University of Texas at El Paso, June 25-28, 2011. Cincinnati, OH: International Environmental Communication Association, 2012.

■ 22. Source quoted in another source (a secondary source)

22. Thomas Wentworth Higginson, *Margaret Fuller Ossoli* (Boston: Houghton Mifflin, 1890), 11, quoted in John Matteson, *The Lives of Margaret Fuller* (New York: Norton, 2012), 7.

Higginson, Thomas Wentworth. *Margaret Fuller Ossoli*. Boston: Houghton Mifflin, 1890, 11. Quoted in John Matteson, *The Lives of Margaret Fuller* (New York: Norton, 2012), 7.

Articles and other short works

▶ Citation at a glance: Article in a journal, **page 250**

▶ Citation at a glance: Article from a database, **page 252**

■ 23. Article in a journal   If an article in a database or on the Web shows only a beginning page, use a plus sign after the page number in the bibliography: 212+.

a. Print

23. Catherine Foisy, "Preparing the Quebec Church for Vatican II: Missionary Lessons from Asia, Africa, and Latin America, 1945-1962," *Historical Studies* 78 (2012): 8.

Foisy, Catherine. "Preparing the Quebec Church for Vatican II: Missionary Lessons from Asia, Africa, and Latin America, 1945-1962." *Historical Studies* 78 (2012): 7-26.

b. Web   If no DOI is available, give the URL for the article.

23. Anne-Lise François, "Flower Fisting," *Postmodern Culture* 22, no. 1 (2011), doi:10.1353/pmc.2012.0004.

François, Anne-Lise. "Flower Fisting." *Postmodern Culture* 22, no. 1 (2011). doi:10.1353/pmc.2012.0004.

c. Database   Give one of the following pieces of information from the database listing, in this order of preference: a DOI for the article; or the name of the database and the article number, if any; or a "stable" or "persistent" URL for the article.

23. Patrick Zuk, "Nikolay Myaskovsky and the Events of 1948," *Music and Letters* 93, no. 1 (2012): 61, Project Muse.

Zuk, Patrick. "Nikolay Myaskovsky and the Events of 1948." *Music and Letters* 93, no. 1 (2012): 61. Project Muse.

Citation at a glance

Article in a journal `Chicago`

To cite an article in a print journal in *Chicago* style, include the following elements:

1 Author(s)
2 Title and subtitle of article
3 Title of journal
4 Volume and issue numbers
5 Year of publication
6 Page number(s) cited (for notes); page range of article (for bibliography)

FIRST PAGE OF ARTICLE

Work, Family, and the Eighteenth-Century History of a Middle Class in the American South   **2**

By EMMA HART   **1**

ON OCTOBER 15, 1800, WIDOW VIOLETTA WYATT APPEARED BEFORE William Hassell Gibbes, the master-in-equity in Charleston District, South Carolina. She commenced an account of her married life, which had begun almost exactly twenty-two years earlier, when she took carpenter John Wyatt as her husband. The daughter of a blacksmith, Violetta had lived and worked in the city of Charleston from childhood,

TITLE PAGE OF JOURNAL

The Journal of **SOUTHERN HISTORY**   **3**

4 VOLUME LXXVIII   **5** AUGUST 2012   **4** NUMBER 3

Contents

2 Work, Family, and the Eighteenth-Century History of a Middle Class in the American South
    1 *By Emma Hart*   551 **6**

A Twice Sacred Circle: Women, Evangelicalism, and Honor in the Deep South, 1784–1860
    By Robert Elder   579

The Free Black Experience in Antebellum Wilmington, North Carolina: Refining Generalizations about Race Relations
    By Richard C. Rohrs   615

Looking the Thing in the Face: Slavery, Race, and the Commemorative Landscape in Charleston, South Carolina, 1865–2010
    By Blain Roberts and Ethan J. Kytle   639

Book Reviews   685

Historical News and Notices   794

NOTE

1. Emma Hart, "Work, Family, and the Eighteenth-Century History of a Middle Class in the American South," *Journal of Southern History* 78, no. 3 (2012): 565.

BIBLIOGRAPHY

Hart, Emma. "Work, Family, and the Eighteenth-Century History of a Middle Class in the American South." *Journal of Southern History* 78, no. 3 (2012): 551-78.

For more on citing articles in *Chicago* style, see items 23–25.

■ **24. Article in a magazine**   Give the month and year for a monthly publication; give the month, day, and year for a weekly publication. If an article in a database or on the Web shows only a beginning page, use a plus sign after the page number in the bibliography: 212+.

a. Print

24. Alan Lightman, "Our Place in the Universe: Face to Face with the Infinite," *Harper's*, December 2012, 34.

Lightman, Alan. "Our Place in the Universe: Face to Face with the Infinite." *Harper's*, December 2012, 33-38.

b. Web   If no DOI is available, include the URL for the article.

24. James Verini, "The Tunnels of Gaza," *National Geographic*, December 2012, http://ngm.nationalgeographic.com/2012/12 /gaza-tunnels /verini-text.

Verini, James. "The Tunnels of Gaza." *National Geographic*, December 2012. http://ngm.nationalgeographic.com/2012/12 /gaza-tunnels/verini-text.

c. Database   Give one of the following from the database listing, in this order of preference: a DOI for the article; or the name of the database and the article number, if any; or a "stable" or "persistent" URL for the article.

24. Ron Rosenbaum, "The Last Renaissance Man," *Smithsonian*, November 2012, 40, OmniFile Full Text Select (83097302).

Rosenbaum, Ron. "The Last Renaissance Man." *Smithsonian*, November 2012, 39-44. OmniFile Full Text Select (83097302).

Citation at a glance

Article from a database *Chicago*

To cite an article from a database in *Chicago* style, include the following elements:

1. Author(s)
2. Title and subtitle of article
3. Title of journal
4. Volume and issue numbers
5. Year of publication
6. Page number(s) cited (for notes); page range of article (for bibliography)
7. DOI; *or* database name and article number; *or* "stable" or "persistent" URL for article

---

Authors: Bell, Adrian[1]   **[1]**
Dale, Richard[2]

[5]   **[4]**   **[6]**

Source: History Today; Jan2013, Vol. 63 Issue 1, p30-37, 8p

[3]

DATABASE RECORD

Searching: OmniFile Full Text Select (H.W. Wilson) | Choose Databases

JN "History Today" AND DT 20130101   in Select a Field (optional)   Search   Clear

AND   in Select a Field (optional)

AND   in Select a Field (optional)   Add Row

Basic Search | Advanced Search | Visual Search | Search History

◄ Result List | Refine Search ◄ 3 of 47 ►

Detailed Record

Check Article Linker for this item's availability. Check Article Linker for more information

Rich Pickings from Medieval Pilgrims. **[2]**

Authors: Bell, Adrian[1]
Dale, Richard[2]

Source: History Today; Jan2013, Vol. 63 Issue 1, p30-37, 8p

Document Type: Article

Subjects: Europe; Christian pilgrims & pilgrimages -- History; Church history -- Middle Ages, space; Christian saints; Miracles; Indulgences; Europe -- Church history -- 600-

Abstract: The article discusses historical accounts of Medieval pilgrims and pilgrimages to Europe. It considers how sites of holy relics and remains marketed their mirac members to travel to their sites. Other topics include plenary indulgences, ad Saints' days or through special church attendance, and books issued listing in in cities such as Rome, Italy. Shrines discussed include the tomb of Saint Thoi the tomb of Saint Martin in Tours, France; and the remains of Sainte Foy at L

Author Affiliations: [1]Professor, History of Finance and Head of School, ICMA Centre, Henley Busin [2]Professor Emeritus of International Banking, University of Southampton

Full Text Word Count: 3892

ISSN: 00182753

Accession Number: 84769933

Database: OmniFile Full Text Select (H.W. Wilson)

◄ Result List | Refine Search ◄ 3 of 47 ►

Accession Number: 84769933 **[7]**

Database: OmniFile Full Text Select (H.W. Wilson)

$\overset{1}{\overbrace{\hspace{4cm}}}$ $\overset{2}{\overbrace{\hspace{4cm}}}$

1. Adrian Bell and Richard Dale, "Rich Pickings from Medieval

$\overset{3}{\overbrace{\hspace{2cm}}}$ $\overset{4}{\overbrace{\hspace{1.5cm}}}$ $\overset{5}{\overbrace{\hspace{0.8cm}}}$ $\overset{6}{\overbrace{\hspace{0.5cm}}}$ $\overset{7}{\overbrace{\hspace{2cm}}}$

Pilgrims," *History Today* 63, no. 1 (2013): 33, OmniFile Full Text

$\overset{}{\overbrace{\hspace{3cm}}}$

Select (84769933).

BIBLIOGRAPHY

$\overset{1}{\overbrace{\hspace{4cm}}}$ $\overset{2}{\overbrace{\hspace{4cm}}}$

Bell, Adrian, and Richard Dale. "Rich Pickings from Medieval

$\overset{3}{\overbrace{\hspace{2cm}}}$ $\overset{4}{\overbrace{\hspace{1.5cm}}}$ $\overset{5}{\overbrace{\hspace{0.8cm}}}$ $\overset{6}{\overbrace{\hspace{0.8cm}}}$ $\overset{7}{\overbrace{\hspace{2cm}}}$

Pilgrims." *History Today* 63, no. 1 (2013): 30–37. OmniFile Full

$\overset{}{\overbrace{\hspace{4cm}}}$

Text Select (84769933).

For more on citing articles from databases in *Chicago* style, see items 23–25.

■ **25. Article in a newspaper**   Page numbers are not necessary; a section letter or number, if available, is sufficient.

a. Print

25. Alissa J. Rubin, "A Pristine Afghan Prison Faces a Murky Future," *New York Times*, December 18, 2012, sec. A.

Rubin, Alissa J. "A Pristine Afghan Prison Faces a Murky Future." *New York Times*, December 18, 2012, sec. A.

b. Web   Include the URL for the article; if the URL is very long, use the URL for the newspaper's home page.

25. David Brown, "New Burden of Disease Study Shows World's People Living Longer but with More Disability," *Washington Post*, December 13, 2012, http://www.washingtonpost.com/.

Brown, David. "New Burden of Disease Study Shows World's People Living Longer but with More Disability." *Washington Post*, December 13, 2012. http://www.washingtonpost.com/.

c. Database   Give one of the following from the database listing, in this order of preference: a DOI for the article; or the name of the database and the number assigned by the database; or a "stable" or "persistent" URL for the article.

25. "Safe in Sioux City at Last: Union Pacific Succeeds in Securing Trackage from the St. Paul Road," *Omaha Daily Herald*, May 16, 1889, America's Historical Newspapers.

"Safe in Sioux City at Last: Union Pacific Succeeds in Securing Trackage from the St. Paul Road." *Omaha Daily Herald*, May 16, 1889. America's Historical Newspapers.

■ **26. Unsigned newspaper article** In the note, begin
with the title of the article. In the bibliography entry,
begin with the title of the newspaper.

26. "Rein in Charter Schools," *Chicago Sun-Times*, December
13, 2012, http://www.suntimes.com/.

Chicago Sun-Times. "Rein in Charter Schools." December 13, 2012.
http://www.suntimes.com/.

■ **27. Article with a title in its title** Use italics for titles of
long works such as books and for terms that are normally
italicized. Use single quotation marks for titles of short
works and terms that would otherwise be placed in double
quotation marks.

27. Karen Garner, "Global Gender Policy in the 1990s: Incorporating
the 'Vital Voices' of Women," *Journal of Women's History* 24, no. 4
(2012): 130.

Garner, Karen. "Global Gender Policy in the 1990s: Incorporating the
'Vital Voices' of Women." *Journal of Women's History* 24, no. 4
(2012): 121-48.

■ **28. Review**

28. David Denby, "Dead Reckoning," review of *Zero Dark
Thirty*, directed by Kathryn Bigelow, *New Yorker*, December 24/31,
2012, 130.

Denby, David. "Dead Reckoning." Review of *Zero Dark Thirty*,
directed by Kathryn Bigelow. *New Yorker*, December 24/31,
2012, 130-32.

28. David Eggleton, review of *Stalking Nabokov*, by Brian Boyd,
New Zealand Listener, December 13, 2012, http://www.listener.co.nz
/culture/books/stalking-nabokov-by-brian-boyd-review/.

Eggleton, David. Review of *Stalking Nabokov*, by Brian Boyd. *New
Zealand Listener*, December 13, 2012. http://www.listener
.co.nz/culture/books/stalking-nabokov-by-brian-boyd-review/.

■ **29. Letter to the editor** Do not use the letter's title,
even if the publication gives one.

29. Andy Bush, letter to the editor, *Economist*, December 15,
2012, http://www.economist.com/.

Bush, Andy. Letter to the editor. *Economist*, December 15, 2012.
http://www.economist.com/.

■ **30. Article in a reference work (encyclopedia, dictionary, wiki)**   Reference works such as encyclopedias do not require publication information and are usually not included in the bibliography. The abbreviation "s.v." is for the Latin *sub verbo* ("under the word").

> 30. *Encyclopaedia Britannica*, 15th ed., s.v. "Monroe Doctrine."

> 30. *Wikipedia*, s.v. "James Monroe," last modified December 19, 2012, http://en.wikipedia.org/wiki/James_Monroe.

> 30. Bryan A. Garner, *Garner's Modern American Usage*, 3rd ed. (Oxford: Oxford University Press, 2009), s.v. "brideprice."

Garner, Bryan A. *Garner's Modern American Usage*. 3rd ed. Oxford: Oxford University Press, 2009.

■ **31. Letter in a published collection**   Use the day-month-year form for the date of the letter. If the letter writer's name is part of the book title, begin the note with only the last name but begin the bibliography entry with the full name.

> ► Citation at a glance: Letter in a published collection, **page 256**

> 31. Dickens to Thomas Beard, 1 June 1840, in *The Selected Letters of Charles Dickens*, ed. Jenny Hartley (New York: Oxford University Press, 2012), 65.

Dickens, Charles. *The Selected Letters of Charles Dickens*. Edited by Jenny Hartley. New York: Oxford University Press, 2012.

Web sources   For most Web sites, include an author if a site has one, the title of the site, the sponsor, the date of publication or the modified (update) date, and the site's URL. Do not italicize a Web site title unless the site is an online book or periodical. Use quotation marks for the titles of sections or pages in a Web site. If a site does not have a date of publication or a modified date, give the date you accessed the site ("accessed January 3, 2013").

■ **32. An entire Web site**

> 32. Chesapeake and Ohio Canal National Historical Park, National Park Service, last modified November 25, 2012, http://www.nps.gov/choh/index.htm.

Chesapeake and Ohio Canal National Historical Park. National Park Service. Last modified November 25, 2012. http://www.nps.gov/choh/index.htm.

Citation at a glance

Letter in a published collection `Chicago`

To cite a letter in a published collection in *Chicago* style, include the following elements:

1. Author of letter
2. Recipient of letter
3. Date of letter
4. Title of collection
5. Editor of collection
6. City of publication
7. Publisher
8. Year of publication
9. Page number(s) cited (for notes); page range of letter (for bibliography)

TITLE PAGE

[TO HIS EXCELLENCY
THOMAS JEFFERSON

······ *Letters to a President* ······

JACK
McLAUGHLIN

AVON BOOKS ◆ NEW YORK]

AVON BOOKS ◆ NEW YORK

FROM COPYRIGHT PAGE

Copyright © 1991 by Jack McLaughlin
Cover painting by Giraudon/Art Resource, New York
Published by arrangement with W.W. Norton & Company, Inc.
Library of Congress Catalog Card Number: 90-27824
ISBN: 0-380-71964-9

NOTE

1. John O'Neill to Thomas Jefferson, October 30, 1805, in *To His Excellency Thomas Jefferson: Letters to a President*, ed. Jack McLaughlin (New York: Avon Books, 1991), 61.

BIBLIOGRAPHY

O'Neill, John. John O'Neill to Thomas Jefferson, 30 October 1805. In *To His Excellency Thomas Jefferson: Letters to a President*, edited by Jack McLaughlin, 59-61. New York: Avon Books, 1991.

For another citation of a letter in *Chicago* style, see item 31.

■ **33. Short work from a Web site**

▶ Citation at a glance: Primary source from a Web site, **page 260**

33. Dan Archer, "Using Illustrated Reportage to Cover Human Trafficking in Nepal's Brick Kilns," Poynter, last modified December 18, 2012, http://www.poynter.org/.

Archer, Dan. "Using Illustrated Reportage to Cover Human Trafficking in Nepal's Brick Kilns." Poynter, last modified December 18, 2012. http://www.poynter.org/.

■ **34. Blog post**   Italicize the name of the blog. Insert "blog" in parentheses after the name if the word *blog* is not part of the name. If the blog is part of a larger site, add the title of the site after the blog title (see item 35). Do not list the blog post in the bibliography; but if you cite the blog frequently in your paper, you may give a bibliography entry for the entire blog.

34. Gregory LeFever, "Skull Fraud 'Created' the Brontosaurus," *Ancient Tides* (blog), December 16, 2012, http://ancient-tides .blogspot.com/2012/12/skull-fraud-created-brontosaurus.html.

LeFever, Gregory. *Ancient Tides* (blog). http://ancient-tides .blogspot.com/.

■ **35. Comment on a blog post**   In the bibliography entry here, the blog is given by title only because the blog has many contributors, not a single author.

35. Didomyk, comment on B.C., "A New Spokesman," *Pomegranate: The Middle East* (blog), *Economist*, December 18, 2012, http://www.economist .com/blogs/pomegranate/2012/12 /christians-middle-east.

Pomegranate: The Middle East (blog). *Economist*. http://www .economist.com/blogs/pomegranate/.

Audio, visual, and multimedia sources

■ **36. Podcast**

36. Peter Limb, "Economic and Cultural History of the Slave Trade in Western Africa," Episode 69, Africa Past and Present, African Online Digital Library, podcast audio, December 12, 2012, http://afripod.aodl .org/.

Limb, Peter. "Economic and Cultural History of the Slave Trade in Western Africa." Episode 69. Africa Past and Present. African Online Digital Library. Podcast audio. December 12, 2012. http://afripod.aodl.org/.

■ **37. Online audio or video** If the source is a download-able file, identify the file format or medium before the URL.

37. Tom Brokaw, "Global Warming: What You Need to Know," Discovery Channel, January 23, 2012, http://www.youtube.com /watch?v=xcVwLrAavyA.

Brokaw, Tom. "Global Warming: What You Need to Know." Discovery Channel, January 23, 2012. http://www.youtube.com /watch?v=xcVwLrAavyA.

■ **38. Published or broadcast interview**

38. Jane Goodall, interview by Suza Scalora, *Origin*, n.d., http://www .originmagazine.com/2012/12/07/dr-jane-goodall-interview-with -suza-scalora.

Goodall, Jane. Interview by Suza Scalora. *Origin*, n.d. http://www .originmagazine.com/2012/12/07/dr-jane-goodall-interview -with-suza-scalora.

38. Julian Castro and Joaquin Castro, interview by Charlie Rose, *Charlie Rose Show*, WGBH, Boston, December 17, 2012.

Castro, Julian, and Joaquin Castro. Interview by Charlie Rose. *Charlie Rose Show*. WGBH, Boston, December 17, 2012.

■ **39. Film (DVD, BD, or other format)**

39. *Argo*, directed by Ben Affleck (Burbank, CA: Warner Bros. Pictures, 2012).

Argo. Directed by Ben Affleck. Burbank, CA: Warner Bros. Pictures, 2012.

39. *The Dust Bowl*, directed by Ken Burns (Washington, DC: PBS, 2012), DVD.

The Dust Bowl. Directed by Ken Burns. Washington, DC: PBS, 2012. DVD.

■ **40. Sound recording**

40. Gustav Holst, *The Planets*, Royal Philharmonic Orchestra, conducted by André Previn, Telarc 80133, compact disc.

Holst, Gustav. *The Planets*. Royal Philharmonic Orchestra. Conducted by André Previn. Telarc 80133, compact disc.

■ **41. Musical score or composition**

41. Antonio Vivaldi, *L'Estro armonico*, op. 3, ed. Eleanor Selfridge-Field (Mineola, NY: Dover, 1999).

Vivaldi, Antonio. *L'Estro armonico*, op. 3. Edited by Eleanor Selfridge-Field. Mineola, NY: Dover, 1999.

Citation at a glance

Primary source from a Web site `Chicago`

To cite a primary source (or any other document) from a Web site in *Chicago* style, include as many of the following elements as are available:

1 Author(s)
2 Title of document
3 Title of site
4 Sponsor of site

5 Publication date or modified date; date of access (if no publication date)
6 URL of document page

WEB SITE HOME PAGE

FIRST PAGE OF DOCUMENT

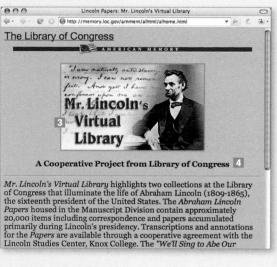

Mr. Lincoln's Virtual Library, The Library of Congress.

For more on citing documents from Web sites in *Chicago* style, see item 33.

▓ 42. Work of art

42. Aaron Siskind, *Untitled (The Most Crowded Block)*, gelatin silver print, 1939, Kemper Museum of Contemporary Art, Kansas City, MO.

Siskind, Aaron. *Untitled (The Most Crowded Block)*. Gelatin silver print, 1939. Kemper Museum of Contemporary Art, Kansas City, MO.

▓ 43. Performance

43. Jackie Sibblies Drury, *Social Creatures*, directed by Curt Columbus, Trinity Repertory Company, Providence, RI, March 15, 2013.

Drury, Jackie Sibblies. *Social Creatures*. Directed by Curt Columbus. Trinity Repertory Company, Providence, RI, March 15, 2013.

Personal communication and social media

▓ 44. Personal communication
Personal communications are not included in the bibliography.

44. Sara Lehman, e-mail message to author, August 13, 2012.

▓ 45. Online posting or e-mail
If an online posting has been archived, include a URL. E-mails that are not part of an online discussion are treated as personal

communication (see item 44). Online postings and e-mails are not included in the bibliography.

> 45. Ruth E. Thaler-Carter to Copyediting-L discussion list, December 18, 2012, https://list.indiana.edu/sympa/arc/copyediting-l.

■ **46. Facebook post**   Facebook posts are not included in the bibliography.

> 46. US Department of Housing and Urban Development's Facebook page, accessed October 15, 2012, http://www.facebook.com/HUD.

■ **47. Twitter post (tweet)**   Tweets are not included in the bibliography.

> 47. National Geographic's Twitter feed, accessed December 18, 2012, https://twitter.com/NatGeo.

44   *Chicago* manuscript format; sample pages

44a *Chicago* manuscript format

The following guidelines for formatting a *Chicago*-style paper and preparing its endnotes and bibliography are based on *The Chicago Manual of Style*, 16th ed. (Chicago: University of Chicago Press, 2010). For pages from a sample paper, see 44b.

Formatting the paper

Font   If your instructor does not require a specific font, choose one that is standard and easy to read (such as Times New Roman).

Title page   Include the full title of your paper, your name, the course title, the instructor's name, and the date. See page 266 for a sample title page.

Pagination   Using arabic numerals, number the pages in the upper right corner. Do not number the title page but count it in the manuscript numbering; that is, the first page of the text will be numbered 2. Depending on your instructor's preference, you may also use a short title or your last name before the page numbers to help identify pages.

Margins, line spacing, and paragraph indents Leave margins of at least one inch at the top, bottom, and sides of the page. Double-space the body of the paper, including long quotations that have been set off from the text. (For line spacing in notes and the bibliography, see p. 265.) Left-align the text.

Indent the first line of each paragraph one-half inch from the left margin.

Capitalization, italics, and quotation marks In titles of works, capitalize all words except articles (*a*, *an*, *the*), prepositions (*at*, *from*, *between*, and *so on*), coordinating conjunctions (*and*, *but*, *or*, *nor*, *for*, *so*, *yet*), and *to* and *as*—unless the word is first or last in the title or subtitle. Follow these guidelines in your paper even if the title is styled differently in the source.

In your text, lowercase the first word following a colon even if the word begins a complete sentence. When the colon introduces a series of sentences or questions, capitalize the first word in all sentences in the series, including the first.

Italicize the titles of books and other long works. Use quotation marks around the titles of periodical articles, short stories, poems, and other short works.

Long quotations You can choose to set off a long quotation of five to ten typed lines by indenting the entire quotation one-half inch from the left margin. (Always set off quotations of ten or more lines.) Double-space the quotation; do not use quotation marks and do not add extra space above or below it. (See also p. 237.)

Visuals *Chicago* classifies visuals as tables and figures (graphs, drawings, photographs, maps, and charts). Keep visuals as simple as possible.

Label each table with an arabic numeral (Table 1, Table 2, and so on) and provide a clear title that identifies the table's subject. The label and the title should appear on separate lines above the table, flush left. For a table that you have borrowed or adapted, give its source in a note like this one, below the table:

> *Source:* Edna Bonacich and Richard P. Appelbaum, *Behind the Label* (Berkeley: University of California Press, 2000), 145.

For each figure, place a label and a caption below the figure, flush left. The label and caption need not appear on separate lines. The word "Figure" may be abbreviated to "Fig."

In the text of your paper, discuss the most significant features of each visual. Place visuals as close as possible to the sentences that relate to them unless your instructor prefers that visuals appear in an appendix.

URLs and DOIs When a URL or DOI (digital object identifier) must break across lines, do not insert a hyphen or break at a hyphen. Instead, break after a colon or a double slash or before any other mark of punctuation. If your word processing program automatically turns URLs into links (by underlining them and changing the color), turn off this feature.

Headings *Chicago* does not provide guidelines for the use of headings in student papers. If you would like to insert headings in a long essay or research paper, check first with your instructor. See page 267 for typical placement and formatting of headings in a *Chicago*-style paper.

Preparing the endnotes Begin the endnotes on a new page at the end of the paper. Center the title "Notes" about one inch from the top of the page, and number the pages consecutively with the rest of the paper. See page 268 for an example.

Indenting and numbering Indent the first line of each note one-half inch from the left margin; do not indent additional lines in the note. Begin the note with the arabic numeral that corresponds to the number in the text. Put a period after the number.

Line spacing Single-space each note and double-space between notes (unless your instructor prefers double-spacing throughout).

Preparing the bibliography Typically, the notes in *Chicago*-style papers are followed by a bibliography, an alphabetically arranged list of all the works cited or consulted. Center the title "Bibliography" about one inch from the top of the page. Number bibliography pages consecutively with the rest of the paper. See page 269 for a sample bibliography.

Alphabetizing the list Alphabetize the bibliography by the last names of the authors (or editors); when a work has no author or editor, alphabetize it by the first word of the title other than *A*, *An*, or *The*.

If your list includes two or more works by the same author, arrange the entries alphabetically by title. Then use six hyphens instead of the author's name in all entries after the first. (See item 6 on p. 244.)

Indenting and line spacing   Begin each entry at the left margin, and indent any additional lines one-half inch. Single-space each entry and double-space between entries (unless your instructor prefers double-spacing throughout).

44b Sample pages from a *Chicago* research paper

Following are pages from a research paper by Ned Bishop, a student in a history class. Bishop used *Chicago*-style endnotes, bibliography, and manuscript format.

hackerhandbooks.com/pocket

e *Chicago* papers > Sample student writing
   > Bishop, "The Massacre at Fort Pillow: Holding Nathan
      Bedford Forrest Accountable" (research)

The Massacre at Fort Pillow:

Holding Nathan Bedford Forrest Accountable

Ned Bishop

History 214

Professor Citro

March 22, 2012

1 Paper title, centered. **2** Writer's name. **3** Course title, instructor's name, date.

(Annotations indicate *Chicago*-style formatting and effective writing.)

Bishop 2

Although Northern newspapers of the time no doubt exaggerated some of the Confederate atrocities at Fort Pillow, most modern sources agree that a massacre of Union troops took place there on April 12, 1864. It seems clear that Union soldiers, particularly black soldiers, were killed after they had stopped fighting or had surrendered or were being held prisoner. Less clear is the role played by Major General Nathan Bedford Forrest in leading his troops. Although we will   **1** never know whether Forrest directly ordered the massacre, evidence suggests that he was responsible for it.

What happened at Fort Pillow?   **2**

Fort Pillow, Tennessee, which sat on a bluff overlooking the Mississippi River, had been held by the Union for two years. It was garrisoned by 580 men, 292 of them from United States Colored Heavy and Light Artillery regiments, 285 from the white Thirteenth Tennessee Cavalry. Nathan Bedford Forrest commanded about 1,500 troops.[1]

The Confederates attacked Fort Pillow on April 12, 1864, and had virtually surrounded the fort by the time Forrest arrived on the battlefield. At 3:30 p.m., Forrest demanded the surrender of the Union forces: "The conduct of the officers and men garrisoning Fort Pillow has been such as to entitle them to being treated as prisoners of war. . . . Should my demand be refused, I cannot be responsible for the fate of your command."[2] Union Major William Bradford, who had replaced   **3** Major Booth, killed earlier by sharpshooters, asked for an hour to consider the demand. Forrest, worried that vessels in the river were bringing in more Union troops, "shortened the time to twenty minutes."[3] Bradford refused to surrender, and Forrest quickly ordered the attack.

The Confederates charged to the fort, scaled the parapet, and fired on

1 Writer's thesis. **2** Headings (centered) guide readers.
3 Quotation cited with endnote.

Sample *Chicago* endnotes

Notes

1   1. John Cimprich and Robert C. Mainfort Jr., eds., "Fort Pillow Revisited: New Evidence about an Old Controversy," *Civil War History* 28, no. 4 (1982): 293-94.

2   2. Quoted in Brian Steel Wills, *A Battle from the Start: The Life of Nathan Bedford Forrest* (New York: HarperCollins, 1992), 182.

    3. Ibid., 183.

    4. Shelby Foote, *The Civil War, a Narrative: Red River to Appomattox* (New York: Vintage, 1986), 110.

    5. Nathan Bedford Forrest, "Report of Maj. Gen. Nathan B. Forrest, C. S. Army, Commanding Cavalry, of the Capture of Fort Pillow," Shotgun's Home of the American Civil War, accessed March 6, 2012, http://www.civilwarhome.com/forrest.htm.

3   6. Jack Hurst, *Nathan Bedford Forrest: A Biography* (New York: Knopf, 1993), 174.

    7. Foote, *Civil War*, 111.

4   8. Cimprich and Mainfort, "Fort Pillow," 295.

    9. Ibid., 305.

    10. Ibid., 299.

    11. Foote, *Civil War*, 110.

    12. Quoted in Wills, *Battle from the Start*, 187.

5   13. Albert Castel, "The Fort Pillow Massacre: A Fresh Examination of the Evidence," *Civil War History* 4, no. 1 (1958): 44-45.

    14. Cimprich and Mainfort, "Fort Pillow," 300.

---

1 First line of note indented ½". **2** Note number not raised, followed by period. **3** Authors' names not inverted. **4** Last names and shortened title refer to earlier note by same authors. **5** Single-space notes; double-space between them.

Sample *Chicago* bibliography

Bibliography

Castel, Albert. "The Fort Pillow Massacre: A Fresh Examination of the   **1**
    Evidence." *Civil War History* 4, no. 1 (1958): 37-50.

Cimprich, John, and Robert C. Mainfort Jr., eds. "Fort Pillow Revisited:
    New Evidence about an Old Controversy." *Civil War History* 28,
    no. 4 (1982): 293-306.

Cornish, Dudley Taylor. *The Sable Arm: Black Troops in the Union Army,*   **2**
    1861-1865. Lawrence: University Press of Kansas, 1987.

Foote, Shelby. *The Civil War, a Narrative: Red River to Appomattox*. New
    York: Vintage, 1986.

Forrest, Nathan Bedford. "Report of Maj. Gen. Nathan B. Forrest,
    C. S. Army, Commanding Cavalry, of the Capture of Fort Pillow."
    Shotgun's Home of the American Civil War. Accessed March 6,
    2012. http://www.civilwarhome.com/forrest.htm.

Hurst, Jack. *Nathan Bedford Forrest: A Biography*. New York: Knopf,   **3**
    1993.

McPherson, James M. *Battle Cry of Freedom: The Civil War Era*. New
    York: Oxford University Press, 1988.

Wills, Brian Steel. *A Battle from the Start: The Life of Nathan Bedford
    Forrest*. New York: HarperCollins, 1992.

1 Alphabetize by authors' last names. **2** First line of each entry
at left margin; additional lines indented ½". **3** Single-space
entries; double-space between them.

CSE Papers

45 CSE documentation style 271

Directory to CSE in-text citation models 271

Directory to CSE reference list models 274

46 CSE manuscript format 284

45   CSE documentation style

In many science classes, you may be asked to use one of three systems of documentation recommended by the Council of Science Editors (CSE) in *Scientific Style and Format: The CSE Manual for Authors, Editors, and Publishers*, 8th ed. (Chicago: Council of Science Editors, 2014).

45a   CSE documentation systems

The three CSE documentation systems specify the ways that sources are cited in the text of the paper and in the reference list at the end of the paper.

In the citation-sequence system, each source is given a superscript number the first time it appears in the paper. Any subsequent references to that source are marked with the same number. At the end of the paper, a list of references provides full publication information for each numbered source. Entries in the reference list are numbered in the order in which they are mentioned in the paper.

In the citation-name system, the list of references is created first, with entries alphabetized by authors' last names. The entries are numbered according to their alphabetical order, and the numbers are used in the text to cite the sources from the list.

In the name-year system, the author of the source is named in the text or in parentheses, and the date is given in parentheses. The reference list at the end of the paper is arranged alphabetically by authors' last names.

Sections 45b and 45c describe formatting of in-text citations and the reference list, respectively, in all three systems.

Directory to CSE in-text citation models

1. Basic format   272
2. Author named in the text   272
3. Specific part of source   272
4. Work by two authors   272
5. Work by three or more authors   273
6. Multiple works by one author   273
7. Organization as author   274

45b CSE in-text citations

In-text citations in all three CSE systems refer readers to the reference list at the end of the paper. The reference list is organized differently in the three systems (see 45c).

■ 1. Basic format

Citation-sequence or citation-name

Scientists are beginning to question the validity of linking genes to a number of human traits and disorders.[1]

Name-year

Scientists are beginning to question the validity of linking genes to a number of human traits and disorders (Allen 2009).

■ 2. Author named in the text

Citation-sequence or citation-name

Smith,[2] studying three species of tree frogs, identified variations in coloring over a small geographic area.

Name-year

Smith (2010), studying three species of tree frogs, identified variations in coloring over a small geographic area.

■ 3. Specific part of source

Citation-sequence or citation-name

Our data differed markedly from Markam's study[3(Figs. 2,7)] on the same species in North Dakota.

Researchers observed an immune response in "19 of 20 people who ate a potato vaccine aimed at the Norwalk virus," according to Langridge.[4(p. 68)]

Name-year

Our data differed markedly from Markam's study (2010, Figs. 2, 7) on the same species in North Dakota.

Researchers observed an immune response in "19 of 20 people who ate a potato vaccine aimed at the Norwalk virus," according to Langridge (2009, p. 68).

■ 4. Work by two authors
See item 2 on page 275 for a work with multiple authors in the reference list.

Citation-sequence or citation-name

Follow item 1, 2, or 3 on page 272, depending on how you use the source in your paper. Use "and" between the two authors' names in parentheses or in the text.

Name-year

Use "and" between the two authors' names in parentheses or in the text.

Self-organization plays a complex role in the evolution of biological systems (Johnson and Lam 2010).

Johnson and Lam (2010) explored the complex role of self-organization in evolution.

■ **5. Work by three or more authors** See item 2 on page 275 for a work with multiple authors in the reference list.

Citation-sequence or citation-name

Follow item 1, 2, or 3 on page 272, depending on how you use the source in your paper.

Name-year

Give the first author's name followed by "et al." in parentheses or in the text.

Orchid seed banking is a promising method of conservation to preserve species in situ (Seaton et al. 2010).

Seaton et al. (2010) provided a range of in situ techniques for orchid seed banking as a method of conservation of species.

■ **6. Multiple works by one author**

Citation-sequence or citation-name

Gawande's work[4,5,6] deals not just with the practice of modern medicine but more broadly with the way we rely on human expertise in every aspect of society.

Name-year: works in different years

Gawande's work (2003, 2007, 2009) deals not just with the practice of modern medicine but more broadly with the way we rely on human expertise in every aspect of society.

Name-year: works in the same year

The works are arranged in the reference list in chronological order, the earliest first. The letters "a," "b," and so on are added after the year, in both the reference list and the in-text citation. (See also the name-year model on p. 277.)

Scientists have investigated the role of follicle stimulating hormone (FSH) in the growth of cancer cells beyond the ovaries and testes (Seppa 2010a).

■ 7. Organization as author

Citation-sequence or citation-name

Follow item 1, 2, or 3 on page 272, depending on how you use the source in your paper.

Directory to CSE reference list models

BASIC GUIDELINES

1.	Single author	275
2.	Two or more authors	275
3.	Organization as author	276
4.	Two or more works by the same author	276
5.	Two or more works by the same author in the same year	276

ARTICLES AND OTHER SHORT WORKS

6.	Article in a print journal	277
7.	Article in a print magazine	277
8.	Article in a print newspaper	278
9.	Selection or chapter in an edited book	278

BOOKS AND OTHER LONG WORKS

10.	Print book	278
11.	Book with an editor	278
12.	Edition other than the first	279
13.	Report from an organization or a government agency	279
14.	Conference proceedings	279

ONLINE SOURCES

15.	Entire Web site	280
16.	Short work from a Web site	280
17.	Online book	280
18.	Article in an online journal or magazine	281
19.	Article from a database	281
20.	Blog post	282
21.	Social media	282
22.	E-mail or other personal communication	282

AUDIO, VISUAL, AND MULTIMEDIA SOURCES

23.	CD, DVD, or Blu-ray Disc	282
24.	Online video	283
25.	Podcast	283

Name-year

Developing standards for handling and processing biospecimens is essential to ensure the validity of cancer research and, ultimately, treatment (OBBR 2010).

The reference list entry gives the abbreviation for the organization's name, followed by the full name of the organization (Office of Biorepositories and Biospecimen Research); only the abbreviation is used in the in-text citation. (See item 3 on p. 276.)

45c CSE reference list

In the citation-sequence system, entries in the reference list are numbered in the order in which they appear in the text of the paper. In the citation-name system, entries in the reference list are put into alphabetical order and then numbered in that order. In the name-year system, entries are listed alphabetically in the reference list; they are not numbered. See 45b for examples of in-text citations using all three systems. See 46b for details about formatting the reference list.

Basic guidelines

■ 1. Single author

Citation-sequence or citation-name

1. Bliss M. The making of modern medicine: turning points in the treatment of disease. Chicago (IL): University of Chicago Press; 2011.

Name-year

Bliss M. 2011. The making of modern medicine: turning points in the treatment of disease. Chicago (IL): University of Chicago Press.

■ 2. Two or more authors
For a source with two to ten authors, list all authors' names; for a source with more than ten authors, list the first ten authors followed by a comma and "et al." (for "and others").

Citation-sequence or citation-name

2. Seaton PT, Hong H, Perner H, Pritchard HW. Ex situ conservation of orchids in a warming world. Bot Rev. 2010;76(2):193-203.

Name-year

Seaton PT, Hong H, Perner H, Pritchard HW. 2010. Ex situ conservation of orchids in a warming world. Bot Rev. 76(2):193-203.

■ 3. Organization as author

Citation-sequence or citation-name

3. American Cancer Society. Cancer facts and figures for African
    Americans 2005-2006. Atlanta (GA): The Society; 2005.

Name-year

Give the abbreviation of the organization name in brackets at the beginning of the entry; alphabetize the entry by
the first word of the full name. (For an in-text citation, see
the name-year model in item 7 on p. 277.)

[ACS] American Cancer Society. 2005. Cancer facts and figures for
    African Americans 2005-2006. Atlanta (GA): The Society.

■ 4. Two or more works by the same author

Citation-sequence or citation-name

In the citation-sequence system, list the works in the order
in which they appear in the paper. In the citation-name
system, order the works alphabetically by title. (The following examples are presented in the citation-name system.)

4. Gawande A. Better: a surgeon's notes on performance. New York
    (NY): Metropolitan; 2007.

5. Gawande A. The checklist manifesto: how to get things right.
    New York (NY): Metropolitan; 2009.

6. Gawande A. Complications: a surgeon's notes on an imperfect
    science. New York (NY): Picador; 2003.

Name-year

List the works chronologically, the earliest first.

Gawande A. 2003. Complications: a surgeon's notes on an imperfect
    science. New York (NY): Picador.

Gawande A. 2007. Better: a surgeon's notes on performance. New
    York (NY): Metropolitan.

Gawande A. 2009. The checklist manifesto: how to get things right.
    New York (NY): Metropolitan.

■ 5. Two or more works by the same author in the same year

Citation-sequence or citation-name

In the citation-sequence system, list the works in the order
in which they appear in the paper. In the citation-name

system, order the works alphabetically by title. (The following examples are presented in the citation-sequence system.)

5. Seppa N. Protein implicated in many cancers. Sci News. 2010 Oct 20 [accessed 2011 Jan 22]. http://www.sciencenews.org/view/generic/id/64426.

8. Seppa N. Anticancer protein might combat HIV. Sci News. 2010 Nov 20:9.

Name-year

List the works in chronological order, the earliest first, and add the letters "a," "b," and so on after the year. If the works have only a year but not exact dates, arrange the entries alphabetically by title.

Seppa N. 2010a Jul 31. Fish oil may fend off breast cancer: other supplements studied show no signs of protection. Sci News. 13.

Seppa N. 2010b. Sep 25. Ovary removal boosts survival: procedure shown to benefit women with BRCA mutations. Sci News. 12.

Articles and other short works

Use the basic format for an article in print publications when citing articles or other short works in most other media. See also "Online sources" on page 280.

■ 6. Article in a print journal

Citation-sequence or citation-name

6. Wasserman EA, Blumberg MS. Designing minds: how should we explain the origins of novel behaviors. Am Sci. 2010;98(3):183-185.

Name-year

Wasserman EA, Blumberg MS. 2010. Designing minds: how should we explain the origins of novel behaviors. Am Sci. 98(3):183-185.

■ 7. Article in a print magazine

Citation-sequence or citation-name

7. Quammen D. Great migrations. Natl Geogr. 2010 Nov:31-51.

Name-year

Quammen D. 2010 Nov. Great migrations. Natl Geogr. 31-51.

■ 8. Article in a print newspaper

Citation-sequence or citation-name

8. Wald M. Scientists call for new sources of critical elements.
   New York Times (New York Ed.). 2011 Feb 19;B5 (col. 1).

Name-year

Wald M. 2011 Feb 19. Scientists call for new sources of critical
   elements. New York Times (New York Ed.). B5 (col. 1).

■ 9. Selection or chapter in an edited book

Citation-sequence or citation-name

9. Underwood AJ, Chapman MG. Intertidal ecosystems. In: Levin
   SA, editor. Encyclopedia of biodiversity. Vol. 3. San Diego (CA):
   Academic Press; 2000. p. 485-499.

Name-year

Underwood AJ, Chapman MG. 2000. Intertidal ecosystems. In: Levin
   SA, editor. Encyclopedia of biodiversity. Vol. 3. San Diego (CA):
   Academic Press; p. 485-499.

Books and other long works

Use the basic format for a print book when citing books
and other long works in most other media. See also
"Online sources" on page 280.

■ 10. Print book

Citation-sequence or citation-name

10. Tobin M. Endangered: biodiversity on the brink. Golden (CO):
    Fulcrum; 2010.

Name-year

Tobin M. 2010. Endangered: biodiversity on the brink. Golden (CO):
    Fulcrum.

■ 11. Book with an editor

Citation-sequence or citation-name

11. Kurimoto N, Fielding D, Musani A, editors. Endobronchial
    ultrasonography. New York (NY): Wiley-Blackwell; 2011.

Name-year

Kurimoto N, Fielding D, Musani A, editors. 2011. Endobronchial
    ultrasonography. New York (NY): Wiley-Blackwell.

◼ 12. Edition other than the first

Citation-sequence or citation-name

12. Mai J, Paxinos G, Assheuer J. Atlas of the human brain. 2nd ed.
    Burlington (MA): Elsevier; 2004.

Name-year

Mai J, Paxinos G, Assheuer J. 2004. Atlas of the human brain. 2nd ed.
    Burlington (MA): Elsevier.

◼ 13. Report from an organization or a government agency

Citation-sequence or citation-name

13. National Institute on Drug Abuse (US). Inhalant abuse.
    Bethesda (MD): National Institutes of Health (US); 2010
    Jul. NIH Pub. No.: 10-3818. Available from: National
    Clearinghouse on Alcohol and Drug Information, Rockville,
    MD 20852.

13. National Institute on Drug Abuse (US). Inhalant abuse.
    Bethesda (MD): National Institutes of Health (US); [accessed
    2011 Jan 23]. NIH Pub. No.: 10-3818. http://www.drugabuse
    .gov/ResearchReports/Inhalants/inhalants.html.

Name-year

[NIDA] National Institute on Drug Abuse (US). 2010 Jul. Inhalant
    abuse. Bethesda (MD): National Institutes of Health (US). NIH
    Pub. No.: 10-3818. Available from: National Clearinghouse on
    Alcohol and Drug Information, Rockville, MD 20852.

[NIDA] National Institute on Drug Abuse (US). 2010 Jul. Inhalant
    abuse. Bethesda (MD): National Institutes of Health (US);
    [accessed 2010 Jan 23]. NIH Pub. No.: 10-3818. http://www
    .drugabuse.gov/ResearchReports/Inhalants/inhalants.html.

◼ 14. Conference proceedings
Cite a paper or presentation from the conference proceedings as you would a selection in an edited book (see item 9).

Citation-sequence or citation-name

14. Proceedings of the 2004 National Beaches Conference; 2004
    Oct 13-15; San Diego, CA. Washington (DC): Environmental
    Protection Agency (US); 2005 Mar. Document No.:
    EPA-823-R-05-001.

■ 14. Conference proceedings (*cont.*)

Name-year

Proceedings of the 2004 National Beaches Conference. 2005 Mar.
  2004 Oct 13-15; San Diego, CA. Washington (DC): Environmental
  Protection Agency (US). Document No.: EPA-823-R-05-001.

Online sources

■ 15. Entire Web site

Citation-sequence or citation-name

15. American Society of Gene and Cell Therapy. Milwaukee (WI):
  The Society; c2000-2011 [accessed 2011 Jan 16]. http://www
  .asgt.org/.

Name-year

[ASGCT] American Society of Gene and Cell Therapy. c2000-2011.
  Milwaukee (WI): The Society; [accessed 2011 Jan 16]. Available
  from: http://www.asgt.org/.

■ 16. Short work from a Web site   Begin with the author
of the short work, if there is one, and include the date
of the short work in brackets as an "updated" or "modified" date. Include the title of the Web site and publishing
information for the Web site.

Citation-sequence or citation-name

16. Butler R. The year in review for rain forests. Mongabay.com.
  Menlo Park (CA): Mongabay; c2011 [updated 2011 Dec 28;
  accessed 2012 Jan 11]. http://news.mongabay.com/2011/
  1228-year_in_rainforests_2011.html.

Name-year

Butler R. c2011. The year in review for rain forests. Mongabay.com.
  Menlo Park (CA): Mongabay. [updated 2011 Dec 28; accessed
  2012 Jan 11]. http://news.mongabay.com/2011/1228-year_in
  _rainforests_2011.html.

■ 17. Online book

Citation-sequence or citation-name

17. Wilson DE, Reeder DM, editors. Mammal species of the world.
  Washington (DC): Smithsonian Institution; 2011 [accessed
  2012 Oct 14]. http://vertebrates.si.edu/msw/mswcfapp/msw/
  index.cfm.

Name-year

Wilson DE, Reeder DM, editors. c2011. Mammal species of the world. Washington (DC): Smithsonian Institution; [accessed 2012 Oct 14]. http://vertebrates.si.edu/msw/mswcfapp/msw/index/cfm.

■ **18. Article in an online journal or magazine**   Give whatever publication information is available as for a print source. End with the URL and DOI (if any).

Citation-sequence or citation-name

18. Leslie M. The power of one. Science. 2011 [accessed 2011 Feb 3];331(6013):24-26. http://www.sciencemag.org/content/331/6013/24.1.summary. doi:10.1126/science.331.6013.24-a.

18. Matson J. Twisted light could enable black hole detection. Sci Am. 2011 Feb 14 [accessed 2011 Feb 28]. http://www.scientificamerican.com/article.cfm?id=twisting-light-oam.

Name-year

Leslie M. 2011. The power of one. Science. [accessed 2011 Feb 3];331(6013):24-26. http://www.sciencemag.org/content/331/6013/24.1.summary. doi:10.1126/science.331.6013.24-a.

Matson J. 2011 Feb 14. Twisted light could enable black hole detection. Sci Am. [accessed 2011 Feb 28]. http://www.scientificamerican.com/article.cfm?id=twisting-light-oam.

■ **19. Article from a database**

Citation-sequence or citation-name

19. Logan CA. A review of ocean acidification and America's response. BioScience. 2010 [accessed 2011 Jun 17];60(10):819-828. General OneFile. http://find.galegroup.com.ezproxy.bpl.org/. Document No.: A241952492.

Name-year

Logan CA. 2010. A review of ocean acidification and America's response. BioScience. [accessed 2011 Jun 17];60(10): 819-828. General OneFile. http://find.galegroup.com.ezproxy.bpl.org/. Document No.: A241952492.

■ 20. Blog post

Citation-sequence or citation-name

20. Salopek P. The river door [blog post]. Out of Eden
    walk: dispatches from the field from Paul Salopek. 2014
    Apr 17 [accessed 2014 May 19]. http://outofedenwalk
    .nationalgeographic.com/.

Name-year

Salopek P. 2014 Apr 17. The river door [blog post]. Out of Eden
    walk: dispatches from the field from Paul Salopek. [accessed
    2014 May 19]. http://outofedenwalk.nationalgeographic.com/.

■ 21. Social media

Citation-sequence or citation-name

21. National Science Foundation. Facebook [organization page].
    2013 Jan 21, 10:31 a.m. [accessed 2013 Jan 22]. https://
    www.facebook.com/US.NSF.

Name-year

National Science Foundation. 2013 Jan 21, 10:31 a.m. Facebook
    [organization page]. [accessed 2013 Jan 22]. https://
    www.facebook.com/US.NSF.

■ 22. E-mail or other personal communication   CSE rec-
ommends not including personal communications such
as e-mail and personal letters in the reference list. A parenthetical note in the text usually suffices: (2010 e-mail to
me; unreferenced).

Audio, visual, and multimedia sources

■ 23. CD, DVD, or Blu-ray Disc

Citation-sequence or citation-name

23. NOVA: secrets beneath the ice [DVD]. Seifferlein B, editor;
    Hochman G, producer. Boston (MA): WGBH Educational
    Foundation; 2010. 1 DVD: 52 min.

Name-year

NOVA: secrets beneath the ice [DVD]. 2010. Seifferlein B,
    editor; Hochman G, producer. Boston (MA): WGBH Educational
    Foundation. 1 DVD: 52 min.

■ 24. Online video

Citation-sequence or citation-name

24. Life: creatures of the deep: nemertean worms and sea
    stars [video]. Gunton M, executive producer; Holmes
    M, series producer. 2010 Mar 21, 2:55 min. [accessed
    2011 Feb 4]. http://dsc.discovery.com/videos/
    life-the-series-videos/?bcid=73073289001.

Name-year

Life: creatures of the deep: nemertean worms and sea stars [video].
    2010 Mar 21, 2:55 min. Gunton M, executive producer; Holmes
    M, series producer. [accessed 2011 Feb 4]. http://dsc.discovery
    .com/videos/life-the-series-videos/?bcid=73073289001.

■ 25. Podcast

Citation-sequence or citation-name

25. Mirsky S, host; Conrad N, interviewee. The spirit of
    innovation: from high school to the moon [podcast].
    Sci Am. 2011 Feb 17, 19:26 min. [accessed 2011 Feb 27].
    http://www.scientificamerican.com/podcast/episode
    .cfm?id=from-high-school-innovation-to-the-11-02-17.

Name-year

Mirsky, S, host; Conrad N, interviewee. 2011 Feb 17, 19:26 min.
    The spirit of innovation: from high school to the moon [podcast].
    Sci Am. [accessed 2011 Feb 27]. http://www.scientificamerican
    .com/podcast/episode.cfm?id=from-high-school-innovation
    -to-the-11-02-17.

46 CSE manuscript format

The guidelines in this section are adapted from advice given in *Scientific Style and Format: The CSE Manual for Authors, Editors, and Publishers*, 8th ed. (Chicago: Council of Science Editors, 2014). When in doubt about the formatting required in your course, check with your instructor.

46a Formatting the paper

Font   If your instructor does not require a specific font, choose one that is standard and easy to read (such as Times New Roman).

Title page   Center all information on the title page: the title of your paper, your name, the course name, and the date.

Pagination   The title page is counted as page 1, although a number does not appear. Number the first page of the text of the paper as page 2. Type a shortened form of the title followed by the page number in the top right corner of each page.

Margins, spacing, and indentation   Leave margins of at least one inch on all sides of the page. Double-space throughout the paper. Indent the first line of each paragraph one-half inch. When a quotation is set off from the text, indent the entire quotation one-half inch from the left margin.

Abstract   An abstract is a single paragraph at the beginning of the paper that summarizes the paper and might include your research methods, findings, and conclusions. Do not include citations in the abstract.

Headings   CSE encourages the use of headings to help readers follow the organization of a paper. Common headings for papers reporting research are Introduction, Methods, Results, and Discussion.

hackerhandbooks.com/pocket

e CSE papers > Sample student writing
> Martin, "Hypothermia, the Diving Reflex, and Survival" (literature review)
> Johnson/Arnold, "Distribution Pattern of Dandelion (*Taraxacum officinale*) on an Abandoned Golf Course" (lab report)

Visuals A visual, such as a table, figure, or chart, should be placed as close as possible to the text that discusses it. In general, try to place visuals at the top of a page.

Appendixes Appendixes may be used for relevant information that is too long to include in the body of the paper. Label each appendix and give it a title (for example, Appendix 1: Methodologies of Previous Researchers).

Acknowledgments An acknowledgments section is common in scientific writing because research is often conducted with help from others. Place the acknowledgments at the end of the paper before the reference list.

46b Formatting the reference list

Basic format Begin on a new page. Center the title "References" and then list the works you have cited in the paper. Double-space throughout.

Organization of the list In the citation-sequence system, number the entries in the order in which they appear in the text.

In the citation-name system, first alphabetize all the entries by authors' last names (or by organization name or by title for works with no author, ignoring any initial *A*, *An*, or *The*); for two or more works by the same author, arrange the entries alphabetically by title.

In both systems, number the entries in the order in which they appear in the list. Make the first line flush with the left margin, and indent subsequent lines one-quarter inch. In both systems, use the number from the reference list whenever you refer to the source in the text of the paper.

In the name-year system, alphabetize the entries by authors' last names (or by organization name or by title for works with no author, ignoring any initial *A*, *An*, or *The*). Place the year after the last author's name, followed by a period. For two or more works by the same author, arrange the entries by year, the earliest first. For two or more works by the same author in the same year, see item 5 on page 276. Type the first line of each entry flush left, and indent any additional lines one-quarter inch.

Authors' names Give the last name first; use initials for first and middle names, with no periods after the initials and no space between them. Do not use a comma between the last name and the initials. For a work with up to ten authors, use all authors' names; for a work with eleven or more authors, list the first ten names followed by a comma and "et al." (for "and others").

Titles of books and articles   Capitalize only the first word and all proper nouns in the title and subtitle of a book or an article. Do not underline or italicize titles of books; do not place titles of articles in quotation marks.

Titles of journals   Abbreviate titles of journals that consist of more than one word. Omit the words *the* and *of* and apostrophes. Capitalize all the words or abbreviated words in the title; do not underline or italicize the title: Science, Sci Am, N Engl J Med, Womens Health.

Page ranges   Do not abbreviate page ranges for articles in journals or periodicals or for chapters in edited works. When an article appears on discontinuous pages, list all pages or page ranges, separated by commas: 145-149, 162-174. For chapters in edited volumes, use the abbreviation "p." before the numbers (p. 63-90).

Breaking a URL or DOI   When a URL or a DOI (digital object identifier) must be divided, break it before or after a double slash, a slash, or any other mark of punctuation. Do not insert a hyphen.

Appendixes

Glossary of usage 288

Glossary of grammatical terms 298

Checklist for global revision 306

Checklist for visiting the writing center 307

Glossary of usage

This glossary includes words commonly confused, words commonly misused, and words that are nonstandard. It also lists colloquialisms that may be appropriate in informal speech but are inappropriate in formal writing.

a, an   Use *an* before a vowel sound, *a* before a consonant sound: *an apple, a peach.* Problems sometimes arise with words beginning with *h* or *u.* If the *h* is silent, the word begins with a vowel sound, so use *an: an hour, an heir, an honest senator.* If the *h* is pronounced, the word begins with a consonant sound, so use *a: a hospital, a historian, a hotel.* Words such as *university* and *union* begin with a consonant sound, so use *a: a union.* Words such as *uncle* and *umbrella* begin with a vowel sound, so use *an: an underground well.* When an abbreviation or acronym begins with a vowel sound, use *an: an EKG, an MRI.*

accept, except   *Accept* is a verb meaning "to receive." *Except* is usually a preposition meaning "excluding." *I will accept all the packages except that one. Except* is also a verb meaning "to exclude." *Please except that item from the list.*

adapt, adopt   *Adapt* means "to adjust or become accustomed"; it is usually followed by *to. Adopt* means "to take as one's own." *Our family adopted a Vietnamese child, who quickly adapted to his new life.*

adverse, averse   *Adverse* means "unfavorable." *Averse* means "opposed" or "reluctant"; it is usually followed by *to. I am averse to your proposal because it could have an adverse impact on the economy.*

advice, advise   *Advice* is a noun, *advise* a verb. *We advise you to follow John's advice.*

affect, effect   *Affect* is usually a verb meaning "to influence." *Effect* is usually a noun meaning "result." *The drug did not affect the disease, and it had adverse side effects. Effect* can also be a verb meaning "to bring about." *Only the president can effect such a change.*

all ready, already   *All ready* means "completely prepared." *Already* means "previously." *Susan was all ready for the concert, but her friends had already left.*

all right   *All right,* written as two words, is correct. *Alright* is nonstandard.

all together, altogether   *All together* means "everyone gathered." *Altogether* means "entirely." *We were not altogether sure that we could bring the family all together for the reunion.*

allusion, illusion An *allusion* is an indirect reference; an *illusion* is a misconception or false impression. *Did you catch my allusion to Shakespeare? Mirrors give the room an illusion of depth.*

a lot *A lot* is two words. Do not write *alot*.

among, between Ordinarily, use *among* with three or more entities, *between* with two. *The prize was divided among several contestants. You have a choice between carrots and beans.*

amoral, immoral *Amoral* means "neither moral nor immoral"; it also means "not caring about moral judgments." *Immoral* means "morally wrong." *Many business courses are taught from an amoral perspective. Murder is immoral.*

amount, number Use *amount* with quantities that cannot be counted; use *number* with those that can. *This recipe calls for a large amount of sugar. We have a large number of toads in our garden.*

an See *a, an*.

and/or Avoid *and/or* except in technical or legal documents.

anxious *Anxious* means "worried" or "apprehensive." In formal writing, avoid using *anxious* to mean "eager." *We are eager* (not *anxious*) *to see your new house.*

anybody, anyone See pages 23 and 33.

anyone, any one *Anyone*, an indefinite pronoun, means "any person at all." *Any one* refers to a particular person or thing in a group. *Anyone in the class may choose any one of the books to read.*

anyways, anywheres *Anyways* and *anywheres* are nonstandard for *anyway* and *anywhere*.

as *As* is sometimes used to mean "because." But do not use it if there is any chance of ambiguity. *We canceled the picnic because* (not *as*) *it began raining. As* here could mean "because" or "when."

as, like See *like, as*.

averse See *adverse, averse*.

awful The adjective *awful* and the adverb *awfully* are too colloquial for formal writing.

awhile, a while *Awhile* is an adverb; it can modify a verb, but it cannot be the object of a preposition such as *for*. The two-word form *a while* is a noun preceded by an article and therefore can be the object of a preposition. *Stay awhile. Stay for a while.*

back up, backup   *Back up* is a verb phrase. *Back up the car carefully. Be sure to back up your hard drive. Backup* is a noun often meaning "duplicate of electronically stored data." *Keep your backup in a safe place. Backup* can also be used as an adjective. *I regularly create backup disks.*

bad, badly   *Bad* is an adjective, *badly* an adverb. *They felt bad about being early and ruining the surprise. Her arm hurt badly after she slid into second.* See section 13.

being as, being that   *Being as* and *being that* are non-standard expressions. Write *because* instead.

beside, besides   *Beside* is a preposition meaning "at the side of" or "next to." *Annie sleeps with a flashlight beside her bed. Besides* is a preposition meaning "except" or "in addition to." *No one besides Terrie can have that ice cream. Besides* is also an adverb meaning "in addition." *I'm not hungry; besides, I don't like ice cream.*

between   See *among, between.*

bring, take   Use *bring* when an object is being transported toward you, *take* when it is being moved away. *Please bring me a glass of water. Please take these magazines to Mr. Scott.*

can, may   *Can* is traditionally reserved for ability, *may* for permission. *Can you speak French? May I help you?*

capital, capitol   *Capital* refers to a city, *capitol* to a building where lawmakers meet. *The residents of the state capital protested the development plans. The capitol has undergone extensive renovations. Capital* also refers to wealth or resources.

censor, censure   *Censor* means "to remove or suppress material considered objectionable." *Censure* means "to criticize severely." *The school's policy of censoring books has been censured by the media.*

cite, site   *Cite* means "to quote as an authority or example." *Site* is usually a noun meaning "a particular place." *He cited the zoning law in his argument against the proposed site of the gas station.* Locations on the Internet are usually referred to as *sites.*

coarse, course   *Coarse* means "crude" or "rough in texture." *The hand-knit sweater had a coarse weave. Course* usually refers to a path, a playing field, or a unit of study. *I plan to take a course in car repair this summer.* The expression *of course* means "certainly."

complement, compliment   *Complement* is a verb meaning "to go with or complete" or a noun meaning "something that completes." As a verb, *compliment* means "to flatter"; as a noun, it means "flattering remark." *Her skill at rushing the net complements his skill at volleying. Sheiying's music arrangements receive many compliments.*

conscience, conscious *Conscience* is a noun meaning "moral principles"; *conscious* is an adjective meaning "aware or alert." *Let your conscience be your guide. Were you conscious of his love for you?*

continual, continuous *Continual* means "repeated regularly and frequently." *She grew weary of the continual telephone calls. Continuous* means "extended or prolonged without interruption." *The broken siren made a continuous wail.*

could care less *Could care less* is a nonstandard expression. Write *couldn't care less* instead.

could of *Could of* is nonstandard for *could have.*

council, counsel A *council* is a deliberative body, and a *councilor* is a member of such a body. *Counsel* usually means "advice" and can also mean "lawyer"; a *counselor* is one who gives advice or guidance. *The councilors met to draft the council's position paper. The pastor offered wise counsel to the troubled teenager.*

criteria *Criteria* is the plural of *criterion*, which means "a standard, rule, or test on which a judgment or decision can be based." *The only criterion for the scholarship is ability.*

data *Data* is a plural noun meaning "facts or results." But *data* is increasingly being accepted as a singular noun. *The new data suggest* (or *suggests*) *that our theory is correct.* (The singular *datum* is rarely used.)

different from, different than Ordinarily, write *different from. Your sense of style is different from Jim's.* However, *different than* is acceptable to avoid an awkward construction. *Please let me know if your plans are different than* (to avoid *from what*) *they were six weeks ago.*

don't *Don't* is the contraction for *do not. I don't want milk. Don't* should not be used as the contraction for *does not,* which is *doesn't. He doesn't* (not *don't*) *want milk.*

due to *Due to* is an adjective phrase and should not be used as a preposition meaning "because of." *The trip was canceled because of* (not *due to*) *lack of interest. Due to* is acceptable as a subject complement and usually follows a form of the verb *be. His success was due to hard work.*

each See pages 23 and 33.

effect See *affect, effect.*

either See pages 23 and 33.

elicit, illicit   *Elicit* is a verb meaning "to bring out" or "to evoke." *Illicit* is an adjective meaning "unlawful." *The reporter was unable to elicit any information from the police about illicit drug traffic.*

emigrate from, immigrate to   *Emigrate* means "to leave one place to settle in another." *My great-grandfather emigrated from Russia to escape the religious pogroms. Immigrate* means "to enter another place and reside there." *Thousands of Bosnians immigrated to the United States in the 1990s.*

enthused   As an adjective, *enthusiastic* is preferred. *The children were enthusiastic* (not *enthused*) *about going to the circus.*

etc.   Avoid ending a list with *etc.* It is more emphatic to end with an example, and usually readers will understand that the list is not exhaustive. When you don't wish to end with an example, *and so on* is more graceful than *etc.*

everybody, everyone   See pages 23 and 33.

everyone, every one   *Everyone* is an indefinite pronoun. *Everyone wanted to go. Every one*, the pronoun *one* preceded by the adjective *every*, means "each individual or thing in a particular group." *Every one* is usually followed by *of. Every one of the missing books was found.*

except   See *accept, except.*

farther, further   *Farther* describes distances. *Further* suggests quantity or degree. *Detroit is farther from Miami than I thought. You extended the curfew further than necessary.*

fewer, less   *Fewer* refers to items that can be counted; *less* refers to items that cannot be counted. *Fewer people are living in the city. Please put less sugar in my tea.*

firstly   *Firstly* sounds pretentious, and it leads to the ungainly series *firstly, secondly, thirdly, fourthly*, and so on. Write *first, second, third* instead.

further   See *farther, further.*

good, well   See page 41.

graduate   Both of the following uses of *graduate* are standard: *My sister was graduated from UCLA last year. My sister graduated from UCLA last year.* It is nonstandard to drop the word *from: My sister graduated UCLA last year.*

grow   Phrases such as *to grow a business* are jargon. Usually the verb *grow* is intransitive (it does not take a direct object). *Our business has grown very quickly.* When *grow* is used in a transitive sense, with a direct object, it means "to cultivate" or "to allow to grow." *We plan to grow tomatoes. John is growing a beard.* (See also pp. 300 and 304.)

hanged, hung   *Hanged* is the past-tense and past-participle form of the verb *hang,* meaning "to execute." *The prisoner was hanged at dawn. Hung* is the past-tense and past-participle form of the verb *hang,* meaning "to fasten or suspend." *The stockings were hung by the chimney with care.*

hardly   Avoid expressions such as *can't hardly* and *not hardly,* which are considered double negatives. *I can* (not *can't*) *hardly describe my elation at getting the job.*

he   At one time *he* was used to mean "he or she." Today such usage is inappropriate. See pages 19 and 33 for alternative constructions.

hisself   *Hisself* is nonstandard. Use *himself.*

hopefully   *Hopefully* means "in a hopeful manner." *We looked hopefully to the future.* Some usage experts object to the use of *hopefully* as a sentence adverb, apparently on grounds of clarity. To be safe, avoid using *hopefully* in sentences such as the following: *Hopefully, your son will recover soon.* Instead, indicate who is doing the hoping: *I hope that your son will recover soon.*

however   Some writers object to *however* at the beginning of a sentence, but experts advise placing the word according to the meaning and emphasis intended. Any of the following sentences is correct, depending on the intended contrast. *Pam decided, however, to attend the lecture. However, Pam decided to attend the lecture.* (She had been considering other activities.) *Pam, however, decided to attend the lecture.* (Unlike someone else, Pam opted for the lecture.)

hung   See *hanged, hung.*

illusion   See *allusion, illusion.*

immigrate   See *emigrate from, immigrate to.*

immoral   See *amoral, immoral.*

imply, infer   *Imply* means "to suggest or state indirectly"; *infer* means "to draw a conclusion." *John implied that he knew all about computers, but the interviewer inferred that John was inexperienced.*

in, into   *In* indicates location or condition; *into* indicates movement or a change in condition. *They found the lost letters in a box after moving into the house.*

in regards to   Use either *in regard to* or *as regards. In regard to* (or *As regards*) *the contract, ignore the first clause.*

irregardless   *Irregardless* is nonstandard. Use *regardless.*

is when, is where   See section 6c.

its, it's   *Its* is a possessive pronoun; *it's* is a contraction for *it is. It's always fun to watch a dog chase its tail.*

kind of, sort of   Avoid using *kind of* or *sort of* to mean "somewhat." *The movie was a little* (not *kind of*) *boring.* Do not put *a* after either phrase. *That kind of* (not *kind of a*) *salesclerk annoys me.*

lay, lie   See page 27.

lead, led   *Lead* is a metallic element; it is a noun. *Led* is the past tense of the verb *lead. He led me to the treasure.*

learn, teach   *Learn* means "to gain knowledge"; *teach* means "to impart knowledge." *I must teach* (not *learn*) *my sister to read.*

leave, let   *Leave* means "to exit." Avoid using it with the nonstandard meaning "to permit." *Let* (not *Leave*) *me help you with the dishes.*

less   See *fewer, less.*

let, leave   See *leave, let.*

liable   *Liable* means "obligated" or "responsible." Do not use it to mean "likely." *You're likely* (not *liable*) *to trip if you don't tie your shoelaces.*

lie, lay   See page 27.

like, as   *Like* is a preposition, not a subordinating conjunction. It should be followed only by a noun or a noun phrase. *As* is a subordinating conjunction that introduces a subordinate clause. In casual speech, you may say *She looks like she has not slept.* But in formal writing, use *as. She looks as if she has not slept.*

loose, lose   *Loose* is an adjective meaning "not securely fastened." *Lose* is a verb meaning "to misplace" or "to not win." *Did you lose your only loose pair of work pants?*

may   See *can, may.*

maybe, may be   *Maybe* is an adverb meaning "possibly"; *may be* is a verb phrase. *Maybe the sun will shine tomorrow. Tomorrow may be a brighter day.*

may of, might of   *May of* and *might of* are nonstandard for *may have* and *might have.*

media, medium   *Media* is the plural of *medium. Of all the media that cover the Olympics, television is the medium that best captures the spectacle of the events.*

must of   *Must of* is nonstandard for *must have.*

myself   *Myself* is a reflexive or intensive pronoun. Reflexive: *I cut myself.* Intensive: *I will drive you myself.* Do not use *myself* in place of *I* or *me: He gave the plants to Melinda and me* (not *myself*).

neither   See pages 23 and 33.

none   See page 23.

nowheres   *Nowheres* is nonstandard for *nowhere.*

number   See *amount, number.*

off of   *Off* is sufficient. Omit *of.*

passed, past   *Passed* is the past tense of the verb *pass. Emily passed me a slice of cake. Past* usually means "belonging to a former time" or "beyond a time or place." *Our past president spoke until past 10:00. The hotel is just past the station.*

plus   *Plus* should not be used to join independent clauses. *This raincoat is dirty; moreover* (not *plus*), *it has a hole in it.*

precede, proceed   *Precede* means "to come before." *Proceed* means "to go forward." *As we proceeded up the mountain, we saw evidence that some hikers had preceded us.*

principal, principle   *Principal* is a noun meaning "the head of a school or an organization" or "a sum of money." It is also an adjective meaning "most important." *Principle* is a noun meaning "a basic truth or law." *The principal expelled her for three principal reasons. We believe in the principle of equal justice for all.*

proceed, precede   See *precede, proceed.*

quote, quotation   *Quote* is a verb; *quotation* is a noun. Avoid using *quote* as a shortened form of *quotation. Her quotations* (not *quotes*) *from Shakespeare intrigued us.*

real, really   *Real* is an adjective; *really* is an adverb. *Real* is sometimes used informally as an adverb, but avoid this use in formal writing. *She was really* (not *real*) *angry.* See also section 13.

reason . . . is because   See section 6c.

reason why   The expression *reason why* is redundant. *The reason* (not *The reason why*) *Jones lost the election is clear.*

respectfully, respectively   *Respectfully* means "showing or marked by respect." *He respectfully submitted his opinion. Respectively* means "each in the order given." *John, Tom, and Larry were a butcher, a baker, and a lawyer, respectively.*

sensual, sensuous   *Sensual* means "gratifying the physical senses," especially those associated with sexual pleasure. *Sensuous* means "pleasing to the senses," especially involving art, music, and nature. *The sensuous music and balmy air led the dancers to more sensual movements.*

set, sit   *Set* means "to put" or "to place"; *sit* means "to be seated." *She set the dough in a warm corner of the kitchen. The cat sits in the warmest part of the room.*

should of   *Should of* is nonstandard for *should have.*

since   Do not use *since* to mean "because" if there is any chance of ambiguity. *Because* (not *Since*) *we won the game, we have been celebrating. Since* here could mean "because" or "from the time that."

sit   See *set, sit.*

site, cite   See *cite, site.*

somebody, someone, something   See pages 23 and 33.

suppose to   Write *supposed to.*

sure and   *Sure and* is nonstandard for *sure to. Be sure to* (not *sure and*) *bring a gift for the host.*

take   See *bring, take.*

than, then   *Than* is a conjunction used in comparisons; *then* is an adverb denoting time. *That pizza is more than I can eat. Tom laughed, and then we recognized him.*

that   See *who, which, that.*

that, which   Many writers reserve *that* for restrictive clauses, *which* for nonrestrictive clauses. (See p. 60.)

theirselves   *Theirselves* is nonstandard for *themselves.*

them   The use of *them* in place of *those* is nonstandard. *Please send those* (not *them*) *letters to the sponsors.*

then   See *than, then.*

there, their, they're   *There* is an adverb specifying place; it is also an expletive (placeholder). Adverb: *Sylvia is sitting there patiently.* Expletive: *There are two plums left.* (See also p. 300.) *Their* is a possessive pronoun. *Fred and Jane finally washed their car. They're* is a contraction of *they are. They're late today.*

to, too, two   *To* is a preposition; *too* is an adverb; *two* is a number. *Too many of your shots slice to the left, but the last two were right on the mark.*

toward, towards   *Toward* and *towards* are generally interchangeable, although *toward* is preferred in American English.

try and   *Try and* is nonstandard for *try to. I will try to* (not *try and*) *be better about writing to you.*

unique   See page 42.

use to   Write *used to*. *We used to live in an apartment.*

utilize   *Utilize* is often a pretentious substitute for *use*; in most cases, *use* is sufficient. *I used* (not *utilized*) *the best workers to get the job done fast.*

wait for, wait on   *Wait for* means "to be in readiness for" or "await." *Wait on* means "to serve." *We're waiting for* (not *waiting on*) *Ruth before we can leave.*

ways   *Ways* is colloquial when used in place of *way* to mean "distance." *The city is a long way* (not *ways*) *from here.*

weather, whether   The noun *weather* refers to the state of the atmosphere. *Whether* is a conjunction indicating a choice between alternatives. *We wondered whether the weather would clear up in time for our picnic.*

well, good   See page 41.

where   Do not use *where* in place of *that*. *I heard that* (not *where*) *the crime rate is increasing.*

which   See *that, which* and *who, which, that.*

while   Avoid using *while* to mean "although" or "whereas" if there is any chance of ambiguity. *Although* (not *While*) *Gloria lost money in the slot machine, Tom won it at roulette.* Here *While* could mean either "although" or "at the same time that."

who, which, that   Use *who*, not *which*, to refer to persons. Generally, use *that* to refer to things or, occasionally, to a group or class of people. *The player who* (not *that* or *which*) *made the basket at the buzzer was named MVP. The team that scores the most points in this game will win the tournament.*

who, whom   See section 12d.

who's, whose   *Who's* is a contraction of *who is*; *whose* is a possessive pronoun. *Who's ready for more popcorn? Whose coat is this?*

would of   *Would of* is nonstandard for *would have*.

you   See page 35.

your, you're   *Your* is a possessive pronoun; *you're* is a contraction of *you are*. *Is that your bike? You're in the finals.*

Glossary of grammatical terms

This glossary gives definitions for parts of speech, such as nouns; parts of sentences, such as subjects; and types of sentences, clauses, and phrases.

If you are looking up the name of an error (sentence fragment, for example), consult the index or the table of contents instead.

absolute phrase   A word group that modifies a whole clause or sentence, usually consisting of a noun followed by a participle or participial phrase: *Her words echoing in the large arena, the senator mesmerized the crowd.*

active vs. passive voice   When a verb is in the active voice, the subject of the sentence does the action: *Hernando caught* the ball. In the passive voice, the subject receives the action: The *ball was caught* by Hernando. Often the actor does not appear in a passive-voice sentence: The *ball was caught.* See also section 2.

adjective   A word used to modify (describe) a noun or pronoun: the *frisky* horse, *rare old* stamps, *sixteen* candles. Adjectives usually answer one of these questions: Which one? What kind of? How many or how much? See also section 13.

adjective clause   A subordinate clause that modifies a noun or pronoun. An adjective clause begins with a relative pronoun (*who, whom, whose, which, that*) or a relative adverb (*when, where*) and usually appears right after the word it modifies: The book *that goes unread* is a writer's worst nightmare.

adverb   A word used to modify a verb, an adjective, or another adverb: rides *smoothly, unusually* attractive, *very* slowly. An adverb usually answers one of these questions: When? Where? How? Why? Under what conditions? To what degree? See also section 13.

adverb clause   A subordinate clause that modifies a verb (or occasionally an adjective or adverb). An adverb clause begins with a subordinating conjunction such as *although, because, if, unless,* or *when* and usually appears at the beginning or the end of a sentence: *When the sun went down,* the hikers prepared their camp. See also *subordinate clause; subordinating conjunction.*

agreement   See sections 10 and 12.

antecedent   A noun or pronoun to which a pronoun refers: When the *battery* wears down, we recharge *it.* The noun *battery* is the antecedent of the pronoun *it.*

appositive   A noun or noun phrase that renames a nearby noun or pronoun: Bloggers, *conversationalists at heart*, are the online equivalent of talk show hosts.

article   The word *a, an, or the*, used to mark a noun. Also see section 16b.

case   See sections 12c and 12d.

clause   A word group containing a subject, a verb, and any objects, complements, or modifiers. See *independent clause; subordinate clause*.

collective noun   See sections 10e and 12a.

common noun   See section 22a.

complement   See *object complement; subject complement*.

complex sentence   A sentence consisting of one independent clause and one or more subordinate clauses. In the following example, the subordinate clause is italicized: We walked along the river *until we came to the bridge*.

compound-complex sentence   A sentence consisting of at least two independent clauses and at least one subordinate clause: Jan dictated a story, and the children wrote whatever he said. In the preceding sentence, the subordinate clause is *whatever he said*. The two independent clauses are *Jan dictated a story* and *the children wrote whatever he said*.

compound sentence   A sentence consisting of two independent clauses. The clauses are usually joined with a comma and a coordinating conjunction (*and, but, or, nor, for, so, yet*) or with a semicolon: The car broke down, *but* a rescue van arrived within minutes. A shark was spotted near shore; people left the water immediately.

conjunction   A joining word. See *conjunctive adverb; coordinating conjunction; correlative conjunction; subordinating conjunction*.

conjunctive adverb   An adverb used with a semicolon to connect independent clauses: The bus was stuck in traffic; *therefore*, the team was late for the game. The most commonly used conjunctive adverbs are *consequently, furthermore, however, moreover, nevertheless, then, therefore*, and *thus*. See page 65 for a longer list.

coordinating conjunction   One of the following words, used to join elements of equal grammatical rank: *and, but, or, nor, for, so, yet*.

correlative conjunction   A pair of conjunctions connecting grammatically equal elements: *either . . . or, neither . . . nor, whether . . . or, not only . . . but also*, and *both . . . and*. See also section 3b.

count noun See page 50.

demonstrative pronoun A pronoun used to identify or point to a noun: *this, that, these, those. This* is my favorite chair.

direct object A word or word group that receives the action of the verb: The hungry cat clawed *the bag of dry food.* The complete direct object is *the bag of dry food.* The simple direct object is always a noun or a pronoun, in this case *bag.*

expletive The word *there* or *it* when used at the beginning of a sentence to delay the subject: *There* are eight planes waiting to take off. *It* is healthy to eat breakfast every day. The delayed subjects are the noun *planes* and the infinitive phrase *to eat breakfast every day.*

gerund A verb form ending in *-ing* used as a noun: *Reading* aloud helps children appreciate language. The gerund *reading* is used as the subject of the verb *helps.*

gerund phrase A gerund and its objects, complements, or modifiers. A gerund phrase always functions as a noun, usually as a subject, a subject complement, or a direct object. In the following example, the phrase functions as a direct object: We tried *planting tulips.*

helping verb One of the following words, when used with a main verb: *be, am, is, are, was, were, being, been; has, have, had; do, does, did; can, will, shall, should, could, would, may, might, must.* Helping verbs always precede main verbs: *will work, is working, had worked.* See also *modal verb.*

indefinite pronoun A pronoun that refers to a nonspecific person or thing: *Something* is burning. The most common indefinite pronouns are *all, another, any, anybody, anyone, anything, both, each, either, everybody, everyone, everything, few, many, neither, nobody, none, no one, nothing, one, some, somebody, someone, something.* See also pages 23 and 33.

independent clause A word group containing a subject and a verb that can or does stand alone as a sentence. In addition to at least one independent clause, many sentences contain subordinate clauses that function as adjectives, adverbs, or nouns. See also *clause; subordinate clause.*

indirect object A noun or pronoun that names to whom or for whom the action of a sentence is done: We gave *her* some leftover yarn. An indirect object always precedes a direct object, in this case *some leftover yarn.*

infinitive The word *to* followed by the base form of a verb: *to think, to dream.*

infinitive phrase An infinitive and its objects, complements, or modifiers. An infinitive phrase can function as a noun, an adjective, or an adverb. Noun: *To live without health* *insurance* is risky. Adjective: The Nineteenth Amendment gave women the right *to vote*. Adverb: Volunteers knocked on doors *to rescue people from the flood*.

intensive or reflexive pronoun   A pronoun ending in *-self* (or *-selves*): *myself, yourself, himself, herself, itself, ourselves, yourselves, themselves*. An intensive pronoun emphasizes a noun or another pronoun: I *myself* don't have a job. A reflexive pronoun names a receiver of an action identical with the doer of the action: Did Paula cut *herself*?

interjection   A word expressing surprise or emotion: *Oh! Wow! Hey! Hooray!*

interrogative pronoun   A pronoun used to introduce a question: *who, whom, whose, which, what. What* does history teach us?

intransitive verb   See *transitive and intransitive verbs*.

irregular verb   See *regular and irregular verbs*. See also section 11a.

linking verb   A verb that links a subject to a subject comple-ment, a word or word group that renames or describes the subject: The winner *was* a teacher. The cherries *taste* sour. The most common linking verbs are forms of *be: be, am, is, are, was, were, being, been*. The following sometimes function as linking verbs: *appear, become, feel, grow, look, make, seem, smell, sound, taste*. See also *subject complement*.

modal verb   A helping verb that cannot be used as a main verb. There are nine modals: *can, could, may, might, must, shall, should, will,* and *would*. We *must* shut the windows before the storm. The verb phrase *ought to* is often classified as a modal as well. See also *helping verb*.

modifier   A word, phrase, or clause that describes or quali-fies the meaning of a word. Modifiers include adjectives, adverbs, prepositional phrases, participial phrases, some infinitive phrases, and adjective and adverb clauses.

mood   See section 11c.

noncount noun   See pages 51–52.

noun   The name of a person, place, thing, or concept (*free-dom*): The *lion* in the *cage* growled at the *zookeeper*.

noun clause   A subordinate clause that functions as a noun, usually as a subject, a subject complement, or a direct object. In the following sentence, the italicized noun clause functions as the subject: *Whoever leaves the house last* must lock the door. Noun clauses usually begin with *how, who, whom, whoever, that, what, whatever, whether,* or *why*.

noun equivalent   A word or word group that functions like a noun: a pronoun, a noun and its modifiers, a gerund phrase, some infinitive phrases, or a noun clause.

object   See *direct object; indirect object.*

object complement   A word or word group that renames or describes a direct object. It always appears after the direct object: The kiln makes clay *firm and strong.*

object of a preposition   See *prepositional phrase.*

participial phrase   A present or past participle and its objects, complements, or modifiers. A participial phrase always functions as an adjective describing a noun or pronoun. Usually it appears before or after the word it modifies: *Being a weight-bearing joint,* the knee is often injured. Plants *kept in moist soil* will thrive.

participle, past   A verb form usually ending in *-d, -ed, -n, -en,* or *-t: asked, stolen, fought.* Past participles are used with helping verbs to form perfect tenses (had *spoken*) and the passive voice (were *required*). They are also used as adjectives (the *stolen* car).

participle, present   A verb form ending in *-ing.* Present participles are used with helping verbs in progressive forms (is *rising,* has been *walking*). They are also used as adjectives (the *rising* tide).

parts of speech   A system for classifying words. Many words can function as more than one part of speech. See *adjective, adverb, conjunction, interjection, noun, preposition, pronoun, verb.*

passive voice   See *active vs. passive voice.*

personal pronoun   One of the following pronouns, used to refer to a specific person or thing: *I, me, you, she, her, he, him, it, we, us, they, them.* After Julia won the award, *she* gave half of the prize money to a literacy program. See also *antecedent.*

phrase   A word group that lacks a subject, a verb, or both. Most phrases function within sentences as adjectives, as adverbs, or as nouns. See *absolute phrase; appositive; gerund phrase; infinitive phrase; participial phrase; prepositional phrase.*

possessive case   See section 19a.

possessive pronoun   A pronoun used to indicate ownership: *my, mine, your, yours, her, hers, his, its, our, ours, your, yours, their, theirs.* The guest made *his* own breakfast.

predicate   A verb and any objects, complements, and modifiers that go with it: The horses *exercise in the corral every day.*

preposition A word placed before a noun or noun equivalent to form a phrase modifying another word in the sentence. The preposition indicates the relation between the noun (or noun equivalent) and the word the phrase modifies. The most common prepositions are *about, above, across, after, against, along, among, around, at, before, behind, below, beside, besides, between, beyond, by, down, during, except, for, from, in, inside, into, like, near, of, off, on, onto, out, outside, over, past, since, than, through, to, toward, under, unlike, until, up, with, within,* and *without.*

prepositional phrase A phrase beginning with a preposition and ending with a noun or noun equivalent (called the *object of the preposition*). Most prepositional phrases function as adjectives or adverbs. Adjective phrases usually come right after the noun or pronoun they modify: The road *to the summit* was treacherous. Adverb phrases usually appear at the beginning or the end of the sentence: *To the hikers*, the brief shower was a welcome relief. The brief shower was a welcome relief *to the hikers.*

progressive verb forms See pages 30–31 and 48–49.

pronoun A word used in place of a noun. Usually the pronoun substitutes for a specific noun, known as the pronoun's *antecedent*. In the following example, *alarm* is the antecedent of the pronoun *it*: When the *alarm* rang, I reached over and turned *it* off. See also *demonstrative pronoun; indefinite pronoun; intensive or reflexive pronoun; interrogative pronoun; personal pronoun; possessive pronoun; relative pronoun.*

proper noun See section 22a.

regular and irregular verbs When a verb is regular, both the past tense and the past participle are formed by adding *-ed* or *-d* to the base form of the verb: *walk, walked, walked*. The past tense and past participle of irregular verbs are formed in a variety of other ways: *ride, rode, ridden; begin, began, begun; go, went, gone;* and so on. Also see section 11a.

relative adverb The word *when* or *where*, when used to introduce an adjective clause. The park *where* we had our picnic closes on October 1. See also *adjective clause.*

relative pronoun One of the following words, when used to introduce an adjective clause: *who, whom, whose, which, that*. The writer *who* won the award refused to accept it.

sentence A word group consisting of at least one independent clause. See also *complex sentence; compound sentence; compound-complex sentence; simple sentence.*

simple sentence   A sentence consisting of one independent clause and no subordinate clauses: Without a passport, Eva could not visit her parents in Poland.

subject   A word or word group that names who or what the sentence is about. In the following example, the complete subject (the simple subject and all of its modifiers) is italicized: *The devastating effects of famine* can last for many years. The simple subject is *effects*. See also *subject after verb; understood subject*.

subject after verb   Although the subject normally precedes the verb, sentences are sometimes inverted. In the following example, the subject *the sleepy child* comes after the verb *sat*: Under the table *sat the sleepy child*. When a sentence begins with the expletive *there* or *it*, the subject always follows the verb. See also *expletive*.

subject complement   A word or word group that follows a linking verb and either renames or describes the subject of the sentence. If the subject complement renames the subject, it is a noun or a noun equivalent: That signature may be *a forgery*. If it describes the subject, it is an adjective: Love is *blind*.

subjunctive mood   See section 11c.

subordinate clause   A word group containing a subject and a verb that cannot stand alone as a sentence. Subordinate clauses function within sentences as adjectives, adverbs, or nouns. They begin with subordinating conjunctions such as *although, because, if,* and *until* or with relative pronouns such as *who, which,* and *that*. See *adjective clause; adverb clause; independent clause; noun clause*.

subordinating conjunction   A word that introduces a subordinate clause and indicates the relation of the clause to the rest of the sentence. The most common subordinating conjunctions are *after, although, as, as if, because, before, even though, if, since, so that, than, that, though, unless, until, when, where, whether,* and *while*. Note: The relative pronouns *who, whom, whose, which,* and *that* also introduce subordinate clauses.

tenses   See section 11b.

transitive and intransitive verbs   Transitive verbs take direct objects, nouns or noun equivalents that receive the action. In the following example, the transitive verb *wrote* takes the direct object *a story*: Each student *wrote* a story. Intransitive verbs do not take direct objects: The audience *laughed*. If any words follow an intransitive verb, they are adverbs or word groups functioning as adverbs: The audience *laughed* at the talking parrot.

understood subject   The subject *you* when it is understood but not actually present in the sentence. Understood subjects occur in sentences that issue commands or advice: [*You*] Put your clothes in the hamper.

verb   A word that expresses action (*jump, think*) or being (*is, was*). A sentence's verb is composed of a main verb possibly preceded by one or more helping verbs: The band *practiced* every day. The report *was* not *completed* on schedule. Verbs have five forms: the base form, or dictionary form (*walk, ride*); the past-tense form (*walked, rode*); the past participle (*walked, ridden*); the present participle (*walking, riding*); and the *-s* form (*walks, rides*).

verbal phrase   See *gerund phrase; infinitive phrase; participial phrase.*

Checklist for global revision

Focus

▶ Is your thesis stated clearly enough? Is it placed where readers will notice it?

▶ Does each idea support the thesis?

Organization

▶ Can readers easily follow the structure? Would headings help?

▶ Do topic sentences signal new ideas?

▶ Do you present ideas in a logical order?

Content

▶ Are your supporting ideas persuasive?

▶ Do you fully develop important ideas?

▶ Is the draft concise enough—free of irrelevant or repetitious material?

Style

▶ Is your tone appropriate—not too stuffy, not too casual?

▶ Are your sentences clear, direct, and varied?

Use of sources

▶ Which sources inform, support, or extend your argument?

▶ Have you varied the function of sources—to provide background, explain concepts, lend authority, and counter objections? Do you introduce sources with signal phrases that indicate these functions?

▶ Is it clear how your sources relate to your argument?

▶ Do you analyze sources in your own words?

▶ Is your own argument easy to identify and to understand, with or without your sources?

▶ Is the draft free of plagiarism? Are summaries and paraphrases in your own words? Is quoted material enclosed in quotation marks or set off from the text?

▶ Have you documented source material that is not common knowledge?

Checklist for visiting the writing center

Step 1: Gather your materials.

▶ Gather materials your instructor has provided: the assignment, sample papers, your syllabus.

▶ Gather your own materials: a copy of your draft, copies of texts you have cited in your paper, previous papers with instructor comments.

Step 2: Organize your materials and prepare questions.

▶ Reread the assignment. If you are confused, ask your instructor to clarify the assignment before you visit the writing center.

▶ Look at previous papers with instructor comments. Can those comments help you think about your current paper?

▶ Create a list of specific questions to focus your writing center conversation.

Step 3: Visit the writing center.

▶ Be on time and treat your tutor or consultant with courtesy and respect.

▶ Participate actively by asking questions and taking notes.

▶ Understand the limitations of your visit. Be prepared to cover one or two major issues.

▶ Understand the purpose of your visit. Most writing center staff are trained to give you suggestions and feedback, but they will not write or edit your paper for you.

Step 4: Reflect on your visit.

▶ As soon as possible after your visit, make sure you understand your notes from the session and add anything you didn't have time to write during your visit.

▶ As you revise, apply your notes to your entire paper. Don't focus only on the parts of your paper you looked at in the session.

▶ Do not feel obligated to follow advice that you disagree with. Writing center staff are trained to provide helpful feedback, but you are the author; you decide which changes will help you best express your meaning.

▶ As you revise, keep track of questions or goals for your next writing center visit.

Index

A

a, an, 50–52, 288. *See also the*
Abbreviations, 82–83
  in APA reference list,
    194–95
  capitalizing, 81
  Latin, 74, 83
  in MLA works cited list,
    136–37
  parentheses with, 76
  periods with, 74
  plurals of, 69
  for titles with proper
    names, 82
  for units of measurement, 83
Absolute concepts (such as
  unique), 42
Absolute phrases, 298
  commas with, 61
Abstracts
  in APA papers, 219, 223
  citing, 147 (MLA); 203 (APA)
  in CSE papers, 284
  in databases, 95
accept, except, 288
Acknowledgments, in CSE
  papers, 285
Active verbs, 5–7
Active voice, 6–7, 50, 298
adapt, adopt, 288
AD, BC (CE, BCE), 82
Addresses. *See also* URLs
  commas with, 62–63
  e-mail, 89
  numbers in, 84
Adjective clauses
  avoiding repetition in, 54
  defined, 298
  punctuation of, 60
Adjective phrases, punctuation
  of, 60
Adjectives
  and adverbs, 40–42
  commas with coordinate,
    58–59
  comparative forms (with
    -er or *more*), 41–42
  defined, 298
  hyphens with, 88–89
  after linking verbs (subject
    complements), 40
  no commas with
    cumulative, 59

  with prepositions
    (idioms), 55
  punctuation of, 58–59
  as subject complements, 40
  superlative forms (with *-est*
    or *most*), 41–42
adopt. See adapt, adopt, 288
Adverb clauses, 298
Adverbs
  and adjectives, 40–42
  comparative forms (with
    -er or *more*), 41–42
  conjunctive, 65, 299
  defined, 298
  introducing clauses, 54
  relative, 54, 303
  repetition of, avoiding, 54
  superlative forms (with *-est*
    or *most*), 41–42
adverse, averse, 288
advice, advise, 288
affect, effect, 288
Agreement of pronoun and
    antecedent, 32–34
  with collective nouns (*audi-
    ence, family*, etc.), 34
  with generic nouns, 33–34
  with indefinite pronouns, 33
  and sexist language, avoid-
    ing, 19, 33
Agreement of subject and verb,
    22–26
  with collective nouns (*audi-
    ence, family*, etc.), 24
  with indefinite pronouns, 23
  with subject after verb, 24
  with subjects joined with
    and, 23
  with subjects joined with
    or or *nor*, 23
  with *who, which, that*,
    24–25
  with words between subject
    and verb, 22–23
Aircraft, italics for names of, 85
all (singular or plural), 23
all ready, already, 288
all right (not *alright*), 288
all together, altogether, 288
allusion, illusion, 289
almost, placement of, 12–13
a lot (not *alot*), 289
*already. See all ready,
    already*, 288

alright (nonstandard). See *all right*, 288

altogether. See *all together, altogether*, 288

American Psychological Association. *See* APA papers

among, between, 289

amoral, immoral, 289

amount, number, 289

a.m., p.m., AM, PM, 82

am vs. *is* or *are*, 22

an, a. See a, an

and
    comma with, 57
    as coordinating conjunction, 57, 299
    no comma with, 57, 63
    no semicolon with, 66
    parallelism and, 7–8
    and subject-verb agreement, 23

and/or, 77, 289

Annotated bibliography, 101–02

Anonymous. *See* Unknown author

Antecedent
    agreement of pronoun and, 32–34
    defined, 298
    pronoun reference, 34–36
    of *who, which, that*, 24–25

Anthology (collection), selection in
    APA citation of, 207
    Chicago citation of, 247, 256–57
    citation at a glance, 154–55 (MLA); 256–57 (*Chicago*)
    CSE citation of, 278
    MLA citation of, 129–30, 152–53, 154–55

anxious, 289

any (singular or plural), 23

anybody (singular), 23, 33

anyone (singular), 23, 33

anyone, any one, 289

anyways, anywheres, 289

APA papers, 175–229
    abstracts in, 219, 223
    citation at a glance
        article from a database, 202
        article in a journal or magazine, 200–01

        book, 206
        section in a Web document, 212–13
    citations, in-text, 185–91
        directory to models for, 185
        models for, 185–91
    DOIs (digital object identifiers) in, 195, 198–99, 221
    evidence for, 176–77
    footnotes in, 219, 224
    keywords in, 219, 223
    manuscript format, 217–21
    numbers in, 83
    plagiarism in, avoiding, 177–80
    reference list, 191–217
        directory to models for, 192–93
        DOIs (digital object identifiers) in, 195, 198–99, 221
        formatting, 220–21
        general guidelines for, 194–95
        models for, 195–217
        sample, 226
        URLs in, 195, 210–17, 221
    sample pages, 222–29
    signal phrases in, 182–84, 185–91
    sources
        citing, 177–80, 185–217
        integrating, 180–84
        uses of, 176–77
    tenses in, 183, 185
    thesis in, 175–76
    title page, 218, 222, 227
    URLs in, 195, 210–17, 221
    visuals in, 211, 213–16, 220, 225

Apostrophes, 67–70

Appendixes, in CSE papers, 285

Appositives (nouns that rename other nouns)
    case of pronouns with, 37
    colon with, 66
    defined, 299
    punctuation with, 60–61, 75
    as sentence fragments, 43

Appropriate language (avoiding jargon, slang, etc.), 17–20

Apps, citing, 161 (MLA); 214–15 (APA)

are vs. *is*. *See* Agreement of
subject and verb
Arguments, evaluating,
99–101
Article from a database,
citing. *See also* Articles
in periodicals
APA style, 199
Chicago style, 249, 251–53
citation at a glance, 146
(MLA); 202 (APA); 252–53
(*Chicago*)
CSE style, 280
MLA style, 143–47
Articles (*a, an, the*), 50–53, 299.
See also a, an; the
Articles in periodicals. *See also*
Article from a database
abstracts of, 95
capitalizing titles of, 80; 136,
168 (MLA); 194, 218, 221
(APA); 263 (*Chicago*); 286
(CSE)
citation at a glance, 144
(MLA); 200–01 (APA);
250–51 (*Chicago*)
citing, 142–49 (MLA);
198–204 (APA); 249–55
(*Chicago*); 278–80 (CSE)
finding, 92–94
previewing, 98
quotation marks for titles of,
71; 136, 168 (MLA); 194,
221 (APA); 263 (*Chicago*);
286 (CSE)
Artwork, italics for title of, 84
as
ambiguous use of, 289
parallelism and, 7–8
pronoun after, 38
as, like. *See like, as,* 294
at, in idioms (common
expressions), 55
audience. *See* Collective nouns
Audience (readers)
appropriate voice for, 17
purpose and, evaluating, 101
thesis and, 107–09 (MLA);
175–76 (APA); 231–32
(*Chicago*)
Authors
citing, 125–28, 137–42
(MLA); 186–89, 195–98
(APA); 243–45 (*Chicago*)

identifying, 140
vs. narrators or speakers, 121
Auxiliary verbs. *See* Helping
verbs
averse. See *adverse, averse,* 288
awful, 289
awhile, a while, 289

B

back up, backup, 290
bad, badly, 40, 290
Base form of verb, 26, 47–48
to form tenses, 47–49
modal verbs (*can, might,* etc.)
with, 49–50
BC, AD (*CE, BCE*), 82
be, forms of
vs. active verbs, 5–6
and agreement with
subject, 22
in conditional sentences, 32
as helping verbs, 47–49
as irregular verbs, 27, 30
as linking verbs, 40, 53, 301
in passive voice, 50
in progressive forms, 48, 49
and subjunctive mood, 32
in tenses, 30–31
as weak verbs, 5–6
because, avoiding after *reason
is,* 12
Beginning of sentences
capitalizing words at, 81
numbers at, 83
varying, 16–17
being as, being that (nonstandard), 290
beside, besides, 290
between, among. See *among,
between,* 289
Bias, signs of, 99–100
Biased language, avoiding,
19–20
Bible. *See* Sacred texts (Bible,
Qur'an)
Bibliography. *See also* Reference
list (APA); Reference
list (CSE); Works cited list
(MLA)
annotated, 101–02
Chicago style, 240–62,
264–65, 269

for finding sources, 94
working, 103
Block quotation. *See* Quotations, long (indented)
Blog, citing, 158 (MLA); 211 (APA); 258 (*Chicago*)
Blu-ray Disc (BD), citing, 160 (MLA); 213 (APA); 259 (*Chicago*); 282 (CSE)
Book catalog, 93
Books
    capitalizing titles of, 80; 136, 168 (MLA); 194, 218, 221 (APA); 263 (*Chicago*); 286 (CSE)
    citation at a glance, 151, 154–55 (MLA); 206 (APA); 246 (*Chicago*)
    citing, 150–56 (MLA); 205–10 (APA); 245–49 (*Chicago*); 277–78 (CSE)
    finding, 92–94
    italics for titles of, 84–85; 136, 168 (MLA); 194, 218, 221 (APA); 241, 263 (*Chicago*); 286 (CSE)
Borrowed language and ideas. *See* Citing sources; Plagiarism, avoiding
Boundaries. *See* Dropped quotations, avoiding
Brackets, 76–77; 115 (MLA); 181 (APA); 237 (*Chicago*)
bring, take, 290
but
    comma with, 57
    as coordinating conjunction, 57, 299
    no comma with, 57, 63
    no semicolon with, 66
    parallelism and, 7–8

C

can, as modal verb, 49–50
can, may, 290
capital, capitol, 290
Capitalization, 79–81
    of abbreviations, 81
    after colon, 66, 81; 168 (MLA); 218 (APA); 263 (*Chicago*)
    of first word of sentence, 81
    of Internet terms, 80
    in quotations, 81
    of titles of persons, 80
    of titles of works, 80; 136, 168 (MLA); 194, 218, 221 (APA); 263 (*Chicago*); 286 (CSE)
capitol. See *capital, capitol*, 290
Captions, for figures and visuals, 131, 168–69 (MLA); 211, 213–16, 220 (APA); 263–64 (*Chicago*)
Case. *See* Pronoun case
Catalog, library, 93
censor, censure, 290
Central idea. *See* Thesis
Charts. *See* Visuals
Checklists
    for global revision, 306
    for visiting the writing center, 307
Chicago Manual of Style, The, 240, 262
Chicago papers, 231–69
    bibliography
        directory to models for, 242–43
        formatting, 264–65
        models for, 243–62
        sample, 269
    citation at a glance
        article in a journal, 250–51
        book, 246
        journal article from a database, 252–53
        letter in a published collection, 256–57
        primary source from a Web site, 260–61
    DOIs (digital object identifiers) in, 243, 264
    evidence for, 232–33
    footnotes or endnotes, 233–34, 240–41
        directory to models for, 242–43
        ibid. in, 241
        models for, 243–62
        sample, 268
    manuscript format, 262–65
    numbers in, 83

Chicago papers (*cont.*)
  plagiarism in, avoiding,
    233–36
  sample pages, 266–69
  signal phrases in, 238–40
  sources in
    citing, 233–36, 240–62
    integrating, 236–40
    uses of, 232–33
  supporting arguments in,
    232–33
  tenses in, 239
  thesis in, 231–32
  URLs in, 243, 255,
    258–62, 264
Choppy sentences, 15–16
Citation at a glance
  APA style
    article from a database,
      202
    article in a journal or
      magazine, 200–01
    book, 206
    section in a Web
      document, 212–13
  Chicago style
    article in a journal,
      250–51
    book, 246
    journal article from a
      database, 252–53
    letter in a published
      collection, 256–57
    primary source from a
      Web site, 260–61
  MLA style
    article from a database,
      146
    article in a journal, 144
    book, 151
    selection from an anthol-
      ogy or a collection,
      154–55
    short work from a Web
      site, 159
Citation-name system (CSE),
  271, 285
Citations, for finding sources, 94
Citation-sequence system
  (CSE), 271, 285
cited in, for source quoted in
  another source, 191. *See
  also quoted in* (*qtd. in*)
cite, site, 290

Citing sources. *See also* Citation
  at a glance; Plagiarism,
  avoiding; Quotations
  APA style, 177–80,
    185–217
  Chicago style, 233–36,
    240–62
  common knowledge, 110–11
    (MLA); 177–78 (APA); 233
    (*Chicago*)
  CSE style, 272–83
  general guidelines for,
    104–05
  MLA style, 110–13, 124–66
class. See Collective nouns
Clauses, 299. *See also* Independent clauses; Subordinate
  clauses
Clichés, avoiding, 18–19
coarse, course, 290
Collection. *See* Anthology
  (collection), selection in
Collective nouns (*audience,
  family*, etc.)
  agreement of pronouns
    with, 34
  agreement of verbs with, 24
Colons, 66–67
  capitalization after, 66, 81;
    168 (MLA); 218 (APA);
    263 (*Chicago*)
  to fix run-on sentences, 46
  introducing quotations, 72
Combining sentences
  (coordination and
  subordination), 15–16
Commands. *See* Imperative
  mood
Commas, 57–64
  with absolute phrases, 61
  in addresses, 62–63
  with *and, but*, etc., 57
  with contrasted elements,
    62
  between coordinate
    adjectives, 58–59
  before coordinating
    conjunctions, 57
  in dates, 62
  with interrogative tags, 62
  with interruptions (*he said*
    etc.), 61–62
  after introductory
    elements, 58

with items in a series, 58

with mild interjections, 62

with nonrestrictive (non-
essential) elements,
59–60

with nouns of direct
address, 62

with parenthetical
expressions, 61

to prevent confusion, 57

with quotation marks, 62,
71, 72–73

with semicolons, 64–65

to set off words or phrases,
59–62

with titles after names, 63

with transitional
expressions, 61

unnecessary, 63–64

with *yes* and *no*, 62

Comma splices. *See* Run-on
sentences

Comments, in online articles,
citing, 148 (MLA); 205
(APA)

committee. See Collective nouns

Common knowledge, 110–11
(MLA); 177–78 (APA); 233
(*Chicago*)

Common nouns, 79–80

Company names, agreement of
verb with, 25–26

Comparative form of adjectives
and adverbs (with *-er* or
more), 41–42

Comparisons
with adjectives and adverbs,
41–42

needed words in, 9–10

parallel elements in, 7–8

with pronoun following *than*
or *as*, 38

complement, compliment, 290–91

Complements, object, 302

Complements, subject. *See*
Subject complements

Complex sentences, 299

compliment. See *complement,
compliment*, 290–91

Compound-complex
sentences, 299

Compound elements
case of pronoun in, 36–39

comma with, 57

needed words in, 8–9

no comma with, 57, 63

parallelism and, 7–8

Compound nouns. *See*
Compound words

Compound numbers, hyphens
with, 89

Compound sentences
comma in, 57

defined, 299

semicolon in, 64–65

Compound subjects, agreement
of verb with, 23

Compound words (*father-in-
law, cross section*, etc.)
hyphens with, 88–89

plural of, 87

Conciseness, 4–5

Conditional sentences. *See*
Subjunctive mood

Conjunctions, 299. *See also*
Conjunctive adverbs;
Coordinating con-
junctions; Correlative
conjunctions

Conjunctive adverbs (*however,
therefore*, etc.)
comma with, 61

defined, 299

semicolon with, 65

conscience, conscious, 291

Consistency. *See* Shifts,
avoiding

Context, establishing, 119
(MLA); 183–84 (APA);
239–40 (*Chicago*)

continual, continuous, 291

Contractions (*can't, won't*,
etc.), 69

Contrary-to-fact clauses, 32

Conversations, research, 91,
99. *See also* Synthesizing
sources

Coordinate adjectives, comma
with, 58–59

Coordinating conjunctions
comma with, 57

coordination and, 16

defined, 299

to fix run-on sentences,
45–46

no comma with, 57, 63

no semicolon with, 66

parallelism and, 7–8

Coordination
  comma and coordinating
    conjunction for, 57
  for fixing choppy sentences,
    16
  for fixing run-on sentences,
    44–46
Correlative conjunctions
  defined, 299
  parallelism with, 7–8
could, as modal verb, 49–50
could care less (nonstandard),
  291
could of (nonstandard), 291
council, counsel, 291
Council of Science Editors. *See*
  CSE papers
Counterarguments, 110 (MLA);
  177 (APA); 232–33
  (*Chicago*)
Count nouns, articles (*a, an,
  the*) with, 50–51
couple. See Collective nouns
course. See coarse, course, 290
Course materials, citing, 158
  (MLA); 190, 216 (APA)
Credibility, of sources, 95,
  100–01
criteria, 291
Critical reading, 94–95,
  99–101
crowd. See Collective nouns
CSE papers, 271–86
  abstracts in, 284
  acknowledgments in, 285
  appendixes in, 285
  citations, in-text, 272–75
    directory to models
      for, 271
    models for, 272–75
  documentation systems
    in, 271
  DOIs (digital object
    identifiers) in, 286
  manuscript format,
    284–86
  numbers in, 83
  reference list, 275–83
    directory to models
      for, 274
    formatting, 285–86
    models for, 275–83
  title page, 284
  URLs in, 286

Cumulative adjectives, no
  comma with, 59, 63
Currency, of sources, 95,
  100–01

D

-d, -ed, verb ending, 26
Dangling modifiers, 13–14
Dashes, 75
data, 291
Database, article from. *See*
  Article from a database,
  citing
Databases, for finding
  sources, 93
Dates
  abbreviations in, 82
  capitalization of, 79
  commas with, 62
  numbers in, 84
Definite article. *See the*
Demonstrative pronouns,
  300
Dependent clauses. *See*
  Subordinate clauses
Diction. *See* Words
different from, different than, 291
Digital object identifier. *See*
  DOI (digital object
  identifier)
Direct objects
  case of pronouns as, 36–39
  defined, 300
Directories, to documentation
  models
  APA style, 185, 192–93
  Chicago style, 242–43
  CSE style, 271, 274
  MLA style, 125, 134–35
Division of words, 89
do
  as helping verb, 300
  irregular forms of, 28
  and subject-verb agreement,
    22–26
Documenting sources. *See*
  Citing sources
does vs. *do*, 22–26
DOI (digital object identifier),
  195, 198–99, 221 (APA);
  243, 264 (*Chicago*); 286
  (CSE)

don't vs. *doesn't*, 22–26, 291

Dots, ellipsis. *See* Ellipsis mark

Double negatives, avoiding. *See hardly*, 293

Double subjects, avoiding, 54

Drawings. *See* Visuals

Dropped quotations, avoiding, 116 (MLA); 182 (APA); 238 (*Chicago*)

due to, 291

E

each (singular), 23, 33

E-books, citing, 147, 150 (MLA); 207 (APA); 245 (*Chicago*)

-ed, verb ending, 26

effect. See *affect, effect*, 288

e.g. ("for example"), 83

either (singular), 23, 33

either . . . or, 7–8, 299

-elect, hyphen with, 89

Electronic sources. *See* Web sources

elicit, illicit, 292

Ellipsis mark, 77; 114–15 (MLA); 180–81 (APA); 236–37 (*Chicago*)

E-mail addresses, division of, 89

emigrate from, immigrate to, 292

Emphasis, subordination for, 15–16

Empty phrases, avoiding, 4–5

Endnotes. *See Chicago* papers, footnotes or endnotes; Information notes (MLA)

End punctuation, 74–75

enthused, 292

-er ending (*faster, stronger*), 41–42

ESL (English as a second language). *See* Multilingual grammar concerns

-es, -s

    spelling rules, for plurals, 86–87

    as verb ending, 22

-est ending (*fastest, strongest*), 41–42

et al. ("and others"), 83; 127, 138 (MLA); 187 (APA); 244 (*Chicago*); 273, 275 (CSE)

etc. ("and so forth"), 83, 292

Evaluating sources, 94–102

even, placement of, 12–13

everybody, everyone, everything (singular), 23, 33

everyone, every one, 292

Evidence, 109–10 (MLA); 176–77 (APA); 232–33 (*Chicago*)

ex-, hyphen with, 89

except. See *accept, except*, 288

Exclamation points, 74–75

    and MLA citation, 126

    no comma with, 64

    with quotation marks, 72

Exclamations. *See* Interjections

Executive summary, MLA citation of, 147

Expletives *there, it*, 300

    and subject following verb, 24, 54

    and subject-verb agreement, 24

    and wordy sentences, 5

F

Facebook. *See* Social media, citing

Facts

    integrating, 117–19 (MLA); 184 (APA); 240 (*Chicago*)

    scientific, and verb tense, 31

family. See Collective nouns

farther, further, 292

fewer, less, 292

Figures. *See* Numbers; Visuals

Files, managing, 103, 105

firstly, 292

First-person point of view, 10

Focus, of paper, 91, 306

Footnotes or endnotes, 166–67 (MLA); 219, 224 (APA); 233–34, 240–41, 264 (*Chicago*)

for. See Coordinating conjunctions; Prepositions

Foreign words, italics for, 85

for example, no colon after, 67

Format, manuscript, 167–69
(MLA); 217–21 (APA);
262–65 (*Chicago*); 284–86
(CSE)
Fractions, 84, 89
Fragments, sentence, 42–44
Full stop. *See* Periods
further. *See* *farther, further*, 292
Fused sentences. *See* Run-on
sentences
Future perfect tense, 30, 49
Future progressive forms, 31,
48–49
Future tense, 30, 48

G

Gender, and pronoun
agreement, 19, 33
Gender-neutral language, 19–20
Generic *he*, 19–20, 293
Generic nouns, 33–34
Geographic names, *the* with, 53
Gerund phrases, 300
Gerunds, 38–39, 300
Global revision, checklist
for, 306
Glossary of grammatical terms,
298–305
Glossary of usage, 288–97
good, well, 41
graduate, 292
Grammar, multilingual
concerns with. *See* Multi-
lingual grammar concerns
Graphic narrative, MLA citation
of, 141
Graphs. *See* Visuals
grow, 292

H

hanged, hung, 293
hardly, 12–13, 293
has vs. *have*. *See* Agreement of
subject and verb
have
forming tenses with, 49
irregular forms of, 28
and perfect tenses, 30–31, 49
and subject-verb agreement,
22–26

Headings, in paper, 168 (MLA);
219–20 (APA); 264
(*Chicago*); 285 (CSE)
he, him, his, sexist use of,
19–20, 33, 293
Helping verbs
defined, 300
and forming verb tenses, 30
multilingual concerns with,
47–49
her vs. *she*, 36–39
he said, she said, comma with,
62, 72–73
he/she, his/her, 77
he vs. *him*, 36–39
hisself (nonstandard), 293
hopefully, 293
however
at beginning of sentence,
293
comma with, 61
semicolon with, 65
Humanities, writing in. *See*
Chicago papers; MLA
papers
hung. *See* *hanged, hung*, 293
Hyphens, 88–89
in e-mail addresses, 89
in URLs, 89; 168, 169 (MLA);
221 (APA); 264 (*Chicago*);
286 (CSE)
in word divisions, 89

I

I
vs. *me*, 36–39
point of view, 10
shifts with *you, he*, or *she*,
avoiding, 10
ibid. ("in the same place"), 241
Idioms (common expressions),
55
i.e. ("that is"), 83
-ie, -ei, spelling rule, 86
if clauses, 32
illicit. *See* *elicit, illicit*, 292
illusion. *See* *allusion,
illusion*, 289
Illustrated work, MLA citation
of, 141
immigrate. *See* *emigrate from,
immigrate to*, 292

immoral. See *amoral, immoral*,
     289
Imperative mood, 32
imply, infer, 293
in, in idioms (common
     expressions), 55
Incomplete comparison, 9–10
Incomplete construction, 8–10
Incomplete sentences. *See*
     Fragments, sentence
Indefinite articles. *See a, an*
Indefinite pronouns
     agreement of verb with, 23
     as antecedents, 33
     apostrophe with, 68
     defined, 300
Indenting
     in APA reference list, 220–21
     in *Chicago* bibliography, 265
     in *Chicago* notes, 264
     in CSE reference list, 285
     of long quotations, 71;
          115, 122–23, 168 (MLA);
          181–82, 218 (APA); 237,
          263 (*Chicago*); 284 (CSE)
     in MLA works cited list, 169
Independent clauses
     colon between, 66
     and comma with coordinat-
          ing conjunction, 57
     defined, 300
     and run-on sentences,
          44–47
     semicolon between,
          64–65
Indicative mood, 32
Indirect objects, 37, 300
Indirect questions, 74
Indirect quotations, 71, 73
Indirect sources, 131–32, 142
     (MLA); 191 (APA); 249
     (*Chicago*)
infer. See *imply, infer*, 293
Infinitive phrases, 300
Infinitives
     case of pronouns with, 38
     defined, 300
     split, 14–15
Inflated phrases, avoiding,
     4–5
Information, for essay. *See also*
     Sources
     finding, 92–94
     managing, 102–03

Information notes (MLA),
     166–67
-ing verb ending. *See* Gerunds;
     Present participles
in, into, 293
in regards to, 293
Inserted material, in quota-
     tions. *See* Brackets
Integrating sources, 104–05;
     113–24 (MLA); 180–84
     (APA); 236–40
     (*Chicago*)
Intensive pronouns, 301
Interjections (exclamations),
     62, 301
Internet. *See also* URLs; Web
     sources
     capitalization of terms
          for, 80
     scanning, 98–99
     searching, 93–94
Interrogative pronouns,
     39, 301
In-text citations. *See also*
     Footnotes or endnotes;
     Integrating sources
     APA style, 185–91
     Chicago style, 240–62
     CSE style, 272–75
     MLA style, 124–33
     parentheses with, 76
into. See *in, into*, 293
Intransitive and transitive
     verbs, 50, 304
Introductory word groups,
     comma with, 58
Inverted sentence order
     with expletives *there, it*,
          24, 54
     and subject-verb agreement,
          24
irregardless, 293
Irregular verbs, 26–29,
     47–48, 303
Issue and volume numbers
     in APA reference list, 195,
          200, 202
     in *Chicago* notes and
          bibliography, 250, 252
     in MLA works cited,
          142–44, 146
is vs. *are*. See Agreement of
     subject and verb
is when, is where, avoiding, 12

it
  as expletive (placeholder), 54, 300
  indefinite use of, 35
  as subject of sentence, 53–54
Italics, 84–85; 136, 168 (MLA); 194, 218, 221 (APA); 263 (*Chicago*); 286 (CSE)
its, it's, 69, 70, 294

J

Jargon, avoiding, 17–18
Journal articles. *See* Articles in periodicals
Journals. *See* Periodicals
jury. See Collective nouns
just, placement of, 12–13

K

Keywords, in APA abstracts, 219, 223
kind of, sort of, 294

L

Labels. *See also* Captions, for figures and visuals
  for people, using with caution, 20
Language
  appropriate, 17–20
  biased, avoiding, 19–20
  borrowed. *See* Citing sources; Plagiarism, avoiding
  clichés, avoiding, 18–19
  direct, 4–5
  idioms (common expressions), 55
  jargon, avoiding, 17–18
  offensive, avoiding, 20
  plain, 4–5
  sexist, avoiding, 19–20
  slang, avoiding, 19
  wordy, 4–5
Latin abbreviations, 74, 83
lay, lie; laying, lying, 27
lead, led, 294
learn, teach, 294
leave, let, 294

less. See fewer, less, 292
let. See leave, let, 294
Letter in a published collection
  Chicago citation of, 255
  citation at a glance, 256–57
Letters of the alphabet
  capitalizing, 79–81
  as letters, italics for, 85
  as letters, plural of, 69
liable, 294
Library resources, 92–94. *See also* Web sources
lie, lay; lying, laying, 27
like, no comma after, 63
like, as, 294
Limiting modifiers (*only, almost*, etc.), 12–13
Line spacing, 167 (MLA); 218 (APA); 263 (*Chicago*); 284 (CSE)
Linking verbs
  adjectives after, 40
  defined, 301
  pronouns after, 37
List of sources. *See* Bibliography, *Chicago* style; Reference list (APA); Reference list (CSE); Works cited list (MLA)
Lists. *See also* Series
  with colon, 66
  with dash, 75
Literary present tense, 11, 31, 122
Literature, writing about. *See also* MLA papers, literary quotations in sample pages, 172–73
Literature review (APA style), sample pages from, 222–26
Long quotations. *See* Indenting, of long quotations
loose, lose, 294
-ly ending, on adverbs, 40
lying vs. *laying*, 27

M

Magazine articles. *See* Articles in periodicals
Magazines. *See* Periodicals

Main clauses. *See* Independent clauses
Main point. *See* Thesis
Main verbs, 47–48, 305. *See also* Verbs
man, mankind, sexist use of, 20
Manuscript formats, 167–69 (MLA); 217–21 (APA); 262–65 (*Chicago*); 284–86 (CSE)
Maps. *See* Visuals
Margins, 167 (MLA); 218 (APA); 263 (*Chicago*); 284 (CSE)
Mass nouns. *See* Noncount nouns
mathematics (singular), 25
may. See can, may, 290
may, as modal verb, 49–50
maybe, may be, 294
may of, might of (nonstandard), 294
Measurement, units of
abbreviations for, 83
and subject-verb agreement, 24
media, medium, 294
Medium of publication, in MLA works cited list, 137
Memo, sample, 229
me vs. *I,* 36–39
might, as modal verb, 49–50
might of (nonstandard). See *may of, might of,* 294
Minor ideas. *See* Subordination
Misplaced modifiers, 12–15. *See also* Modifiers
Missing words. *See* Needed words
Mixed constructions, 11–12
MLA Handbook for Writers of Research Papers, 124, 167
MLA papers, 107–73
citation at a glance
article from a database, 146
article in a journal, 144
book, 151
selection from an anthology or a collection, 154–55
short work from a Web site, 159
citations, in-text, 124–33

directory to models for, 125
models for, 125–33
evidence for, 109–10
information notes (optional), 166–67
literary quotations in, 121–24
formatting and citing, 122–24
introducing, 121
present tense for, 31, 122
shifts in tense, avoiding, 122
manuscript format, 167–69
numbers in, 83
plagiarism, avoiding, 110–13
sample pages, 170–73
signal phrases in, 116–19, 124–33
sources in
citing, 110–13, 124–66
integrating, 113–24
synthesizing, 119–21
uses of, 109–10
supporting arguments in, 109–10, 119–21
tenses in, 31, 118, 122
thesis in, 107–09
URLs in, 137, 157, 168, 169
works cited list
directory to models for, 134–35
formatting, 169
general guidelines for, 136–37
medium of publication in, 137
models for, 137–66
sample, 171, 173
URLs in, 137, 157, 168, 169
Modal verbs, 49–50, 301. *See also* Helping verbs
Modern Language Association. *See* MLA papers
Modifiers
adjectives as, 40
adverbs as, 41–42
commas with, 58–59
dangling, 13–14
defined, 301
of gerunds, 38–39

Modifiers (*cont.*)
  limiting, 12–13
  misplaced, 12–15
  phrases as, 15–16
  redundant, 4
  restrictive (essential)
    and nonrestrictive
    (nonessential), 59–61
  split infinitives, 14–15
  squinting, 12–13
Mood of verbs, 32
more, *most* (comparative and
  superlative), 41–42
moreover
  comma with, 61
  semicolon with, 65
Multilingual grammar
  concerns, 47–55
  articles (*a*, *an*, *the*), 50–53
  idioms (common
    expressions), 55
  nouns, count and noncount,
    50–52
  omitted subjects, expletives,
    or verbs, 53–54
  prepositions, 55
  repeated subjects, objects, or
    adverbs, 54
  verbs, 47–50
Multimedia sources, citing,
  160–64 (MLA); 211,
  213–16 (APA); 258–61
  (*Chicago*)
must, as modal verb, 49–50
must of (nonstandard), 294
myself, 37, 294–95

N

Name-year system
  in APA papers, 185
  in CSE papers, 271, 285
Narrowing a subject, 91
N.B. ("note well"), 83
n.d. ("no date"), 137, 159
  (MLA); 190, 212 (APA)
nearly, placement of, 12–13
Needed words, 8–10
  articles (*a*, *an*, *the*), 50–53
  in comparisons, 9–10
  in compound structures,
    8–9
  it, 53–54

  in parallel structures, 8
  subjects, 53–54
  that, 9
  there, 54
  verbs, 53
Negatives, double. See
  hardly, 293
neither (singular), 23, 33
neither . . . nor, 7–8, 299
nevertheless
  comma with, 61
  semicolon with, 65
news (singular), 25
Newspapers. See Periodicals
News sites, 94
nobody (singular), 23, 33
Noncount nouns, 51–52
none (singular or plural), 23
Nonrestrictive (nonessential)
  elements, commas with,
  59–61
Nonsexist language,
  19–20
no one (singular), 23, 33
nor
  comma with, 57
  as coordinating conjunction,
    57, 299
  and parallel structure,
    7–8
  and subject-verb agreement,
    23
not, placement of, 12–13
Notes. See APA papers, footnotes in; *Chicago* papers,
  footnotes or endnotes;
  Information notes (MLA)
Note taking, 103–05
not only . . . but also, 7–8, 299
Noun clauses, 301
Noun equivalent, 302
Noun markers, 50
Nouns. See also Nouns, types of
  adjectives with, 40, 298
  articles with, 50–53
  capitalizing, 79–80
  defined, 301
  of direct address, comma
    with, 62
  plural of, 86–87
  renaming other nouns. See
    Appositives
  shifts between singular and
    plural, avoiding, 10

Nouns, types of. *See also* Nouns
    collective (*audience, family,*
        etc.), 24, 34
    common vs. proper, 79–80
    count, 50–51
    generic, 33–34
    noncount, 51–52
    possessive, 68
Novels
    capitalizing titles of, 80
    citing, 122–23
    italics for titles of, 84
    quoting from, 122–23
nowheres (nonstandard), 295
no, yes, commas with, 62
N.p. ("no publisher"), in MLA
        works cited list, 136, 159
n. pag. ("no pagination"), in
        MLA works cited list,
        137, 146
number. See *amount, number,*
        289
Number and person
    shifts in, avoiding, 10
    and subject-verb agreement,
        22–26
Numbering. *See also* Page
        numbers
    of *Chicago* footnotes and
        endnotes, 264
    of CSE references, 271, 285
Numbers
    italics for, 85
    plural of, 69
    spelled out vs. numerals,
        83–84
Nursing practice paper, sample
        pages from, 227–29

O

Object complements, 302
Objective case
    of personal pronouns, 36–39
    whom, 39
Objects
    direct, 300
    indirect, 300
    of infinitives, 38
    objective case for, 36
    of prepositions, 303
    pronouns as, 36
    repetition of, avoiding, 54

Offensive language,
        avoiding, 20
off of (nonstandard), 295
Omissions, indicated by
    apostrophe, 69
    ellipsis mark, 77; 114–15
        (MLA); 180–81 (APA);
        236–37 (*Chicago*)
on, in idioms (common
        expressions), 55
one of the, 25
Online sources. *See* Web sources
only, placement of, 12–13
only one of the, 25
or
    comma with, 57
    as coordinating conjunction,
        57, 299
    parallelism and, 7–8
    and subject-verb agreement,
        23
Organization, 109–10 (MLA);
        176 (APA); 232 (*Chicago*)
ought to, as modal verb, 49–50
Ownership. *See* Possessive case

P

Page numbers
    citing, 111, 124, 137 (MLA);
        178, 185–86, 195, 221
        (APA); 241, 246, 250, 252
        (*Chicago*)
    in papers, 167 (MLA); 218
        (APA); 262 (*Chicago*); 284
        (CSE)
    sources without, 131, 146
        (MLA); 189 (APA)
Paired ideas, parallelism and,
        7–8
Parallelism, 7–8
Paraphrases
    avoiding plagiarism and,
        112–13 (MLA); 179–80
        (APA); 235–36 (*Chicago*)
    integrating, 104–05; 117
        (MLA); 182–84 (APA);
        238–40 (*Chicago*)
    no quotation marks for, 71
    and note taking, 103–05
Parentheses, 76
    capitalizing sentence in, 81
    no comma before, 64

Parenthetical citations. *See*
  In-text citations
Parenthetical elements
  commas with, 61
  dashes with, 75
Participial phrases, 16, 302. *See
  also* Past participles;
  Present participles
Participles. *See* Past participles;
  Present participles
Parts of speech, 302
  adjectives, 298
  adverbs, 298
  conjunctions, 299
  interjections (exclamations),
    301
  nouns, 301
  prepositions, 303
  pronouns, 303
  verbs, 305
passed, *past*, 295
Passive voice
  vs. active voice, 6–7, 50, 298
  appropriate uses of, 6–7
  forming, 50
past. See *passed*, *past*, 295
Past participles
  defined, 302
  of irregular verbs, 26–29
  and passive voice, 50
  and perfect tenses, 49
  of regular verbs, 26
Past perfect tense, 30, 31, 49
Past progressive forms, 31, 48
Past tense, 30
  in APA papers, 183, 185
  and -d, -ed endings, 26
  of irregular verbs, 26–29, 48
  vs. past perfect, 31, 49
  of regular verbs, 26, 48
Patchwriting, avoiding,
    112–13 (MLA); 179–80
    (APA)
Percentages, numerals for, 84
Perfect tenses, 30–31, 49
Periodicals. *See also* Articles in
    periodicals
  capitalizing titles of, 80; 136,
    168 (MLA); 194, 218, 221
    (APA); 286 (CSE)
  italics for titles of, 84; 136,
    168 (MLA); 194 (APA);
    263 (*Chicago*); 286 (CSE)

Periods, 74
  and ellipsis mark, 77; 114
    (MLA); 181 (APA); 237
    (*Chicago*)
  to end a sentence, 74
  with parenthetical citations,
    72; 170 (MLA); 182 (APA)
  with quotation marks, 71–72
Personal pronouns
  case of, 36–39
  defined, 302
Personal titles. *See* Titles of
    persons
Person and number
  shifts in, avoiding, 10
  and subject-verb agreement,
    22–26
Persons, names of. *See* Nouns
Photographs. *See* Visuals
Phrases, 302
  absolute, 298
  appositive, 299
  empty or inflated, 4–5
  fragmented, 43–44
  gerund, 300
  infinitive, 300
  participial, 16, 302
  prepositional, 303
  subordination and, 15–16
physics (singular), 25
Places, names of. *See* Nouns
Plagiarism, avoiding
  in APA papers, 177–80
  in *Chicago* papers, 233–36
  and integrating sources,
    104–05
  in MLA papers, 110–13
  and taking notes, 103–05
  and Web sources, 103, 105
  working bibliography
    for, 103
Plays
  capitalizing titles of, 80
  citing, 123–24
  italics for titles of, 84
  quoting from, 123–24
Plurals. *See also* Agreement of
    pronoun and antecedent;
    Agreement of subject and
    verb; Singular vs. plural
  of abbreviations, 69
  of compound nouns (*father-
    in-law* etc.), 87

of letters used as letters, 69
of numbers used as
    numbers, 69
spelling of, 86–87
of words used as words, 69
plus, 295
p.m., a.m., PM, AM, 82
Podcast, citing, 160 (MLA); 211
    (APA); 258 (*Chicago*); 283
    (CSE)
Poems
    capitalizing titles of, 80
    citing, 123
    quotation marks for titles of,
        71; 136, 168 (MLA); 218,
        221 (APA); 263 (*Chicago*)
    quoting from, 123
Point of view, 10
politics (singular), 25
Popular sources, vs. scholarly, 97
Possessive case
    apostrophe and, 68
    with gerund, 38–39
Possessive pronouns
    defined, 302
    no apostrophe in, 70
precede, proceed, 295
Predicate, 302
Predicate adjective. *See* Subject
    complements
Predicate noun. *See* Subject
    complements
Prefixes, hyphen after, 89
Prepositional phrases, 303
Prepositions
    at, in, on, to show time and
        place, 55
    defined, 303
    in idioms (common
        expressions), 55
    repeating, for parallel
        structure, 8
Present participles
    defined, 302
    and progressive verb forms,
        48, 49
Present perfect tense, 30, 49;
    118 (MLA); 183, 185
    (APA); 239 (*Chicago*)
Present progressive form, 30, 48
Present tense, 30, 48
    in *Chicago* papers, 239
    in MLA papers, 118

subject-verb agreement in,
    22–26
in writing about literature,
    31, 122
in writing about science, 31
Pretentious language, avoiding,
    17–18
Primary source from a Web
    site, *Chicago* citation of,
    260–61
principal, principle, 295
proceed. See precede, proceed, 295
Progressive verb forms, 30–31,
    48, 49
Pronoun/adjectives, 50
Pronoun-antecedent
    agreement, 32–34
Pronoun case, 36–39
    I vs. *me*, etc., 36–39
    who vs. *whom*, 39
    you vs. *your*, etc., 38–39
Pronoun reference, 34–36
Pronouns
    agreement of verbs with,
        22–26
    agreement with antecedent,
        32–34
    as appositives, 37
    case (*I* vs. *me*, etc.), 36–39
    defined, 303
    as objects, 36
    possessive, 68–69, 70
    reference of, 34–36
    shifts in person and number,
        avoiding, 10
    singular vs. plural, 32–34
    as subjects, 36
    who, whom, 39
Proof. *See* Evidence
Proper nouns
    capitalizing, 79–80
    the with, 53
Proposal, sample, 229
*Publication Manual of the
    American Psychological
    Association*, 184, 217. *See
    also* APA papers
Punctuation, 57–77
    apostrophe, 67–70
    brackets, 76–77; 115 (MLA);
        181 (APA); 237 (*Chicago*)
    colon. *See* Colons
    comma. *See* Commas

Punctuation (*cont.*)
  dash, 75
  ellipsis mark, 77; 114–15
    (MLA); 180–81 (APA);
    236–37 (*Chicago*)
  exclamation point. *See*
    Exclamation points
  parentheses, 64, 76, 81
  period. *See* Periods
  question mark. *See* Question
    mark
  quotation marks. *See*
    Quotation marks
  with quotation marks, 71–73
  semicolon. *See* Semicolon
  slash, 77
Purpose and audience,
  evaluating, 101

Q

Quantifiers, with noncount
  nouns, 52
Question mark, 74
  and MLA citations, 126
  no comma with, 64
  with quotation marks, 72
Questions, research, 91–92;
  107–09 (MLA); 175–76
  (APA); 231–32 (*Chicago*)
Quotation marks, 70–73. *See
  also* Quotations
  to avoid plagiarism, 111–12
    (MLA); 178–79 (APA); 234
    (*Chicago*)
  with direct quotations (exact
    language), 70–71
  misuses of, 73
  not used with indented
    (long) quotations, 71
  not used with paraphrases
    and summaries, 71
  other punctuation with,
    71–73
  single, 70
  with titles of works, 71;
    136, 168 (MLA); 194, 218
    (APA); 263 (*Chicago*); 286
    (CSE)
  with words used as words, 71
*quotation, quote. See quote,
  quotation,* 295

Quotations. *See also* Quotation
  marks
  accuracy of, 114–15 (MLA);
    180–81 (APA); 236–37
    (*Chicago*)
  appropriate use of, 113–15
    (MLA); 180–82 (APA);
    236–37 (*Chicago*)
  brackets with, 115 (MLA);
    181 (APA); 237 (*Chicago*)
  capitalization in, 81
  citing. *See* Citing sources
  context for, 119 (MLA);
    183–84 (APA); 239–40
    (*Chicago*)
  direct and indirect,
    70–71
  dropped, avoiding, 116
    (MLA); 182 (APA); 238
    (*Chicago*)
  ellipsis mark with, 77;
    114–15 (MLA); 180–81
    (APA); 236–37 (*Chicago*)
  embedding, 119 (MLA);
    183–84 (APA); 239–40
    (*Chicago*)
  integrating, 104–05; 113–24
    (MLA); 180–84 (APA);
    236–40 (*Chicago*)
  literary, 121–24
  long (indented), 71; 115,
    122–23, 168 (MLA);
    181–82, 218 (APA); 237,
    263 (*Chicago*)
  punctuation of, 62, 70–73
  quotation marks for, 70–71;
    111–12 (MLA); 178–79
    (APA); 234 (*Chicago*)
  within quotations, 70
  sic for errors in, 77; 115
    (MLA); 181 (APA); 237
    (*Chicago*)
  with signal phrase, 182–84
    (APA)
  synthesizing, 119–21
quoted in (qtd. in), for a source
  used in another source,
  131–32, 142 (MLA); 249
  (*Chicago*). *See also* cited in
quote, quotation, 295
Quotes. *See* Quotations
Qur'an. *See* Sacred texts (Bible
  and Qur'an)

R

Ratios, colon with, 66–67
Reading
    active and critical, 99–101
    evaluating sources, 94–102
    previewing sources, 98–99
real, really, 295
reason . . . is because
        (nonstandard), 12
reason why (nonstandard), 295
Redundancies, 4
Reference list (APA), 191–217,
        220–21
    directory to models for,
        192–93
    formatting, 220–21
    general guidelines for,
        194–95
    models for, 195–217
    sample, 226
Reference list (CSE), 275–83
    directory to models for, 274
    documentation systems
        for, 271
    formatting, 285–86
    models for, 275–83
    numbering, 271, 285
    organizing, 285
Reference of pronouns, 34–36
Reference works, 93
Reflexive pronouns, 301
Regular verbs, 26, 47–48, 303.
        See also Verbs
Relative adverbs, 303
    introducing adjective
        clauses, 54
Relative pronouns
    agreement with verbs, 24–25
    defined, 303
    introducing adjective
        clauses, 54
    who, whom, 39
Relevance, of sources, 94,
        100–01
Repetition
    of function words, for
        parallel structure, 8
    unnecessary, 4, 54
Reposted source, MLA citation
        of, 140
Requests, subjunctive mood
        for, 32

Researched writing. *See also*
        Researching a topic
    APA papers, 175–229
    Chicago papers, 231–69
    CSE papers, 271–86
    MLA papers, 107–73
    sample pages, 170–73 (MLA);
        222–29 (APA); 266–69
        (*Chicago*)
Researching a topic, 91–105. *See
        also* Researched writing
    bibliography, working, 103
    evaluating sources, 94–102
    finding sources, 92–94, 100
    getting started, 91–92
    keeping track of sources,
        103, 105
    managing information,
        102–03
    and note taking, 103–05
    reading critically, 99–101
    research questions, 91–92
    search strategy for, 93
respectfully, respectively, 295
Restrictive (essential) elements,
        no commas with, 59–61,
        63
Review of the literature, sample
        pages from (APA), 222–26
Revision, checklist for, 306
Running heads, 167 (MLA);
        218, 222, 227 (APA)
Run-on sentences, 44–47

S

-s
    and apostrophe, 68–70
    and spelling, 86–87
    as verb ending, 22
Sacred texts (Bible, Qur'an)
    citing, 66–67; 133, 153
        (MLA); 191, 210 (APA);
        248 (*Chicago*)
    no italics for, 85
    punctuation with, 67
Sample student writing, 170–73
        (MLA); 222–29 (APA);
        266–69 (*Chicago*)
Scholarly sources
    identifying, 96, 98
    vs. popular sources, 96–97

Science, writing about. *See* CSE
    papers

Scientific facts, and verb tense, 31

*Scientific Style and Format: The
    CSE Manual for Authors,
    Editors, and Publishers*,
    271, 284. *See also* CSE
    papers

Scores, numerals for, 84

Searching for information. *See*
    Researching a topic

Second-person point of
    view, 10

Semicolon, 64–66
    with commas, 64–65
    to fix run-on sentences,
      45, 46
    and independent clauses,
      64–65
    misuse of, 65–66
    with quotation marks, 72
    with series, 65
    transitional expressions
      with, 65

sensual, sensuous, 295

Sentence fragments, 42–44

Sentences. *See also* Sentence
    types
    choppy, combining, 15–16
    defined, 303
    fragments, 42–44
    incomplete, 42–44
    inverted, 54
    logical, 12
    run-on, 44–47
    variety in, 15–17
    wordy, 4–5

Sentence structure
    mixed constructions, 11–12
    multilingual concerns with,
      53–54
    simplifying, 5

Sentence types
    complex, 299
    compound, 299
    compound-complex, 299
    simple, 304

Series. *See also* Lists
    commas with, 58
    parallelism and, 7
    parentheses with, 76
    semicolons with, 65

set, sit, 296

Sexist language, avoiding,
    19–20

shall, as modal verb, 49–50

she, her, hers, sexist use of, 19

she said, he said, comma with,
    62, 72–73

she vs. *her*, 36–39

Shifts, avoiding, 10, 122

Short stories
    capitalizing titles of, 80; 136,
      168 (MLA); 196, 218, 221
      (APA); 263 (*Chicago*)
    citing, 122–23
    quotation marks for titles
      of, 71; 136, 168 (MLA);
      196, 218, 221 (APA); 263
      (*Chicago*)
    quoting from, 122–23

should, as modal verb, 49–50

should of (nonstandard), 296

sic, 77; 115 (MLA); 181 (APA);
    237 (*Chicago*)

Signal phrases, 116–19, 124–33
    (MLA); 182–84, 185–91
    (APA); 238–40 (*Chicago*)

Simple sentences, 304

Simple tenses, 30, 48

since, 296

Singular vs. plural
    antecedents, 32–34
    nouns, 22–26
    pronouns, 32–34
    subjects, 22–26

sit. See *set, sit*, 296

site. See *cite, site*, 290

Slang, avoiding, 19

Slash, 77

so. *See* Coordinating
    conjunctions

Social media, citing, 131,
    165–66 (MLA); 190, 216
    (APA); 261–62 (*Chicago*)

Social sciences, writing in the.
    See APA papers; *Chicago*
    papers

Software. *See* Word processing
    programs

some (singular or plural), 23

somebody, someone, something
    (singular), 23, 33

Songs, quotation marks for
    titles of, 71

sort of. See *kind of, sort of*, 294

Sources. *See also* Web sources
    citing. *See* Citing sources
    documenting. *See* Citing
      sources

evaluating, 94–102
finding, 92–94
integrating, 104–05; 113–24
   (MLA); 180–84 (APA);
   236–40 (*Chicago*)
introducing. *See* Signal
   phrases
keeping track of, 103, 105
list of. *See* Bibliography,
   Chicago style; Reference
   list (APA); Reference list
   (CSE); Works cited list
   (MLA)
popular, 97
quoted in another source,
   131–32, 142 (MLA); 191
   (APA); 249 (*Chicago*)
scholarly, 94, 96, 98
synthesizing, 119–21
uses of, 92–93, 95; 109–10
   (MLA); 176–77 (APA);
   232–33 (*Chicago*)
"So what?" question, 109
Spacing. *See* Line spacing
Specific nouns, *the* with, 51
Spelling, 86–88
Split infinitives, 14–15
Sponsor, of Web site
   in *Chicago* notes and
      bibliography, 255, 260
   and evaluating sources,
      94, 101
   in MLA works cited, 136, 159
Squinting modifiers, 12–13. *See
   also* Misplaced modifiers
Statements contrary to fact, 32
statistics (singular), 25
Stereotypes, avoiding, 19–20
Subject, of research paper,
   focusing, 91–92
Subject, of sentence
   and agreement with verb,
      22–26
   case of, 36, 39
   defined, 304
   following verb, 54, 304
   identifying, 22–23
   of infinitive, 38
   naming the actor (active
      voice), 6, 50
   naming the receiver (passive
      voice), 6–7, 50
   pronoun as, 36
   repeated, avoiding, 54
   required in sentences, 53–54

separated from verb, 22–23
singular vs. plural, 22–26
understood (*you*), 53, 305
Subject complements
   adjectives as, 40
   case of pronouns as, 36, 37
   defined, 304
   with linking verbs, 304
Subjective case, of pronouns, 36
   who vs. *whom*, 39
Subject-verb agreement. *See*
   Agreement of subject and
   verb
Subjunctive mood, 32
Subordinate clauses
   adjective (beginning with
      who, that, etc.), 298
   adverb (beginning with *if,
      when*, etc.), 298
   avoiding repeated elements
      in, 54
   defined, 304
   fragmented, 43
   with independent clauses,
      299
   noun, 301
Subordinating conjunctions,
   304
Subordination
   for combining sentences,
      15–16
   for fixing sentence
      fragments, 42–44
   for sentence variety, 15–16
Subtitles of works. *See* Titles of
   works
such as
   no colon after, 67
   no comma after, 63
Suffixes, hyphen with, 88–89
Summary
   in annotated bibliography,
      101–02
   avoiding plagiarism and,
      112–13 (MLA); 179–80
      (APA); 235–36 (*Chicago*)
   integrating, 104–05; 117
      (MLA); 182 (APA);
      238–40 (*Chicago*)
   no quotation marks for,
      71
   and note taking, 103–05
Superlative form of adjectives
   and adverbs, 41–42
Support. *See* Evidence

suppose to (nonstandard), 296
sure and (nonstandard), 296
Synthesizing sources,
    119–21

T

Tables. *See* Visuals
take. See *bring, take*, 290
teach. See *learn, teach*, 294
team. *See* Collective nouns
Tenses, verb, 29–32
    and agreement with subject,
        22–26
    in APA papers, 183, 185
    in *Chicago* papers, 239
    in literature papers, 11,
        31, 122
    in MLA papers, 118, 122
    multilingual concerns with,
        48–49
    in science papers, 31
    shifts in, avoiding, 11, 122
than
    in comparisons, 9–10
    no comma before, 64
    parallelism with, 7–8
    pronoun after, 38
than, then, 296
that
    agreement of verb with,
        24–25
    needed word, 9
    vague reference of, 35
    vs. *which*, 60, 296, 297
    vs. *who*, 297
the, multilingual concerns with,
        50–53
    with geographic names, 53
    omission of, 51–52
    with proper nouns, 53
their
    misuse of, with singular
        antecedent, 32–34
    vs. *there, they're*, 296
theirselves (nonstandard), 296
them vs. *they*, 36–39
them vs. *those*, 296
then, than. See *than, then*, 296
there
    as expletive (placeholder),
        300
    and subject following verb,
        24, 54

therefore
    comma with, 61
    semicolon with, 65
there, their, they're, 296
Thesis
    in APA papers, 175–76
    in *Chicago* papers, 231–32
    in MLA papers, 107–09
    testing and revising, 108–09
they
    indefinite use of, 35
    vs. *I* or *you*, 10
    misuse of, with singular
        antecedent, 32–34
    vs. *them*, 36–39
they're. See *there, their,
    they're*, 296
Third-person point of view, 10
this, vague reference of, 35
Time
    abbreviations for, 82
    colon with, 66–67
    numerals for, 84
Title page
    for APA papers, 218,
        222, 227
    for *Chicago* papers, 262, 266
    for CSE papers, 284
    for MLA papers (optional),
        167
Titles of persons
    abbreviations with names, 82
    capitalizing, 80
    comma with, 63
Titles of works
    capitalizing, 80; 136, 168
        (MLA); 194, 218, 221
        (APA); 263 (*Chicago*); 286
        (CSE)
    in citations with unknown
        authors, 126, 138–39
        (MLA); 187, 196–97 (APA);
        244 (*Chicago*)
    italics for, 84–85; 136, 168
        (MLA); 194, 218, 221
        (APA); 263 (*Chicago*); 286
        (CSE)
    quotation marks for, 71; 136,
        168 (MLA); 194, 218, 221
        (APA); 263 (*Chicago*); 286
        (CSE)
    treated as singular, 25–26
Topic, of research paper, 91–92
to, too, two, 296
toward, towards, 296

Transitional expressions
  commas with, 61
  list of, 65
  semicolon with, 65
Transitive verbs, 304
Trite expressions. *See* Clichés,
  avoiding
troop. See Collective nouns
try and (nonstandard), 296
Twitter. *See* Social media, citing
two. See *to, too, two,* 296

U

Underlining. *See* Italics
Understood subject (*you*),
  53, 305
unique, 42
Unknown author
  citing in APA papers, 187,
    189, 196–97
  citing in *Chicago* papers, 244
  citing in MLA papers, 126,
    138–39
Uploaded materials, MLA
  citation of, 140
URLs
  breaking, 89; 168, 169
    (MLA); 221 (APA); 264
    (*Chicago*); 286 (CSE)
  in citations, 137, 157 (MLA);
    195, 210–17 (APA); 243,
    255, 258–62 (*Chicago*)
Usage, glossary of, 288–97
use to (nonstandard), 297
Using sources, 92–93, 95
  in APA papers, 176–77
  in *Chicago* papers, 232–33
  in MLA papers, 109–10
us vs. *we,* 36–39
utilize, 297

V

Vague reference of *this, that,*
  which, 35
Variety
  in sentences, 15–17
  in signal phrases, 118 (MLA);
    183 (APA); 239 (*Chicago*)
Verbal phrases, 305
  dangling, 13–14
Verbs. *See also* Verbs, types of

active, 5–7, 298
adverbs as modifiers of, 41
agreement with subjects,
  22–26
be, forms of, vs. active, 5–6
in conditional sentences, 32,
  49–50
-d, -ed ending on, 26
defined, 305
forms of, 47–48
mood of, 32
multilingual concerns with,
  47–50
needed, 53
without objects, 50, 304
passive, 5–7, 298
-s ending on, 22
separated from subjects,
  22–23
shifts in tense, avoiding,
  11, 122
in signal phrases, 118 (MLA);
  183 (APA); 239 (*Chicago*)
with singular vs. plural
  subjects, 22–26
standard forms of, 26–27
strong, vs. *be* and passive
  verbs, 5–6
before subjects (inverted
  sentences), 24, 54
tenses of. *See* Tenses, verb
Verbs, types of. *See also* Verbs
  irregular and regular, 26–29,
    303
  linking, 40, 301
  modal (*can, might,* etc.),
    49–50, 301
  transitive and intransitive, 304
Video, online, citing, 140, 161
  (MLA); 211, 213 (APA);
  259 (*Chicago*); 283 (CSE)
Video game, citing, 161 (MLA);
  215 (APA)
Visuals
  in APA papers, 211, 213–16,
    220
  in *Chicago* papers, 258–62,
    263–64
  in CSE papers, 285
  in MLA papers, 131, 160–64,
    168–69
Voice
  active vs. passive, 6–7, 50
  appropriate, in writing,
    17–20

W

wait for, wait on, 297
was vs. *were*
  and subject-verb agreement, 22
  and subjunctive mood, 32
ways, 297
we
  vs. *us*, 36–39
  vs. *you* or *they*, 10
weather, whether, 297
Web sources. *See also* Internet; Sources
  authors of, identifying, 140
  avoiding plagiarism from, 103, 105
  citation at a glance, 159 (MLA); 212–13 (APA); 260–61 (*Chicago*)
  citing, 131, 140, 157–59 (MLA); 189–90, 195, 210–13 (APA); 255, 258–62 (*Chicago*); 277–78 (CSE)
  evaluating, 94, 100–01
  finding, 93–94
  previewing, 98–99
  saving copies of, 103
well, good, 41
were vs. *was*. See *was* vs. *were*
where vs. *that*, 297
whether . . . or, 7–8, 299
whether, weather. See *weather, whether*, 297
which
  agreement of verb with, 24–25
  vs. *that*, 60, 296, 297
  vague reference of, 35
  vs. *who*, 297
while, 297
who
  agreement of verb with, 24–25
  omission of, 8–9
  vs. *which* or *that*, 297
  vs. *whom*, 39
who's, whose, 70, 297
Wiki, as source, 100
will, as modal verb, 49–50
Wishes, subjunctive mood for, 32
Word groups. *See* Independent clauses; Phrases; Subordinate clauses

Wordiness, 4–5
Word processing programs
  and hyphenation, 89
  and keeping track of files, 103, 105
Words
  compound, 87, 88–89
  confused. *See* Glossary of usage
  division of, 89
  foreign, italics for, 85
  needed. *See* Needed words
  spelling of, 86–88
  unnecessary repetition of, 4, 54
  using your own. *See* Paraphrases; Summary
Words as words
  italics for, 85
  plural of, 69
  quotation marks for, 71
  treated as singular, 25–26
Working bibliography, 103
Working thesis. *See* Thesis
Works cited list (MLA)
  directory to models for, 134–35
  formatting, 169
  general guidelines for, 136–37
  models for, 137–66
  sample, 171, 173
would, as modal verb, 49–50
would of (nonstandard), 297
Writing center, checklist for visiting, 307

Y

yes, no, commas with, 62
yet. *See* Coordinating conjunctions
you
  indefinite use of, 35–36
  vs. *I* or *they*, 10
  and shifts in point of view, avoiding, 10
  understood, 53, 305
  vs. *your*, 38–39
your, you're, 297
YouTube. *See* Video

Revision Symbols

abbr	abbreviation **23a**		" "	quotation marks **20**
adj/adv	adjective or adverb **13**		.	period **21a**
add	add needed word **4**		?	question mark **21b**
agr	agreement **10, 12a**		!	exclamation point **21c**
appr	inappropriate language **9**		—	dash **21d**
art	article **16b**		( )	parentheses **21e**
awk	awkward		[ ]	brackets **21f**
cap	capital letter **22**		...	ellipsis mark **21g**
case	case **12c, 12d**		/	slash **21h**
cliché	cliché **9b**		*pass*	ineffective passive **2b**
cs	comma splice **15**		*pn agr*	pronoun agreement **12a**
dm	dangling modifier **7c**		*ref*	pronoun reference **12b**
-ed	*-ed* ending **11a**		*run-on*	run-on sentence **15**
ESL	English as a second language/ multilingual writers **16**		*-s*	*-s* ending on verb **10, 16a**
frag	sentence fragment **14**		*sexist*	sexist language **9d, 12a**
fs	fused sentence **15**		*shift*	confusing shift **5**
hyph	hyphen **24b**		*sl*	slang **9c**
irreg	irregular verb **11a**		*sp*	misspelled word **24a**
ital	italics **23c**		*sv agr*	subject-verb agreement **10**
jarg	jargon **9a**		*t*	verb tense **11b**
lc	use lowercase letter **22**		*usage*	see glossary of usage
mix	mixed construction **6**		*v*	voice **2**
mm	misplaced modifier **7a–b, 7d**		*var*	sentence variety **8**
mood	mood **11c**		*vb*	problem with verb **11, 16a**
num	numbers **23b**		*w*	wordy **1**
om	omitted word **4, 16c**		*//*	faulty parallelism **3**
p	punctuation		^	insert
︿	comma **17a–i**		*x*	obvious error
no ,	no comma **17j**		#	insert space
;	semicolon **18a**		‿	close up space
:	colon **18b**			
⌄	apostrophe **19**			

Detailed Menu

Introduction 1

Clarity 3

1 Wordy sentences 4

2 Active verbs 5
  a vs. *be* verbs
  b vs. passive verbs

3 Parallelism 7
  a Items in a series
  b Paired ideas

4 Needed words 8
  a In compound structures
  b *that*
  c In comparisons

5 Shifts 10
  a Point of view
  b Tense

6 Mixed constructions 11
  a Mixed grammar
  b Illogical connections
  c *is when, is where, reason . . . is because*

7 Misplaced and dangling modifiers 12
  a Misplaced words
  b Misplaced phrases and clauses
  c Dangling modifiers
  d Split infinitives

8 Sentence variety 15
  a Combining choppy sentences
  b Varying sentence openings

9 Appropriate voice 17
  a Jargon
  b Clichés
  c Slang
  d Sexist language
  e Offensive language

Grammar 21

10 Subject-verb agreement 22
  a Words between subject and verb
  b Subjects with *and*
  c Subjects with *or, nor*
  d Indefinite pronouns such as *someone*
  e Collective nouns such as *jury*
  f Subject after verb
  g *who, which, that*

  h Plural form, singular meaning
  i Titles, company names, words as words

11 Other problems with verbs 26
  a Irregular verbs
  b Tense
  c Mood

12 Pronouns 32
  a Agreement
  b Reference
  c Case (*I* vs. *me* etc.)
  d *who* or *whom*

13 Adjectives and adverbs 40
  a Adjectives
  b Adverbs
  c Comparatives and superlatives

14 Sentence fragments 42
  a Clauses
  b Phrases
  c Acceptable fragments

15 Run-on sentences 44
  a Revision with comma and coordinating conjunction
  b With semicolon (or colon or dash)
  c By separating sentences
  d By restructuring

16 Grammar concerns for multilingual writers 47
  a Verbs
  b Articles (*a, an, the*)
  c Sentence structure
  d Prepositions showing time and place

Punctuation 56

17 The comma 57
  a Independent clauses with coordinating conjunction
  b Introductory elements
  c Items in a series
  d Coordinate adjectives
  e Nonrestrictive elements
  f Transitions, parenthetical expressions, absolute phrases, contrasts
  g Direct address, *yes* and *no*, interrogative tags, interjections
  h *he said* etc.